Interpretation of Bloodstain Evidence at Crime Scenes

ELSEVIER SERIES IN
**PRACTICAL ASPECTS OF CRIMINAL
AND FORENSIC INVESTIGATIONS**

VERNON J. GEBERTH, BBA, MPS, FBINA   *Series Editor*

**Practical Homicide Investigation: Tactics, Procedures, and
  Forensic Techniques**
Vernon J. Geberth

**Friction Ridge Skin: Comparison and Identification of
  Fingerprints**
James F. Cowger

**Gunshot Wounds: Practical Aspects of Firearms, Ballistics,
  and Forensic Techniques**
Vincent J. M. Di Maio

Practical Fire and Arson Investigation
John J. O'Connor

**The Sexual Exploitation of Children: A Practical Guide to
  Assessment, Investigation, and Intervention**
Seth L. Goldstein

Practical Drug Enforcement: Procedures and Administration
Michael D. Lyman

Tire Imprint Evidence
Peter McDonald

Interpretation of Bloodstain Evidence at Crime Scenes
William G. Eckert and Stuart H. James

Interpretation of Bloodstain Evidence at Crime Scenes

WILLIAM G. ECKERT, M.D.
Director
Milton Helpern International Center
  for the Forensic Sciences
Wichita State University
Wichita, Kansas

STUART H. JAMES
Director of Forensic Laboratories
Peter Vallas Associates, Inc.
Fort Lauderdale, Florida
Hackensack, New Jersey

Elsevier
New York · Amsterdam · London

Elsevier Science Publishing Co., Inc.
655 Avenue of the Americas, New York, New York 10010

Sole distributors outside the United States and Canada:
Elsevier Science Publishers B.V.
P.O. Box 211, 1000 AE Amsterdam, The Netherlands

© 1989 by Elsevier Science Publishing Co., Inc.

This book has been registered with the Copyright Clearance Center, Inc. For further information, please contact the Copyright Clearance Center, Inc., Salem, Massachusetts.

This book is printed on acid-free paper.

Library of Congress Cataloging-in-Publication Data

Eckert, William G., 1926–
    Interpretation of bloodstain evidence at crime scenes/William G.
Eckert, Stuart H. James.
        p.   cm.—(Elsevier series in practical aspects of forensic and
criminal investigations)
    Bibliography: p.
    Includes index.
    ISBN 0-444-01463-2
    1. Bloodstains. 2. Forensic hematology. I. James, Stuart H.
II. Title. III. Series: Elsevier series in practical aspects of criminal
and forensic investigations.
RA1061.E26   1989
614'.1—dc19   88-38754
                                                                   CIP

Current printing (last digit):
10 9 8 7 6 5 4 3 2 1

Manufactured in the United States of America

Contents

Dedication

This work is dedicated to those who have contributed to the advancement of the examination of blood and the interpretation of bloodstain evidence. Among those who have worked to this end was Dr. Franz Josef Holzer of Innsbruck, Austria, who worked with Professor Karl Landsteiner, the pioneer investigator of blood groups and with Alexander Weiner, the developer of knowledge of the Rh groups of blood. Holzer developed the basic methods for the testing of blood from crime scenes that proved vital for the identification of blood evidence. A simple and polite man, Dr. Holzer frequently attended international meetings and was always willing to share his knowledge with younger forensic scientists and those in training.

Special recognition is given to Professor Herbert Leon MacDonell, a renowned criminalist of Corning, New York, for his contributions to the advancement of research and applications of bloodstain interpretation. Inspired by the work of the late Dr. Paul Leland Kirk, MacDonell's efforts have brought the science of bloodstain interpretation to a high level of acceptance by the medicolegal community. Because he has shared the current level of information concerning the application of physics to the flight characteristics of human blood with his many students in bloodstain institutes, he has promoted the investigation of bloodstain evidence at crime scenes throughout the world.

We also take this opportunity to recognize the late Dr. James Spencer Bell for his contributions to the advancement of forensic medicine and, more specifically, his contributions to the National Association of Medical Examiners. He was a tireless worker who was totally involved with the cause of forensic medicine in the state of Tennessee and throughout the United States. His memory will always be with us as a high standard for tireless work in the advancement of the forensic sciences.

Preface

This work is intended to be an investigative resource and text for law enforcement officers, laboratory scientists, and medicolegal personnel involved with crime scene reconstruction and the examination of blood and bloodstain evidence. Prosecutors and defense attorneys will also find this text an aid to their understanding of the significance of blood for the preparation of their cases involving the interpretation of bloodstain evidence. The earlier works concerned with the subject of bloodstain pattern interpretation were primarily related to blood spatter and the dynamics of the flight characteristics of blood in motion. We have added a new dimension of medical and physiological facts concerning blood that contribute to the complete examination of blood evidence at the crime scene. The evaluation and measurement of the nature and quantity of bloodshed by a victim at a scene yield important information in helping establish postinjury survival time and in some cases assist with the determination of the postmortem interval. Considerations are given to the clotting and drying time of blood with respect to time intervals and various surface textures. In those cases where a wounded victim has been removed from a bloody crime scene, the observations of the quantity and nature of the blood may provide information as to the nature of the injuries sustained and the possibility of survival. A review of the volume of blood flow through different body areas is presented. This is important to the medicolegal investigator as well as the physician who must treat a patient suffering injuries to a specific body area from an accident, shooting, or stabbing.

The proper techniques of blood collection at crime scenes are emphasized, including the importance of good photography and documentation of the evidence. An overview of blood identification is provided with the emphasis on preliminary testing of blood that can be accomplished at the scene. The individualization of blood is discussed and the population distribution frequencies of the common red cell antigens, isoenzymes, and serum genetic markers are provided for the investigator. The emergence of DNA typing is also discussed as a new tool in blood identification.

Special problems are also addressed and demonstrated, including blood diluted by snow or water and blood-flow patterns relative to the final position of the victim at a crime scene. Several areas of bloodstain interpretation research and development of newer techniques are presented, including examination of bloodstains at fire scenes and the utilization of bloodstain experiments with specific reference to high-velocity forward and backspatter produced by gunshot. Also included is a section on data processing of bloodstain measurements and a computer program designed to draw convergences and points of origin of bloodstains at crime scenes.

The potential exposure of medicolegal personnel to the AIDS virus during crime scene examination, postmortem procedures, and examination of physical evidence has prompted the authors to include a section outlining precautions to be undertaken to minimize exposure to the AIDS virus during these situations. The chapters that provide actual case presentations in which bloodstain evidence and the interpretation of bloodstain patterns were significant to the ultimate outcome of the investigations are very useful additions to this book. Twenty-five cases in which the authors were consulted and in which they provided expert court testimony are presented. The cases chosen for this book represent bloodstain patterns produced by a variety of injuries and activities which occur at scenes of violent crimes.

The international bibliography included at the end of this work represents more than 500 references to scientific publications and texts pertaining to the examination and analysis of human blood. This work is intended to serve as an important resource and reference to be used at crime scenes and to provide a means for better understanding of data in the rather specific and often difficult field of medicolegal investigation.

Acknowledgments

We would like to acknowledge Warren R. Darby, at this time Deputy Chief of Police and formerly Director of the Police Crime Laboratory, Syracuse, New York, and the President of the International Association of Bloodstain Pattern Analysts for his support and assistance with the word-processing format and editing of the manuscript. The excellent artwork was produced by Carol L. Olmstead of Binghamton, New York, and it enhances the quality of our work. We would also like to recognize the contributions of David R. Redsicker of Peter Vallas Associates, Inc., Hackensack, New Jersey, for his excellent research and experimentation regarding blood at fire scenes; William C. Fischer, a private investigator in Binghamton, New York, for his interesting research concerning blood acceleration and resulting stain patterns; Donald R. Schuessler, MS, Forensic Evidence Unit, and Frederick E. Wilson, MS, Research and Development, of the Eugene Public Safety Department in Eugene, Oregon, for their comprehensive research into computer applications with bloodstains; and Henry C. Lee, PhD, Chief Criminalist at the Connecticut State Police Laboratory for his outline for precautions against infectious diseases transmitted through blood. These contributions represent innovative approaches to bloodstain research and applications and, we hope, will stimulate others in the field to pursue additional research in the future. We would also like to recognize the support and recommendations of our wives, Haroldine Eckert and Pauline Moffitt James, who as registered nurses assisted with the areas of bloodshed and injuries producing specific types of bleeding characteristics.

Finally, we extend our thanks and appreciation to Vernon J. Geberth,

BBA, MPS, FBINA, Editor of the Elsevier Series in Practical Aspects of Criminal and Forensic Investigations for his favorable review of our original bloodstain manual, which has been revised and expanded through his helpful recommendations.

WILLIAM G. ECKERT, MD
STUART H. JAMES

Foreword

The success or failure of a criminal investigation often depends on the recognition of potential physical evidence left at a crime scene and the proper interpretation of that evidence. Crime scenes that involve bloodshed often contain a wealth of information in the form of bloodstains. The pattern, size, shape, and the location of such stains may be very useful in the reconstruction of the events that occurred.

Although considered still in its infancy, the science of bloodstain interpretation has grown by leaps and bounds over the past twenty years because of the numerous studies that have examined the significance of bloodstain evidence. Much of this work was inspired by specific cases that led the law enforcement personnel and criminalists involved to conduct experiments and exercises to confirm their theories regarding the blood spatter found at the scene.

As a result of the need for this knowledge to be made available to crime scene personnel, a number of training programs have been developed specifically for bloodstain pattern interpretation. Also, many of the evidence technician and crime scene programs being conducted today include a portion of the curriculum on this important topic.

In 1983, the International Association of Bloodstain Pattern Analysts (IABPA) was formed to promote this body of knowledge, standardize the scientific techniques utilized in such analysis, encourage research in this discipline, and keep its members appraised of the latest techniques, discoveries, and developments in bloodstain pattern interpretation. This Association has grown to over 200 members from around the globe.

I have known the authors of this book for many years and consider them to be highly qualified in their respective areas of forensic science.

William G. Eckert, MD, a forensic pathologist of international renown, is the Director of the Milton Helpern International Center for the Forensic Sciences at Wichita State University in Wichita, Kansas. He founded the organization INFORM, the International Reference Organization in Forensic Medicine and Sciences, based at the Milton Helpern Center. Dr. Eckert is the editor-in-chief of the *American Journal of Forensic Medicine and Pathology*, the organ of the National Association of Medical Examiners. He is a noted writer and educator in forensic medicine, who has developed audiovisual and videotape lecture programs as well as a monograph series in forensic investigation. Dr. Eckert is a past president of the International Association of Forensic Sciences and past vice president of the International Academy of Legal Medicine and the American Academy of Forensic Sciences. He has been a consultant in many major cases including the assassination of Robert Kennedy, the jumbo jet crash in Tenerife, Spain, the Tate-LaBianca homicides in Los Angeles, and the Bird love quadrangle homicides in Kansas.

Stuart H. James is the forensic laboratory director and Death Investigator for the private investigating firm of Peter Vallas Associates, Inc., in the Fort Lauderdale, Florida, and Hackensack, New Jersey, offices of that organization. Prior to joining Peter Vallas Associates, Inc. in 1988, he was a private consulting forensic scientist in Binghamton, New York, where he also had directed the operation of a multicounty crime laboratory which was funded through the Law Enforcement Assistance Administration between 1977 and 1981. In conjunction with his experience in crime scene reconstruction and physical evidence examination, Mr. James has completed both the basic and advanced bloodstain institutes conducted by Herbert L. MacDonell in Elmira, New York. He is a charter member of the International Association of Bloodstain Pattern Analysts and a fellow in the toxicology section of the American Academy of Forensic Sciences. He has instructed courses in forensic science at the State University of New York at Binghamton and Broome Community College in Binghamton, New York. He has also been an assistant instructor at basic bloodstain institutes conducted by MacDonell. Mr. James has given testimony concerning bloodstain interpretation in nine states as well as in the United States Virgin Islands, Canada, and the Republic of South Korea.

The authors have contributed to the study and applications of bloodstain interpretation by looking further at the medical and physiological facts concerning blood to provide a more complete understanding of the significance of bloodstains. This text is embellished by numerous photographs that depict specific bloodstain evidence. The case studies that are included provide excellent examples of how such analysis assisted in solving crimes.

Collectively, the chapters are a superb resource and a definitive guide for law enforcement officers, criminalists, medical examiners, forensic pathologists, and associated investigators. It is a must for all persons who have the responsibility of crime scene evaluation.

WARREN R. DARBY
Deputy Chief of Police
Syracuse, New York
President—IABPA

Interpretation of Bloodstain Evidence at Crime Scenes

General Forensic Aspects of Blood Evidence

1

WILLIAM G. ECKERT, MD, and
STUART H. JAMES

Historical Overview of Blood Identification

Blood evidence is involved in many aspects of forensic investigation. It may be the means of identifying a missing body, the source of toxicological interpretation relating to the immediate cause of death of a victim, or the source of physical evidence that may provide the means of distinguishing among a homicidal, suicidal, accidental, or natural cause of death. Blood identification and interpretation of bloodstain patterns become important factors for crime scene reconstruction and for the linking or exclusion of a suspect to a criminal act. Examination of blood evidence in a given case may involve many areas of expertise including forensic pathology, criminalistics, and forensic toxicology.

The early developments in the forensic investigation of blood were those that established whether or not the stain was in fact blood of human origin. Chemical tests to establish the presence of blood were in use in the late nineteenth century. In 1863, the German scientist Schonbein developed a test for blood that utilized the effervescent reaction of hydrogen peroxide with hemoglobin. By 1868, a true color test for the presence of blood had been discovered by Van Deen in Holland, and independently by Day in Australia. This color test utilized an extract of the West Indian shrub guaiacum. Guaiac, in the presence of hemoglobin and hydrogen peroxide, produces a deep blue color. The guaiac test, though nonspecific for blood, was found to be quite sensitive.

Benzidine, first produced by the Merck Company in 1845, was introduced by Adler and Adler as a presumptive blood-testing reagent for forensic purposes in 1904. Benzidine reacted with blood in a manner similar to that of guaiac in the presence of hydrogen peroxide by producing a blue color. It was more sensitive than guaiac but reacted with such nonblood materials as rust, certain metallic salts, and plant peroxidases salts. The use of benzidine has been discontinued by many forensic laboratories because of its carcinogenicity. Leucomalachite green, also developed by the Adlers in 1904, has been used in the place of benzidine.

Additional presumptive chemical tests for blood that appeared between 1901 and 1939 include phenolphthalein, developed by Kastle and Sheed in 1901 and Meyer in 1903; o-tolidine, developed by Ruttan and Hardisty in 1912; and o-toluidine, developed by Gershenfeld in 1939. Testing for the presence of blood by chemical luminescence was introduced to forensic science in 1937 by the German scientist Walter Specht of Jena. He found that the spraying of bloodstains with the chemical luminol in the dark caused the bloodstains to glow or "luminesce" due to the reaction of luminol with hemoglobin.

Ludwig Teichmann developed a hemin crystal test for the confirmation of blood in the mid-nineteenth century. Hemoglobin, which imparts the color to blood, was demonstrated in stains by spectroscopic analysis toward the end of the nineteenth century.

In 1901, Professor Uhlenhuth at the University of Greifswald in Germany developed a precipitin test for distinguishing animal from human blood. This was the initial application of serology in forensic science. Uhlenhuth successfully tested his precipitin method on extremely small and aged bloodstains.

During 1901, Professor Landsteiner in Vienna discovered the presence in humans of different blood groups known as the ABO system. The first attempt to apply this discovery to cases of dried bloodstains was undertaken in 1902 by Professor Richter at the Institute of Forensic Medicine at the University of Vienna.

It was the renowned scientist Dr. Leone Lattes of Torino, Italy, who first developed a technique for the ABO grouping of dried bloodstains in 1916. His writings pointed out the potential of using this technique in cases of disputed parentage. Lattes applied his methods to the analysis of dried bloodstains in criminal cases and was credited with being the first to apply the Landsteiner blood grouping reactions to forensic science.

In 1930, an esteemed student of Landsteiner, Professor Holzer, who worked at the Institute of Forensic Medicine in Innsbruck, Austria, developed a technique of indirectly demonstrating antigens in dried bloodstains known as absorption–inhibition. This technique was utilized during the investigation of the Franz Mair murder in Austria in which Holzer demonstrated the blood group of the victim in bloodstains present on the trousers of the suspect. Professor Holzer testified at the trial for this homicide in which the victim's stepbrother, Karl Mair, was convicted of first-degree murder. Holzer's techniques were utilized in many important cases in later years.

Landsteiner and Levine discovered the MN and P red blood cell antigens in 1927, which added another dimension to the investigation of paternity cases. Their investigations also demonstrated that, in many people, the blood group antigens could be detected in other body fluids such as saliva and semen. The phenomenon of secretion of blood group antigens into body fluids was independently discovered by Professor Yamakami in Japan at about the same time. In 1940, Landsteiner and Weiner discovered the existence of the Rhesus or Rh factor in blood, thereby enhancing the knowledge of blood individualization. The discovery of the Rh system was also contributory to the prevention and management of the so-called Rh babies whose blood antibodies reacted to antigens from the mother's blood introduced through the fetal circulation often producing fatal complications.

In 1945 in England, Coombs, Mourant, and Race introduced a test now known as the Coombs test to detect the presence of the anti-Rh antibodies. Moreau and Dodinval in Liege, Belgium, further developed the Coombs technique as a test for human blood. After this, new blood groups were discovered and new blood identification techniques appeared including a precipitin test developed in Sweden by Professor Ouchterlony in 1949. This agar gel procedure was adapted for forensic purposes in 1957 by Professor Muller in Lille, France, and was used for species determination of blood. In 1960, Stuart Kind in England introduced an absorption–elution procedure for the detection of blood groups in dried stains. This was based upon the work of Weiner in 1939 and of Coombs in 1955 who found that the pneumococcal bacteria and skin cells absorb anti-A and anti-B human sera in a similar manner to group A and B blood cells. In 1961, Barbara Dodd of the Department of Forensic Medicine at the London Hospital Medical College demonstrated that this technique could be used to determine the blood groups present in minute quantities of dried stains. Dodd and Coombs introduced the mixed agglutination technique in 1961. Fluorescent antibody techniques were developed by Hasebe in Japan in 1962. In New Zealand in 1969, Douglas and Stavely developed automated methods for Rh typing of bloodstains that were improved upon with respect to sensitivity by Pereira in England in 1971.

Electrophoresis was advanced as a technique by Brian Culliford at the Metropolitan Police Laboratory in London during the late 1960s to identify hemoglobin variants, haptoglobins, red cell isoenzymes, and the serum genetic markers which have all greatly enhanced the individualization of human blood. Electrophoretic techniques advanced rapidly during the 1970s and 1980s and have become routine procedures in forensic laboratories throughout the world.

Reliable methods are now available for a newer concept in blood individualization, the detection of DNA polymorphisms through isolation of particular portions of the DNA chain. The British researcher

Alec Jeffreys reported in 1987 that the innovative process of "DNA fingerprinting" could radically change the handling of any case in which identity of a particular person is at issue.

Blood Grouping and Personal Identification

Problems of identification may be helped by blood group determination in establishing the individuality of a person. This may be done to correct a nursery mix-up of infants or to establish verification of an immigrant or a person with a foreign passport as he or she attempts to enter a country. In forensic practice, the identification of an unknown body may be established through blood samples in conjunction with other methods of identification. Occasionally, false insurance claims may be detected by proper identification of a body that has been burned or otherwise mutilated in attempts to mask its identification. Remains that are fragmented, mutilated, or partially destroyed by thermal injury may often be identified by blood individualization techniques.

In the future it may be possible to identify valuable thoroughbred animals by blood individualization techniques. A novel approach to animal identification was reported by Dr. Pierre Finck who utilized immunological techniques to identify a cargo of ovine meat from a sunken ship which had foundered during a Civil War campaign more than 100 years previously.

The Individuality of Blood in Disputed Parentage

The question of disputed parentage should be mentioned as an important application of blood serological studies. Blood groups are an inherited characteristic that is passed on from parents to child according to the Mendelian laws governing the inheritance of most human characteristics.

Rules of inheritance applied to blood groups are:

1. A blood group factor cannot appear in a child unless present in one or both parents.
2. If one or the other parent is homozygous (having two identical allelic genes on two corresponding positions of a pair of chromosomes) for a particular blood group, this must appear in the blood of the child.

When blood is tested in cases of disputed parentage, the mother, child, and suspected father should be tested by the same laboratory. It should be noted that states differ in their acceptance of certain blood grouping systems. For example, in Kansas the courts accept the ABO, Rh, MNS, Duffy, Kidd, and Kell red cell antigenic systems and the human leukocyte antigen (HLA) white cell antigenic system, which can approach 96 percent probability of inclusion. In those states accepting both the red cell isoenzyme and serum genetic marker systems, the probability of paternity approaches 98–99 percent.

As will be described in detail later in this book, the testing of a suspected bloodstain begins with a preliminary, catalytic color test for the presence of blood. These tests are not specific for blood and positive tests for blood must be confirmed with the use of the hematin crystal tests or electrophoresis separation of hemoglobins. Verification of human origin is established with the use of precipitin tests. Further individualization is accomplished with ABO grouping and characterization of the red cell isoenzymes and serum genetic markers. The extent of individualization depends upon age of the bloodstain, sample size, and degree of any contamination that may be present. When more systems are tested, the greater the chance of making the desired degree of distinction. Dodd reported that ABO antigens have been detected in bloodstains that were five years old. Absorption–inhibition techniques have detected the A antigen in blood crusts in floor boards fourteen years after the blood was shed.

Approximately 80 percent of individuals are secretors and produce ABH group-specific substances in high concentration in saliva, seminal fluid, vaginal secretions, and gastric juices. In perspiration, tears, and urine, this concentration is fairly low but often detectable by absorption–elution methods. Identification of blood group substances in skin scrapings and hair have been reported by Swinburne and Lincoln. The development of methods of testing of blood groups in these body fluids and tissues broadens the value of forensic investigations in many other types of crimes.

Development of Bloodstain Pattern Interpretation

A major concern of early crime scene investigators has been the study of the crime scene with respect to the evaluation of the bloodstains and patterns resulting from actions and activities of the victim and the assailant at the scene. The earliest information involving the study of bloodstain patterns at a crime scene was related to the activities of Dr. Paul Jeserich, a forensic chemist in Berlin who examined homicide scenes early in the first decade of this century. In 1939, the French scientist Dr. Victor Balthazard conducted original research and experimentation with bloodstain trajectories and patterns. There were individual cases involving bloodstain pattern interpretation in later years including the 1949 Setty case in England reviewed by the late Dr. Francis Camps of London. In the United States a milestone of bloodstain pattern interpretation was the work performed by the late Dr.

Paul L. Kirk of the University of California at Berkeley pertaining to the Sam Sheppard case in Cleveland, Ohio, in 1955. The first modern publication pertaining to bloodstain pattern interpretation, *Flight Characteristics and Stain Patterns of Human Blood*, appeared in 1971 as a result of research and experimentation performed by MacDonell and Bialousz. More recently, Laber and Epstein, in 1983, published a laboratory manual entitled *Experiments and Practice Exercises in Bloodstain Pattern Analysis*. The importance of bloodstain interpretation at crime scenes is reflected in the increased interest in this specialized area and in the availability of training courses and seminars devoted to the subject. Scientific articles pertaining to aspects of bloodstain pattern interpretation are being seen more frequently in the forensic literature.

An area of particular interest in the examination of bloodstain evidence has been the study conducted by Dr. Henry Lee, Director of the Connecticut State Police Laboratory and a noted serologist, concerning the volume of bloodstains found at crime scenes. This knowledge helps to determine many aspects of the wounding of a victim including rapidity of death, which area of the body has sustained injury in cases where the body has been removed from the scene, and in some cases, the amount of activity of a victim subsequent to sustaining the injuries. Because blood is a very frequent form of evidence at a scene of a violent crime, it should be carefully examined and documented by crime scene investigators and other medicolegal representatives.

Iatrogenic Problems with Blood

From a medicolegal standpoint, iatrogenic problems related to the transfusion of blood and blood by-products for legitimate purposes may create problems arising from either the incompatibility of blood and resultant hemolytic transfusion reactions or the prolonged complications of the transmission of an infectious disease. With the alarming and increasing AIDS epidemic creating worldwide unrest among the population, the complications of blood transfusions have become an increasing concern. Additional infections and problems have involved the transmission of malaria, syphilis, mumps, measles, undulant fever, and, more frequently, a serious increase in hepatitis. Blood banks routinely screen donor blood for hepatitis and AIDS viruses. Many problems in disease transmission may be prevented by careful evaluation of the history of the donor. The complications of human error in the technical and clerical areas of blood processing are primarily the hemolytic transfusion reactions resulting from incompatible blood in which death may result from renal failure. Religious objections have been causing problems in the management of cases where blood is required for proper treatment, and court rulings have allowed the physician to continue this therapy as planned in those cases involving minors. The transmission of hepatitis has been well known and documented in drug addicts who use contaminated needles for the intravenous injection of drugs. An unusual case involving blood was one in which the death of a patient occurred during an operation as a result of a misconnection of a tube into a needle that had been placed into a vein. The junction parted and blood continued to flow out of the body through the attached needle. A large pool of blood was discovered under the surgical drapes beneath the arm of the patient. There was a question brought up by attorneys for the plaintiff as to how much bleeding occurred and whether it had a deleterious effect and contributed to the death of the individual.

Research being conducted by Dr. William Eckert has concentrated on the amount of blood loss that is possible in given time intervals from various bleeding points on the body. Since bleeding is a major factor in many manners of death (homicidal, suicidal, accidental, or natural), it is extremely important that there be proper knowledge developed so that clinical physicians as well as those who are responsible for the investigation of deaths by violence may be properly prepared for the fulfillment of their responsibilities in their respective practices.

Natural Diseases and Blood

Natural diseases may involve the blood and may be seen in the practice of forensic medicine. Sickle cell disease affects the red blood cells and on occasion a severely injured victim may suffer the complications of a sickle cell crisis with fatal outcome. The sickling of red blood cells has been reported during air flight in which states of anoxia were present. Many years ago a case in Norfolk, Virginia, involved the death of an elderly black male working on a Chesapeake Bay steamer. He had been found in a poorly ventilated paint locker that contained a heavy concentration of paint fumes. The autopsy revealed massive sickling and clumping of red blood cells in microscopic tissue sections.

Postmortem Chemistry of Blood and Body Fluids

Assessment of biochemicals present in postmortem blood and body fluids may help solve a variety of medicolegal problems. A cause of death due to natural disease can be established. Postmortem blood glucose levels will establish a hyper- or hypoglycemic condition which may be related to diabetes. High postmortem blood glucose levels may be due to glycolysis and may be related to nondiabetic conditions. Elevated urea nitrogen in postmortem blood may indicate kidney disease. Increased ammonia levels have been associated with liver failure in the absence of a clinical history. Dr. John Coe has extensively studied postmortem chemistries in blood, spinal fluid, and ocular fluid. It has been found that some biochemicals remain quite stable in the blood after death whereas others show varying degrees of change that may not be predictable. There has been an increasing use of ocular fluid or vitreous humor for postmortem chemical analyses. Ocular fluid is isolated and more protected from contamination and trauma than blood or spinal fluid. Coe demonstrated that many substances in ocular fluid possess greater postmortem stability. Approximately 2 ml of fluid can be obtained from each eye which is sufficient for numerous determinations including glucose, urea nitrogen, electrolytes, alcohol, and drug screening. The determination of postmortem ocular fluid potassium levels has been utilized as a chemical indicator of postmortem interval. Potassium levels increase after death arithmetically from an average normal of between 3.5 and 5.0 mEq/liter. Adelson, in 1963, established that the average rate of increase was 0.17 mEq/hour. The accuracy of estimating the postmortem interval by this method is subject to error and should be interpreted with caution with a range of time given. Greatest accuracy is achieved during the initial twelve hours after death.

Toxicological Aspects of Blood

Toxicology is concerned with the chemical and physical properties of toxic substances and the effects they produce on living organisms. Forensic toxicology is the application of the science of toxicology to the determination of the role or contribution of toxic substances in the circumstances relating to the cause of death in medical–legal cases. Biological materials are subjected to qualitative and quantitative analyses to establish the identity and amount of toxic agents present in the body. A forensic autopsy is incomplete without the proper collection of blood, tissue, and other samples for toxicological examination.

Blood samples are routinely screened for the presence of alcohol, carbon monoxide, cyanide, heavy metals, and drugs as well as additional toxic agents in specific situations. Therapeutic, toxic, and numerous chemical and drug tests of blood have been established for the interpretation of results.

Initial observation of the blood may indicate the presence of asphyxiant gasses such as carbon monoxide and cyanide, which attach to the hemoglobin on the red blood cells and deprive the body of oxygen. Significant concentrations of carbon monoxide or cyanide impart a characteristic cherry red color to the blood.

Poisoning with heavy metals such as mercury, lead, and arsenic may produce serious effects on the blood and the blood-forming organs.

Aspirin as well as many prescription drugs may have an adverse effect on blood clotting or, as the result of effects on the red cell enzyme system, produce an increased red cell fragility. Vitamin deficiencies may also affect the clotting of blood and fragility of small blood vessels. Aplastic anemia, leukopenia, and thrombocytopenia, in addition to red cell hemolysis, may be drug induced. The effects of such physical trauma as radiation on blood and hemopoietic tissues may result in an acute course leading to death directly or a chronic course with death the outcome as a result of leukemia or other malignancies. There are also organic chemicals, such as benzene, that may contribute to serious organic diseases including liver or kidney failure as well as blood-clotting problems. Agents affecting the blood-clotting mechanisms may cause death due to excessive internal or external bleeding of a victim who has received an otherwise nonfatal injury.

References

1. Coe, J. 1974. Postmortem chemistry: Practical considerations and literature review. *Journal of Forensic Sciences* 19, 1.
2. Coombs, R., et al. 1945. Detection of weak or incomplete Rh agglutinins. *Lancet* 2, 15.
3. Culliford, B.J. 1971. The examination of and typing of bloodstains in the crime laboratory. National Institute of Law Enforcement and Criminal Justice, December.
4. Dodd, B. 1968. "Immunological Aspects of Forensic Science." In *Clinical Aspects of Immunology*, 2nd Edition, by P. Gell and R. Coombs. Philadelphia: F.A. Davis Company.
5. Feegel, J.R. 1975. "Legal Aspects of Laboratory Medicine." In *Blood Banking*, Boston: Little, Brown, and Company.
6. Finck, P. 1971. Serology of 100 year old ovine tissue. *Am I Vet. Res.* 32(9):1428.
7. Hasebe, H. 1962. Fluorescent antibody technique for ABO groups in dried stains. *Japan Journal of Legal Medicine* 16, 325.
8. Holzer, F.J. 1931. Determination of blood groups in bloodstains. *Deutsch Zeit Ges Gericht Medizin* XVI, 445.
9. Kind, S.S. 1960. Absorption-elution groupings of dried blood smears. *Nature* CLXXXVIII, 397.
10. Laber, T., and Epstein, B. 1983. *Experiments and Practical Exercises in Bloodstain Pattern Analysis*. Minneapolis, MN: Callen Publishing Company.
11. Landsteiner, K. 1901. Agglutination differences of human blood. *Wein Klin Woch* XLVI.
12. ———. 1903. Individual blood differences in forensic practice. *Zeit fur Medizinalbeamte* 16, 3, 85.
13. Landsteiner, K., and Levine, P. 1927. New agglutinable factor differentiating individual human bloods. *Proceedings of Society for Experimental Medicine and Biology* XXIV, 600.
14. Landsteiner, K., and Weiner, A.S. 1940. An agglutinable factor in human blood recognized by immune sera for rhesus blood. *Proceedings of Society for Experimental Medicine and Biology* XLIII, 43.

15. Lattes, L. 1923. Diagnosis of individual blood groups. *Ann. Med. Leg. et Crim.* V.
16. Lee, H.C. 1986. Estimation of original volume of bloodstains. *Identification News*, July.
17. Lincoln, P., and Dodd, B. 1968. ABH groups in hair: mixed agglutination. *Med. Sci. Law* 8:1, 41.
18. MacDonell, H.L. 1971. *Flight Characteristics and Stain Patterns of Human Blood.* USDJ, LEAA, Washington, D.C.
19. Martin, E.W. 1971. "Adverse Drug Reactions—Blood Dyscrasias. In *Hazards of Medication*, p. 338. Philadelphia: J.B. Lippincott, Co.
20. Moreau, P., and Dodinval, D. 1962. Classic methods for identification of blood groups. 29th International Congress of Med. Leg. and Med. Sociale, Marseilles, France.
21. Muller, M. 1958. Antibody-antigen reactions in gel. *Lare Medical* XXX, 4,218.
22. Ouchterlony, A. 1949. Antibody–antigen reactions in gels. *Acta Pathologica, Microbiologica, et Immunologica Scandinavica* XXVI, 507.
23. Pereira, M. 1971. Automated Rh genotyping of dried bloodstains. *Technicon Quarterly 1* III, 16–18.
24. Rotter, R. 1956. Splenic infarct in sickelemia during flight. *Annals of Internal Medicine* 44:257.
25. Swinburne, L.M. 1962. The identification of skin. *Medicine, Science, and the Law* 3:3.
26. Thorwald, J. 1966. "Forensic Serology." In *Crime and Science.* New York: Harcourt, Brace, and World Co.
27. ———. 1964. *Century of the Detective.* New York: Harcourt, Brace, and World Co.
28. Uhlenhuth, P.A. 1961. A method of differentiating blood groups. *Deutsch Med. Woch.* No. 6,7.
29. Yamakami, K. 1926. The individuality of semen with reference to property of inhibiting specifically isohemoagglutination. *Journal of Immunology* XII:186.
30. Zipser, S. 1966. Liability for negligence in blood transfusions. *Federal Insurance Quarterly* 16:3,9.

Bloodstain Pattern Interpretation

2

STUART H. JAMES

General Considerations

Blood is one of the most significant and frequently encountered types of physical evidence associated with the forensic investigation of death and violent crime. The identification of human blood and its classification within the blood group systems (for example, ABO), the characterization of the red cell isoenzymes, and serum group systems known as genetic markers have permitted a high degree of individualization of human blood in many cases.

[The circumstances and nature of violent crimes frequently produce a variety of bloodstains that, when carefully studied and evaluated with respect to their geometry and distribution, may provide information of considerable value to assist the investigator with the reconstruction of the scene. The use of blood grouping techniques to associate bloodstains with particular individuals in concert with the reconstruction of events based upon bloodstain patterns provides mutually valuable sources of physical evidence based upon the study of blood. The proper interpretation of bloodstain evidence has proved crucial in numerous cases where the manner of death is questioned and the issue of homicide, suicide, accident, or natural death must be resolved in a criminal or civil litigation or proceeding.

The study of bloodstain patterns and the consideration of the physical processes in the distribution of these patterns to reconstruct details of activity at scenes of death and violent crime have recently emerged as a recognized forensic skill. Historically, bloodstain interpretation has suffered through a long period of neglect and as a result investigators in death cases frequently have not appreciated the very obvious information available from this source. Dr. Paul Kirk stated in his

well-known text *Crime Investigation*, "No other type of investigation
of blood will yield so much useful information as an analysis of the
blood distribution patterns." The failure to consider the significance of
bloodstain evidence when it is present represents a serious omission in
an investigation. In 1955, Dr. Kirk presented an affidavit regarding his
findings based upon bloodstain evidence to the Court of Common
Pleas in the case of the State of Ohio vs. Samuel Sheppard. This was a
significant milestone in the recognition of bloodstain evidence by the
legal system in that Dr. Kirk was able to establish the relative position
of the attacker and victim at the time of the administration of the
beating. He was able to determine that the attacker administered
blows with a left hand, which was significant in that Dr. Sheppard was
right handed.

The further growth of interest and use of the significance of bloodstain evidence is a direct result of the scientific research and practical
applications of bloodstain theory by Herbert Leon MacDonell of Corning, New York. Through the assistance of a Law Enforcement Assistance Administration (LEAA) grant, MacDonell conducted research
and performed experiments to re-create and duplicate bloodstain patterns observed at crime scenes. This resulted in his publication of the
first modern treatise on bloodstain interpretation, *Flight Characteristics and Stain Patterns of Human Blood* in 1971. This was followed in
1973 by a second publication, *Laboratory Manual on the Geometric
Interpretation of Human Bloodstain Evidence.*

MacDonell organized formal instruction for investigators in bloodstain interpretation through bloodstain institutes conducted throughout the United States and abroad and has trained hundreds of police
investigators, forensic scientists, and crime laboratory personnel at
these institutes. As a direct result of MacDonell's efforts, the state of
the art of bloodstain interpretation and its use as evidence in court has
advanced considerably in the past two decades. Interest in research and
practical applications of bloodstain interpretation in forensic science
has increased considerably and others are making significant contributions to the field in crime scene reconstruction and publications.

At the first Advanced Bloodstain Institute held in Corning, New
York, in 1983, the International Association of Bloodstain Pattern Analysts was organized. This Association now consists of more than 200
members from throughout the United States and Canada and publishes
a quarterly newsletter on current bloodstain topics.

Bloodstain interpretation may be accomplished by direct scene evaluation and/or careful study of scene photographs (preferably color photographs with measuring device in view), in conjunction with detailed
examination of clothing, weapons, and other objects regarded as physical evidence. Details of hospital records, postmortem examination,
and autopsy photographs also provide useful information and should

be included for evaluation and study. In those cases where on-scene investigation is not possible and photographs must be relied upon, detailed sketches, diagrams, reports of crime scene investigators, and laboratory reports should be available for review.

Relative to the reconstruction of a crime scene, bloodstain interpretation may provide information to the investigator in many areas:

1. Origin(s) of the bloodstains.
2. Distances between impact areas of blood spatter and origin at time of bloodshed.
3. Type and direction of impact that produced bloodstain or spatter.
4. Object(s) that produced particular bloodstain patterns.
5. Number of blows, shots, etc., that occurred.
6. Position of victim, assailant, or objects at the scene during bloodshed.
7. Movement and direction of victim, assailant, or objects at scene after bloodshed.
8. Support or contradiction of statements given by suspect or witnesses.
9. Additional criteria for estimation of postmortem interval.
10. Correlation with other laboratory and pathology findings relevant to the investigation.

A combination of training through formal instruction, personal experimentation, and experience with actual case work is necessary before an individual acquires proficiency in the correct interpretation of bloodstain patterns. Contemporaneous experiments to duplicate specific patterns should be considered relative to a given case to support an interpretation or conclusion. Some conservative speculation is permissible during the initial investigative stages of a case. However, final opinions, contents of a written report, and ultimate court testimony must be based on scientific fact with no speculation. Alternate conclusions should be explored thoroughly, with correlation achieved through postmortem and laboratory findings in an investigation. It is important to be conservative and not to overinterpret bloodstain evidence especially when the number of bloodstains is limited. Conclusions based upon crime scene photographs should be conservative when the investigator has not had the opportunity to examine the crime scene personally and must rely upon the photographic expertise of others.

Physical Properties of Blood

Physically, blood can be characterized as a fluid mixture, consisting of cellular components and plasma, that circulates throughout the body. When blood is exposed to the external environment as the result of trauma and subjected to various forces, it will behave in a predictable manner according to the principles of physics. Bloodstains result from exposed blood that has come in contact with an external surface. The application of the physical properties of blood (viscosity, specific gravity, and surface tension) and the principles of fluids in motion form the basis for the study and interpretation of the location, shape, size, and directionality of bloodstains relative to the force or forces that produced them.

Free-Falling Drops of Blood and Drip Patterns on Horizontal Surfaces

Blood can drip from an open wound, saturated clothing, hair, weapons, or any objects that have a sufficient volume of blood to permit the formation of free-falling drops. The separation of these drops from the source of blood is caused by gravitational forces exceeding the forces of surface tension of the blood. Surface tension is the result of the molecular cohesive forces that cause the surface of a liquid to resist penetration and separation. As a drop of blood is falling through air, the surface tension of the liquid drop will minimize surface area and cause the drop to assume a spherical shape rather than a teardrop shape as often characterized by artists (Figure 2-1). This spherical drop will not break up in air unless acted upon by a force other than gravity.

The volume of a single drop of free-falling blood was studied by MacDonell in 1971, and more recently in 1985 by Laber, and has been the subject of some controversy regarding the uniformity of blood volume of drops from different sources of blood. The original experiments conducted by MacDonell measured the average volume of a drop of blood to be approximately 0.05 ml. Laber has demonstrated variations in volumes between 0.013 and 0.16 ml of blood drops falling from different sources including fingertip, knife blade, screwdriver tip, and cloth. The volume of 0.05 ml may represent the average volume of a drop of blood but it should be recognized that this value is not written in stone as a constant and will vary depending upon the source of the blood.

The terminal velocity of a free-falling drop of blood is the maximum speed that the drop of blood can reach in air. This is achieved when the acceleration of the drop is offset by the effects of air resistance. MacDonell has established that for a drop size of approximately 0.05 ml, the terminal velocity of a single drop of free-falling blood is a maximum of about 25 feet per second, which would be achieved with a falling distance of about 20 feet. Smaller drop volumes would have less terminal velocity and larger drop volumes would be higher.

When a free-falling drop of blood strikes or impacts a horizontal surface it will create a more or less circular bloodstain depending upon

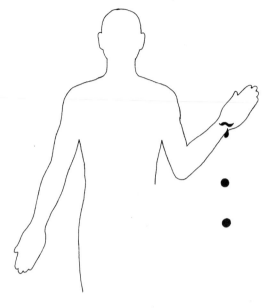

Figure 2-1 Forces on the surface of the blood drop that tend to decrease its surface area and resist penetration are referred to as surface tension.

BLOOD DROPS ASSUME A SPHERICAL

SHAPE WHEN FALLING THROUGH AIR

the nature of the surface. Upon impact with smooth, hard surfaces the surface tension of the blood drop will resist rupture, and a uniformly circular stain will be produced independent of the falling distance. Conversely, a rough-textured surface will overcome the surface tension and cohesiveness of the drop and cause it to rupture upon impact. The resultant bloodstain will exhibit distortion and irregularity in shape and may exhibit spiny edges. Spines are the pointed-edge characteristics of a bloodstain that radiate away from the center of the stain. In addition to spiny edges the stain may exhibit some peripheral spatter. It is important to understand that the degree of distortion of a bloodstain resulting from a free-falling drop is a function of the surface texture of the target rather than the distance fallen (Figure 2-2).

The diameter of the bloodstain produced by a free-falling drop of blood is a function of the volume of the drop, the distance fallen, and

16

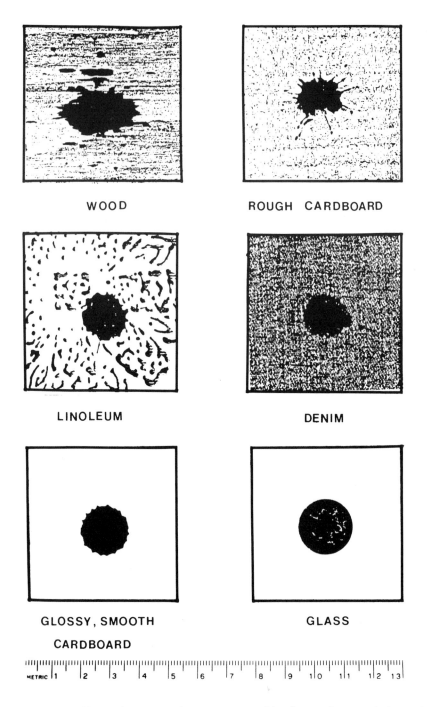

Figure 2-2 Effects of target surface textures on bloodstain characteristics and degree of spatter produced from single drops of blood that fell 12 inches.

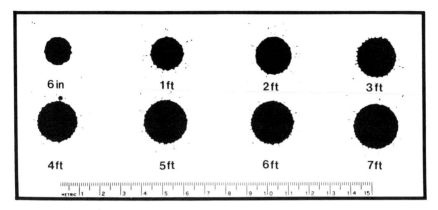

Figure 2-3 Increasing diameter of bloodstains as a function of increasing distance fallen by single drops of blood from fingertip onto smooth cardboard.

the surface texture upon which it impacts. Experimentally, it is easily demonstrated that free-falling drops of blood with an average volume of 0.05 ml will produce bloodstains of increasing diameters when allowed to drop from increasing increments of height onto hard, smooth cardboard (Figure 2-3). The measured diameters range from 13 to 21.5 mm over a dropping range of 6 inches to 7 feet. In excess of 7 feet there is no appreciable increase in diameter (Figure 2-4). Maximum diameters are achieved when the height of the blood source allows the blood drop to reach its terminal velocity. In actual practice at crime scenes, caution must be exercised when attempting to calculate the distance from which a bloodstain has originated based upon the diameter of the resultant stain since the source and thus the exact volume of the blood drop are not known. Larger than average (0.05 ml) blood drops will produce bloodstains with a greater diameter at less falling distance and produce error in interpretation. Conservative estimates based upon experimentation by the investigator that utilize similar impact surfaces and various possible sources of blood relating to the nature of the case are recommended.

From a practical point of view it is important that the investigator be able to recognize the types of bloodstains resulting from free-falling blood drops based upon their size, shape, and distribution at a crime scene and to document their locations. These bloodstains should be categorized relative to the low velocity that produced them and be related to the possible source and movement of the bleeding through recognition of trails and patterns of bloodstains produced by free-falling drops. When there are multiple free-falling drops of blood produced from a stationary source onto a horizontal surface, drip patterns will result from blood drops falling into each other. These drip patterns will

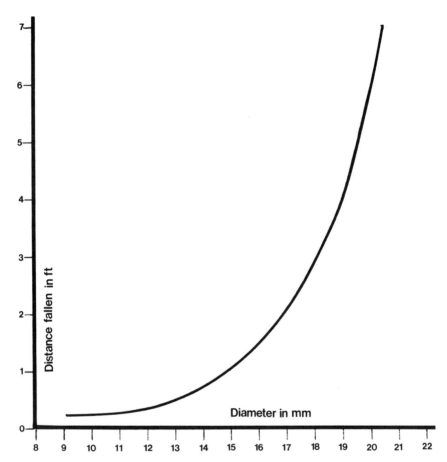

Figure 2-4 Graphical representation of the distance fallen in feet by single drops of blood from fingertip versus diameter in millimeters of bloodstains produced on smooth cardboard.

be large and irregular with small (0.1–1.0 mm), circular to oval satellite spatters in proximity to the central stain (Figures 2-5, 2-6, and 2-7). Satellite spatters are the result of smaller droplets of blood that have detached from the main blood volume at the moment of impact.

Free-Falling Drops of Blood and Drip Patterns on Nonhorizontal Surfaces—Impact Angles

The angle of impact is the internal angle at which blood strikes a target surface. Free-falling blood dropping vertically and impacting a horizontal surface will strike that surface at 90 degrees. The bloodstains produced are essentially circular and dependent upon target surface tex-

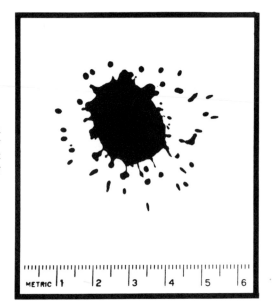

Figure 2-5 Drip pattern with satellite spatter produced by individual blood drops that fell 12 inches into each other onto smooth cardboard.

Figure 2-6 Drip pattern with satellite spatter produced by individual blood drops that fell into each other onto a hardwood floor.

Figure 2-7 Drip pattern with satellite spatter produced by individual blood drops that fell into each other onto a linoleum floor.

ture. Blood drops falling on a surface that is not horizontal will produce more oval, elongated bloodstains relative to the angle of impact. The more acute the angle of impact, the greater the elongation of the bloodstain as its width decreases and its length increases (Figure 2-8). The narrowest end of the parent bloodstain will point in the direction of travel. The angle of impact may be calculated by accurate measurement of the width and length of the bloodstain through the central axis of each dimension (Figure 2-9). Care must be exercised with these measurements especially when there is distortion due to the particular surface texture upon which the bloodstain has impacted. The calculation of the angle of impact may be determined in several ways with the use of the width and length data.

1. Determine length to width ratio (L/W). The angle of impact is determined from graphical representation of the L/W ratio versus known angles of impact from prepared standards of bloodstains (Figure 2-10).
2. Determine width to length ratio (W/L). This ratio value is utilized in the formula:

$$\text{Angle of impact} = \text{arc sin } W/L.$$

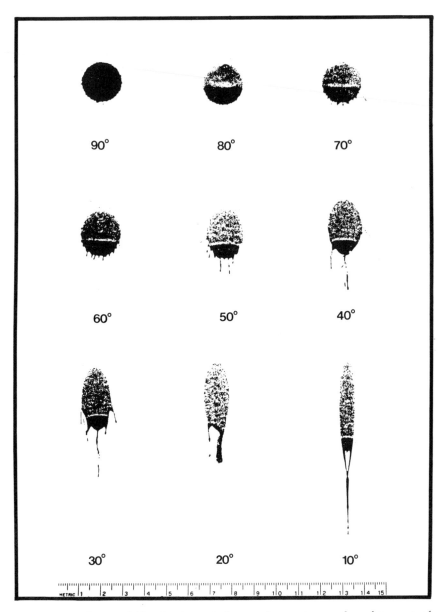

Figure 2-8 Shape of bloodstains relative to decreasing angles of impact of single blood drops falling onto smooth cardboard.

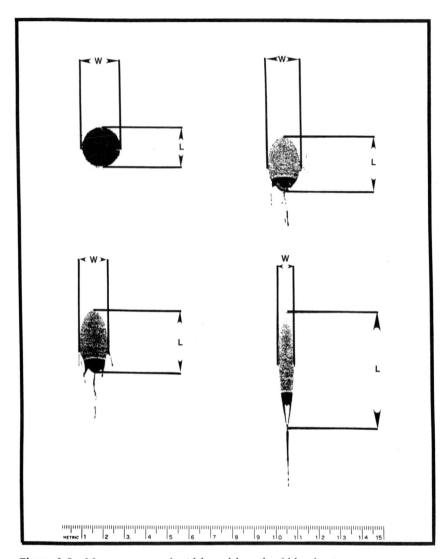

Figure 2-9   Measurement of width and length of bloodstains.

The arc sin value may be determined by use of the trigonometric tables or with the use of a scientific calculator which has the arc sin function.

The angle of impact may also be determined from graphical representation of the W/L ratio as the sine value versus known angles of impact from prepared standards of bloodstains (Figure 2-11).

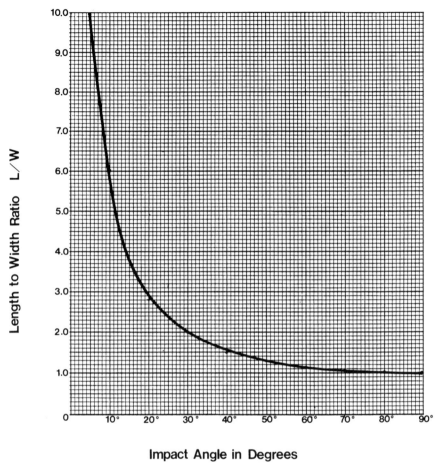

Impact Angle in Degrees

Figure 2-10   Impact angle of a bloodstain as a function of its length to width ratio.

Points of Convergence and Origin of Bloodstains

When a blood source is subjected to a force or impact, the resultant blood droplets may strike a target surface at various impact angles and lines of directionality. A point of convergence is a common point to which individual bloodstains can be traced. This point is determined by tracing the long axis of well-defined bloodstains within the pattern back to a common point or source on a surface as demonstrated in Figure 2-12. This point of convergence is a two-dimensional representation. This may be established at the scene with the use of strings

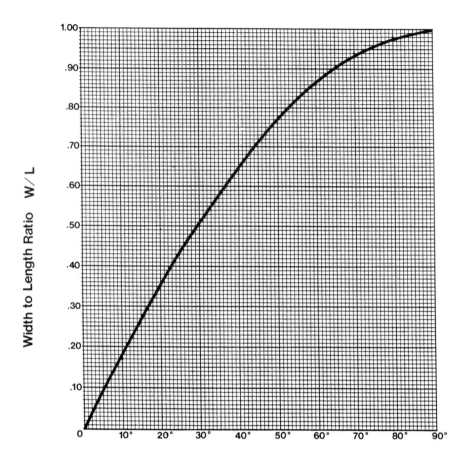

Impact Angle in Degrees

Figure 2-11   Impact angle of a bloodstain as a function of its width to length ratio (sine function).

taped to the target surface extending through the long axis of the individual bloodstains (Figure 2-13). Do not tape over the actual bloodstains, but below them. Graphical representation of the point of convergence is determined by measuring the location of the bloodstains relative to a known set of points, for example, the distance above the floor and distance from the corner of a wall with the angle of directionality on the horizontal surface of the target. Representation of typical bloodstain data including loci, width to length ratios, and impact angles is shown in Table 2-1. The convergence is then plotted on graph paper. Construction of several points of convergence may represent multiple impact sites and movement at the source of the blood.

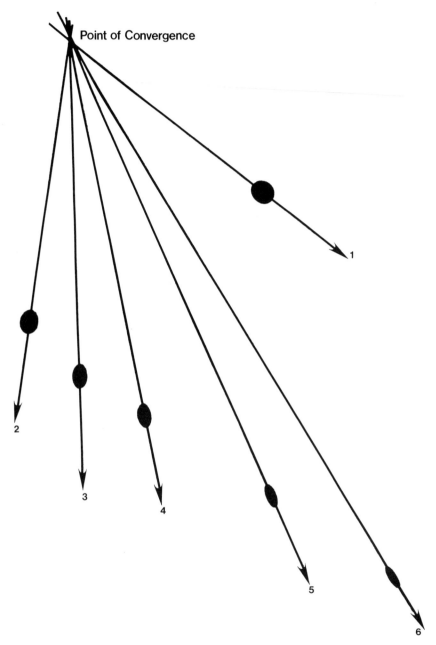

Point of Convergence

1

2

3

4

5

6

Figure 2-12 Determination of the point of convergence of bloodstains.

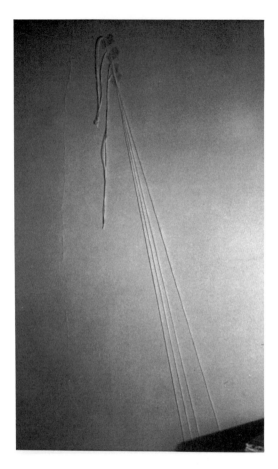

Figure 2-13 Determination of the point of convergence of bloodstains at a scene with the use of strings through the central axis of the bloodstains.

Table 2-1 Representation of Bloodstain Data on South Wall

	Distance from east wall (in)	Height from floor (in)	Width (mm)	Length (mm)	W/L ratio	Impact angle (degrees)
1.	1.0	66.0	3.5	6.0	0.58	35.0
2.	39.5	64.5	2.3	4.0	0.58	35.0
3.	38.3	62.0	2.3	4.0	0.58	35.0
4.	53.0	57.0	2.0	2.7	0.74	47.7
5.	59.0	67.5	1.8	2.5	0.72	46.0
6.	61.5	72.5	3.0	6.8	0.44	26.0
7.	80.0	75.0	2.8	6.0	0.46	27.8
8.	90.5	79.0	2.5	6.0	0.42	24.6
9.	42.0	43.0	2.5	3.2	0.78	51.0
10.	42.5	41.5	2.5	3.2	0.78	51.0

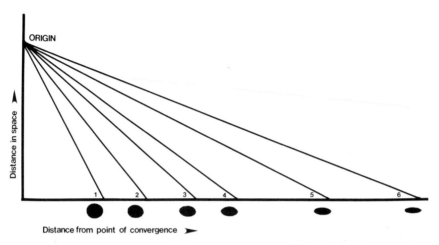

Figure 2-14   Determination of the point of origin of bloodstains by projection of impact angles.

    The point of origin is the location from which the blood that produced a bloodstain originated. This is determined by projecting angles of impact of well-defined bloodstains back to an axis constructed through the established point of convergence (Figure 2-14). At the scene, strings can be projected from each measured bloodstain at its angle of impact back to an axis perpendicular to the plane on which the bloodstains are located and passing through their point of convergence (Figure 2-15). The area of convergence of the strings on this axis will represent in three dimensions a point or points in space from which the bloodstains could have originated. The point of origin may be constructed graphically by plotting the distance from the point of convergence of the bloodstains with their angle of impact on the target surface. The determined point of origin by either method could represent the height above a floor or the distance from a wall, ceiling, or other object to the source of the blood or impact site. When conclusions are drawn a range of possible impact sites should be expressed. Blood droplets have their individual trajectories traveling from impact site to target surface depending upon velocity and distance traveled. When points of origin are determined a range of possible flight paths should be considered that could produce the same angle of impact. Shorter travel distances and higher velocities of blood droplets tend to produce straighter lines of trajectory. Impossible points of origin can also be established which may assist with the reconstruction of the scene and either confirm or refute the description of events by a suspect.

Figure 2-15 Determination of the point of origin of bloodstains at a scene by the projection of impact angles with the use of strings.

Angular Impact Produced by Horizontal Motion

When blood drops are subjected to a force producing horizontal motion as well as the downward effect of gravity, they may have angular impact on vertical or horizontal surfaces. Angle of impact may be established by the width to length ratios on both surfaces by the methods described. Directionality may usually be determined by the stain shape and edge characteristics. A bleeding person in a fast walk or run would provide the source of blood with sufficient horizontal motion to allow the falling drops to impact a horizontal surface such as a floor at an impact angle of less than 90 degrees. A series of bloodstains resulting from free-falling blood drops traveling in a particular direction with some horizontal motion may show a scalloped edge on the side indicating the direction of travel of the source (Figure 2-16). A bleeding person in a slow walk may produce nearly round drops of blood, and directionality based upon edge characteristics of the bloodstains therefore may not be obvious. Vertical surfaces such as walls may receive angular impact when the surface is in proximity to these falling drops. If the source of blood is not an active bleeding site, the quantity of blood available for dripping is limited and the distance of the trail pattern

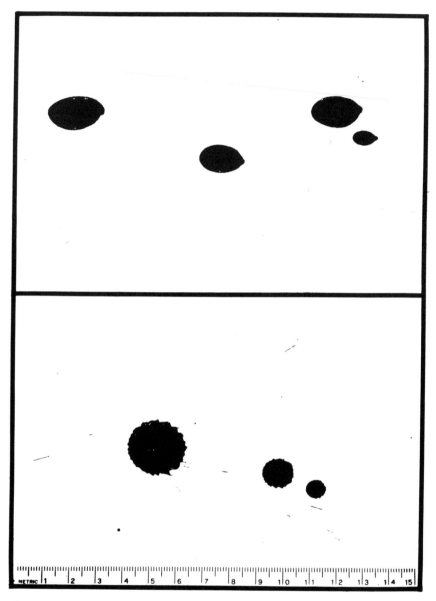

Figure 2-16 Examples of blood drops that fell with horizontal motion left to right onto smooth cardboard.

will be short. This applies to bloody weapons carried from the scene by an assailant.

With sufficient horizontal force or motion, a falling blood drop may rupture upon impact and cast off smaller droplets. The resultant

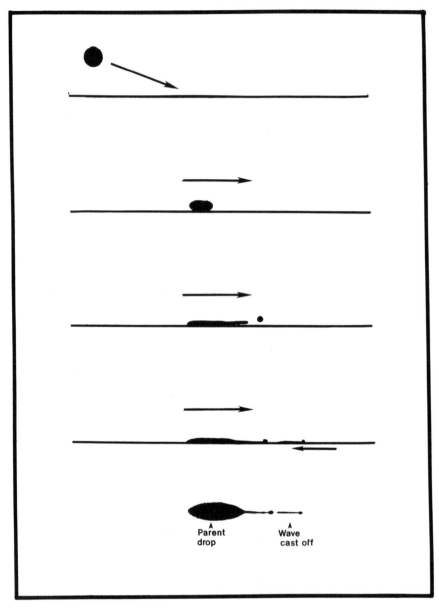

Figure 2-17 Dynamics of wave cast-off formation by a blood drop. The tail of the parent drop points in its direction of travel whereas the tail of the wave cast-off points back to the parent drop.

smaller stains or spatter appear as long, narrow streaks which will point in the direction of the parent drop rather than the direction of their travel. The edge characteristics of the parent drop will show the direction of travel. These smaller droplets are referred to as wave cast-offs, which originate from a parent drop due to the wavelike action of the liquid, in conjunction with striking a target surface at an angle of less than 90 degrees (Figure 2-17).

Splashed, Projected, and Cast-Off Blood

When a quantity of blood in excess of 0.1 ml is subjected to minor or low-velocity impact or is allowed to fall to a surface, a splashed blood-stain pattern will be produced. Splashed bloodstain patterns usually have a large, central area with peripheral spatter appearing as elongated, more oval than round spots (Figure 2-18). This is in contrast to patterns produced by blood dripping into itself where the circular spots predominate.

Secondary blood splashing or ricochet may occur as a result of the deflection of large volumes of blood after impact on a target surface to another target surface. When sufficient blood has been produced, splash patterns may be produced by movement of victim or assailant. These patterns are often produced when pools of blood are disturbed by objects such as a shod foot stepping into blood or by large volumes of blood falling from a source such as a victim's wound. Larger quantities of splashed blood will create more spatter.

Quantities of blood in excess of 0.1 ml acted upon by a force other than low-velocity impact is referred to as projected blood. When blood of sufficient volume is projected horizontally or vertically downward exceeding the gravitational forces, the edges of the resultant blood-stains have numerous, spinelike projections with narrow streaking of the secondary spatter (Figure 2-19). Vomiting of blood is an example of projected blood in large volume. Blood may also be projected from a source or pool by movement of victim or assailant during a phase of violent activity. Movement of a heavy object through a pooled blood source may cause projection of large quantities of blood onto a surface.

Blood exiting the body under pressure as a result of a cut or breached artery is a form of projected blood and is referred to as arterial gushing or spurting. The resulting bloodstain patterns on floors, walls, and other surfaces and objects are very characteristic and identified by their appearance and shape. Frequently, arterial gush patterns appear as clusters of large spots and drip patterns where excess blood has formed flow patterns depending upon the inclination of the target surface (Figures

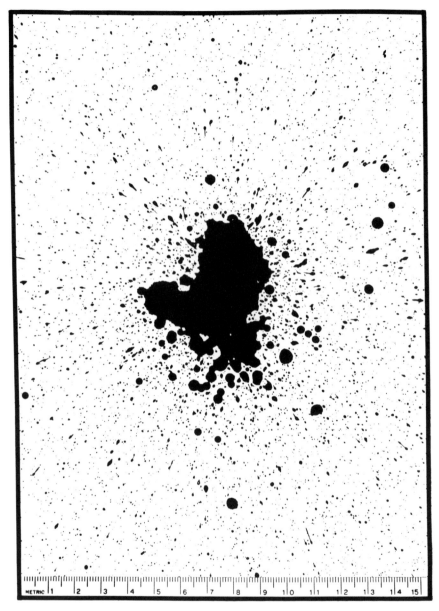

Figure 2-18 Bloodstain pattern produced by 1 ml of blood that fell 72 inches onto smooth cardboard.

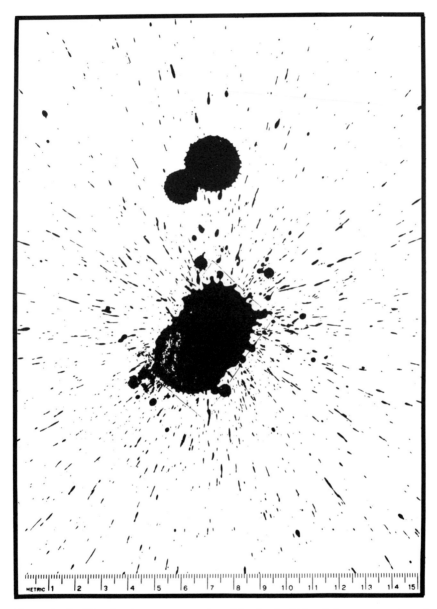

Figure 2-19 Bloodstain pattern produced by 1 ml of blood that was projected downward 36 inches onto smooth cardboard.

Figure 2-20   Arterial spurt bloodstain pattern on wall produced by victim who sustained stab wounds of chest and arms.

2-20, 2-21, and 2-22). In some cases fluctuations of arterial blood pressure may be identified by spurts within the pattern and may bear resemblance to an electrocardiogram tracing. Observation of the distinct bright red color of oxygenated arterial blood may be helpful to discern arterial gush patterns.

Arterial spurt patterns are frequently present at violent scenes where cutting and stabbing injuries have occurred. Arteries in the head area may be traumatized as a result of blunt force injury. An assailant's person and clothing may receive considerable bloodstaining from arterial sources. In death cases where an accidental fall has occurred the scene may be extremely bloody because of the spurting of blood from a cut temporal artery. The resulting patterns of blood may arouse suspicion of foul play unless correctly interpreted.

Cast-off blood patterns occur when blood is projected onto a surface from an object other than the impact site. These patterns are created when blood is flung from a bloody object in motion, such as a beating instrument, owing to a whiplike action (Figure 2-23). A distinction should be made between these cast-off patterns and wave cast-off droplets originating from a parent drop of blood.

In many blunt trauma cases the weapon (crowbar, bat, pipe, fist, etc.) is swung at the victim repeatedly. Once blood has been produced it

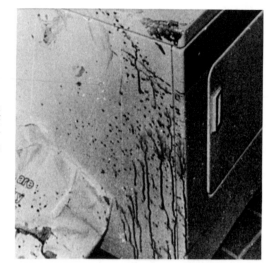

Figure 2-21 Arterial spurt bloodstain pattern on side of clothes dryer produced by victim who sustained stab wounds of chest.

Figure 2-22 Arterial spurt pattern on door of motel produced by victim who sustained stab wounds of the chest including penetration of the heart.

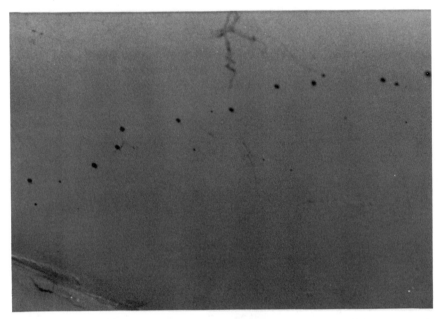

Figure 2-23 Cast-off bloodstain pattern on ceiling produced by overhead swing of blunt weapon during beating of victim.

will adhere to the weapon in varying degrees depending upon the type of weapon and the quantity of blood at the site of injury. During the back swing away from the victim, the blood on the weapon will be thrown off and travel tangentially to the arc of the swing and will impact on nearby surfaces such as walls, ceilings, floors, and other objects in its path. Little blood is cast off during the course of the downward or return swing of the weapon. The initial blood that is cast off from a weapon during the arc of the back swing may strike a target surface and produce circular stains at 90 degrees such as on an overhead ceiling or a nearby wall depending upon the plane of the arc. As the back swing continues the remainder of the blood is cast off a greater distance and will produce more oval-shaped stains due to the angular impact. The size of these cast-off stains is generally in the range of 4–8 mm although they may be larger or smaller depending upon the type of weapon, amount of blood, and forcefulness and length of the arc of the swing. The cast-off bloodstain patterns are often seen as uniformly distributed trails on the impacting surface with the more elongated stains most distant from the source. Determination of the angle of impact and convergence of these cast-off bloodstains will permit projection back to the source of the blood relative to the position of the victim and assailant.

If there are multiple cast-off patterns present, an estimation of the minimum number of blows struck may be made. The number of distinct patterns or trails of cast-off stains would equal the minimum number of blows struck plus one since the first blow generally does not produce sufficient blood on the weapon to produce cast-off droplets. If more than one blow was struck on the same plane, the cast-off patterns may overlap, which is the reason only a minimum number of blows struck may be estimated.

Sometimes the location of cast-off blood patterns may indicate in which hand the weapon was held while being swung. This interpretation should be made with caution with the possibility of two-handed or backhanded delivery in mind.

Other Bloodstain Patterns Associated with Low-Velocity Force

Flow patterns of blood indicate the direction of travel of blood from a source on a victim or other surface that may terminate in a larger quantity referred to as a pool of blood. Flow patterns and pooling of blood are important to recognize for they may yield important information regarding movement of a victim during bloodshed as well as postmortem movement or disturbance of the body and alteration of scene of the death. Flow patterns may be observed on the body or clothing of a victim as well as the surface upon which the victim is found (floor, bed, chair, etc.). Their directionality is governed by gravity unless impeded by an obstruction (Figures 2-24, 2-25, 2-26, 2-27 and 2-28). Inconsistencies of blood flow patterns on the victim's body or clothing relative to the observed position of the victim are easily recognized and may indicate movement of the victim after injury or death (Figure 2-29). The amount of pooling of blood near the victim in association with the blood flow patterns on the victim should be studied with respect to injuries sustained (Figure 2-30). This will help determine whether the victim sustained the injuries in the present scene or was perhaps moved from another location after injury or death.

A smudge is a bloodstain that has been altered or distorted by contact with a nonbloody surface so that further classification of the stain is not possible. However, recognition of smudges of blood may indicate movement of victim or assailant.

A wipe pattern is characterized as a bloodstain created when an object moves through an existing wet bloodstain thereby removing blood from the original stain and altering its appearance (Figure 2-31). The nature of the object producing wipes may be characterized by careful observation of the bloodstain pattern produced such as hand, finger, fabric, etc.

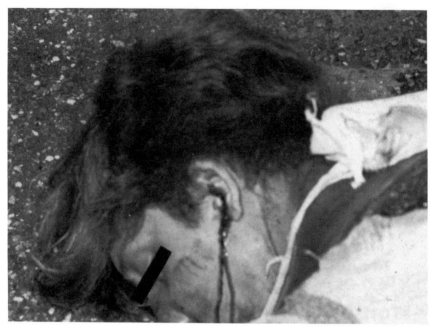

Figure 2-24 Blood flow pattern from ear of victim who sustained fatal skull fractures and brain injury. The flow pattern is consistent with the observed position of the victim on the ground.

Figure 2-25 Blood flow patterns associated with knife wound in back and bleeding from mouth resulting from injured lung consistent with the stabbing occurring in the observed location.

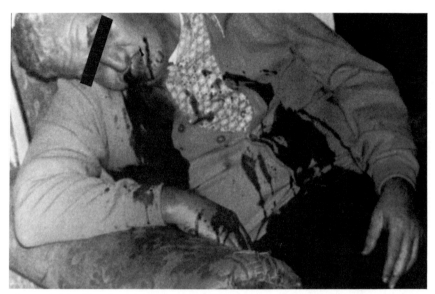

Figure 2-26 Blood projection and flow pattern on chest of victim who sustained two gunshot wounds of the face while sitting in chair. Note the evidence of head movement from left to right after bleeding commenced.

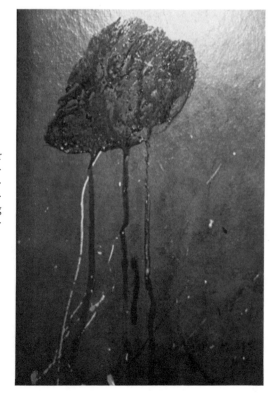

Figure 2-27 Blood transfer and flow pattern on wall produced by contact with bleeding shoulder of gunshot victim as he was descending down stairs prior to fatal collapse.

Figure 2-28 Blood flow patterns created by victim of stabbing leaning against his truck prior to collapsing on ground.

Figure 2-29 Blood flow patterns on rear of jacket and side of face of gunshot victim which are not consistent with his observed position on front seat of vehicle.

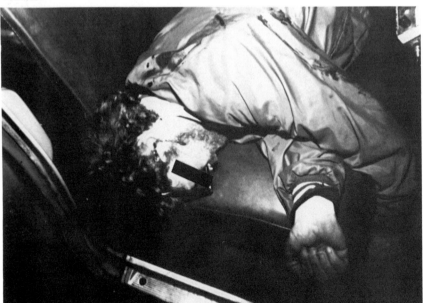

Figure 2-30 Large accumulation and pooling of blood on floor consistent with considerable blood loss in this area. Victim was not moved after fatal injury.

Figure 2-31 Bloodstain pattern resulting from pooling of blood in corner of room with subsequent movement of victim to another location. Note feathering of bloodstain towards foreground.

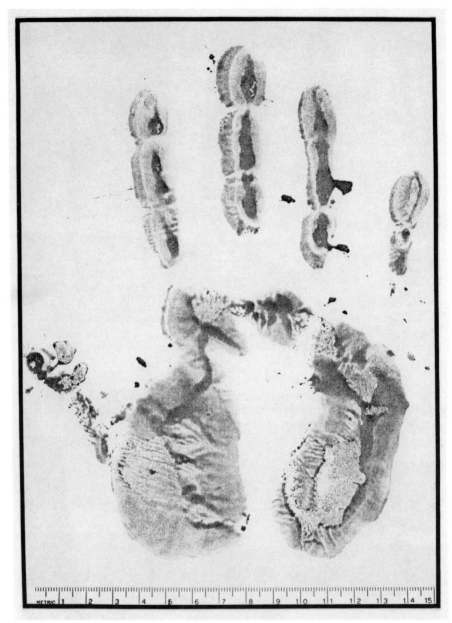

Figure 2-32   Right palmprint transfer in blood produced on smooth cardboard.

A transfer blood pattern is a contact bloodstain created when a wet, bloody surface contacts a secondary surface. A recognizable mirror image of the original surface or a portion of that surface may be produced. Common examples of transfer blood patterns are handprints or fingerprints on walls or doors or other objects, shoeprints or footprints

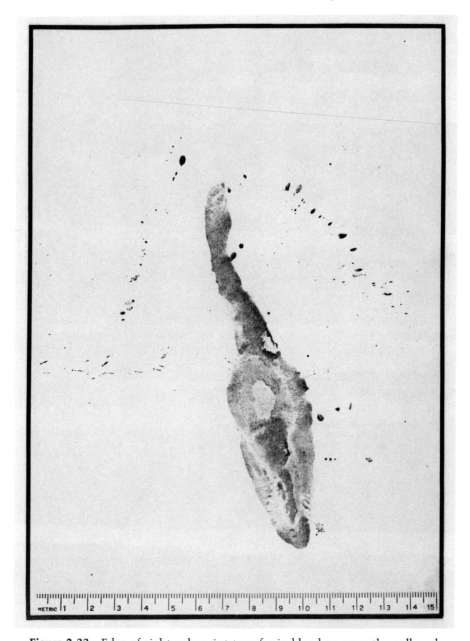

Figure 2-33 Edge of right palmprint transfer in blood on smooth cardboard.

on floors, fabric patterns on various objects, and transfer patterns of bloody weapons such as knives on clothing. Class and/or individual characteristics may be determined from certain transfer blood patterns (Figures 2-32 through 2-45). Bloody hair swipes are a frequent type of transfer blood pattern (Figures 2-46 and 2-47). Smudges, wipes, and

Figure 2-34 Partially smudged handprints in blood around light switches in bathroom produced by assailant after stabbing victim in adjoining motel room.

Figure 2-35 Partial fingerprints transferred in blood on door of motel in same case as Figure 2-34.

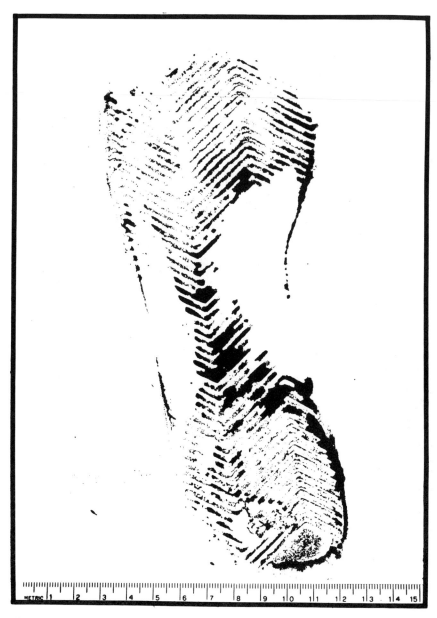

Figure 2-36 Left shoeprint transfer in blood onto smooth cardboard.

Figure 2-37 Partial shoeprint of assailant in blood at scene within chalked body outline of victim.

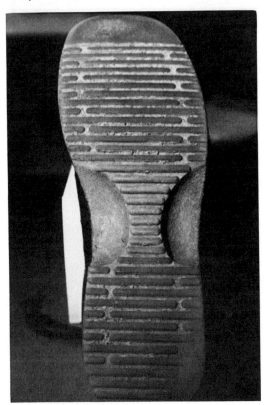

Figure 2-38 Sole of left shoe of suspected assailant in same case as Figure 2-37.

Figure 2-39 Test print in blood of left shoe of assailant produced on identical surface showing similarity to shoeprint in Figure 2-37.

Figure 2-40 Transfer pattern in blood on carpet of partial sneaker shoeprint located near victim at scene of blunt force homicide.

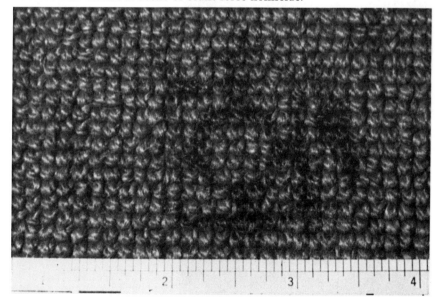

Figure 2-41 Comparison of sneaker tread similar to blood transfer pattern on carpet at scene of Figure 2-40.

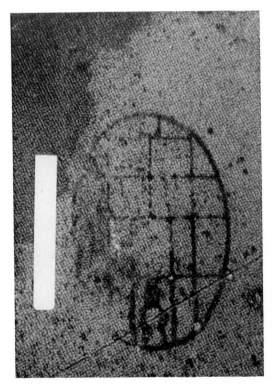

Figure 2-42 Transfer pattern in blood on carpet located near victim of blunt force homicide. Victim was nightwatchman at department store.

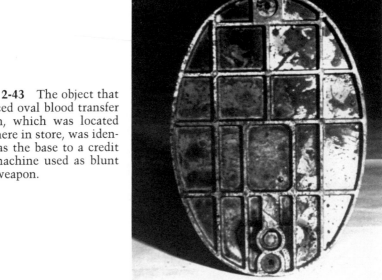

Figure 2-43 The object that produced oval blood transfer pattern, which was located elsewhere in store, was identified as the base to a credit card machine used as blunt force weapon.

Figure 2-44 Transfer of fabric pattern in blood on to bedspread at scene of homicide.

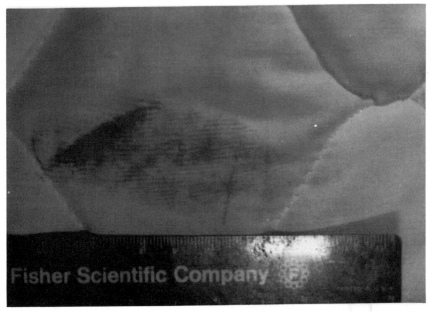

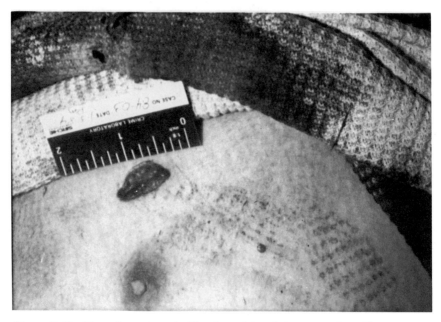

Figure 2-45 Transfer pattern in blood on skin of victim produced by victim's shirt when it was moved after blood had partially dried.

Figure 2-46 Bloodstain pattern produced by transfer of blood from bloody hair when the victim's head was moved across the wall surface.

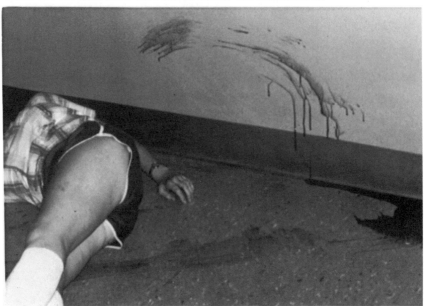

Figure 2-47 Bloodstain pattern on rear seat of vehicle resulting from transport of victim with head injuries. Note hair swipe pattern in upper right area of rear seat.

Figure 2-48 Transfer bloodstain on interior door handle of assailant's vehicle which was identified as victim's blood.

Figure 2-49   Transfer bloodstains on gas pedal of assailant vehicle resulting from contact with shoe of assailant after stepping in blood at the scene of homicide.

transfer blood patterns of victim's blood are frequently created in an assailant's automobile while leaving the scene. Door handles, steering wheel, gearshift apparatus, and floor pedals should be examined carefully when conducting a search of suspect vehicles (Figures 2-48 and 2-49).

Bloodstain Patterns Produced by Medium-Velocity Impact

When a strong force impacts upon an exposed source of blood, the blood is broken up into many small droplets as a result of being subjected to this increased energy. When these droplets strike a target surface they produce bloodstain patterns that are easily distinguishable from patterns produced by dripped, projected, splashed, and cast-off bloodstain patterns, all of which are associated with low-velocity force or impact.

Medium-velocity impact spatter consists of bloodstains produced on a surface when the blood source has been subjected to a force at a velocity between approximately 5 and 25 feet per second. This velocity applies to the impacting object rather than to the speed of the blood droplets in motion. The size of the individual bloodstains produced is usually within the range of 1–4 mm in diameter although smaller and larger bloodstains are not uncommon (Figure 2-50). Directionality, convergence, angle of impact, and origin of these bloodstains are determined by the location and geometry of the stains within the patterns

Figure 2-50   Medium-velocity blood spatter that has impacted onto a vertical smooth cardboard surface at 90 degrees.

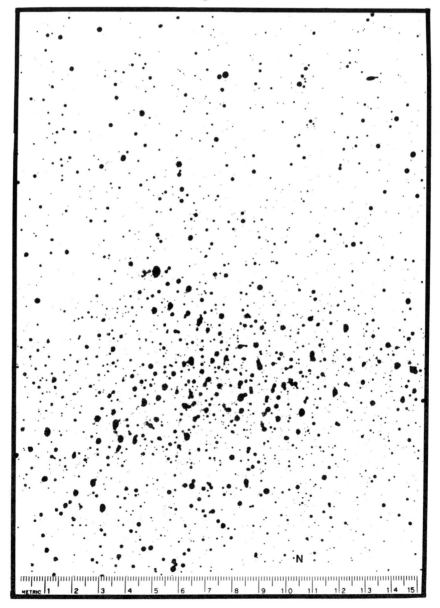

Figure 2-51 Medium-velocity blood spatter that has impacted onto a horizontal smooth cardboard surface creating angular impact.

produced (Figures 2-51 and 2-52). Blows administered to a victim with a blunt instrument (fists, club, hammer, rock, etc.), as well as sharp objects such as knives and axes, will produce medium-velocity blood spatter once a blood source has been exposed (Figure 2-53). A single blow usually is not sufficient to produce significant blood spatter except perhaps in the case of massive crushing injury. The source of blood must be exposed when receiving the impact in order to create spatter.

The study of the distribution of medium-velocity bloodstain patterns and determination of the directionality and origin of the individual bloodstains may determine the relative position of the assailant and victim at the time the blows were delivered. Radial patterns of blood spatter produced by medium-velocity impact are common and are distributed in a fashion not unlike the spokes of a wheel. If the victim is on a floor or other surface during the course of a beating, the spatter may be observed radiating away from the area of impact producing streaking patterns on the victim and floor and impacting at a

Figure 2-52 Medium-velocity blood spatter and arterial spurt pattern on file cabinets produced by severe beating of victim on floor. Note the radial distribution of the blood spatter diverging away from the corner of the file cabinet on two adjacent surfaces.

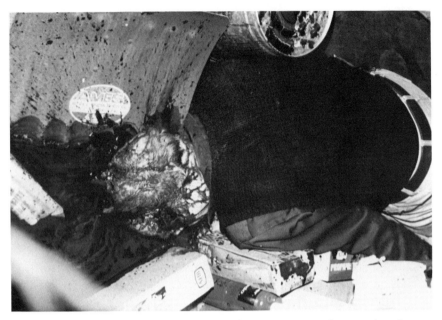

Figure 2-53 Medium-velocity blood spatter on surface of snow shovel converging to area of the head of victim who was beaten on floor in this area.

low level on nearby walls or other objects within range. Sometimes a sector or portion of the radial pattern will appear free of blood. This clean area may represent interception of the blood spatter by the assailant. During events of this type the assailant usually receives significant blood spatter on shoes, trousers, shirt, and other garments. Experience has shown that other objects worn by an assailant may contain blood spatter that may not be apparent to a person attempting to wash bloody clothing to obscure involvement in a homicide. Examples of this are socks, belts, hats, glasses, watches, and other jewelry items. Weapons should also be carefully examined for evidence of medium-velocity blood spatter.

Blood spatter on clothing should be examined carefully especially with respect to estimation of impact angle and spot size. Fabrics can alter the appearance and size of bloodstains. R.B. White researched bloodstain patterns on fabrics and published an article in 1986 entitled "The Effect of Drop Volume, Dropping Height and Impact Angle." Evaluation of bloodstain patterns on clothing is enhanced by dressing the clothing on a manikin for proper orientation and directionality. Blood spatter on clothing may be obscured by the presence of other blood patterns. Also, dark clothing, especially blue jeans, may hinder evaluation of small blood spots due to the lack of contrast. The use of a stereomicroscope is helpful in many cases.

It should be recognized that events other than beatings can produce medium-velocity-sized blood spatter at a crime scene. The slapping of a hand or other object in a blood source and coughing and wheezing of blood frequently produce blood spatter. The occurrence of these events can often be recognized and distinguished appropriately during careful examination of the entire scene, the victim's injuries, and clothing. The investigator should be alerted for the presence of bloodstain patterns resulting from coughing and exhalation of blood in those cases where the victim has sustained injuries of the mouth, nose, sinus cavities, and lungs (Figures 2-54, 2-55, and 2-56).

Conclusions should be considered carefully when there are a limited number of small bloodstains available for evaluation. It is also critical to evaluate an entire bloodstain pattern when evaluating the origin of blood spatters. Frequently, a small area of spatter may be the result of blood dripping into itself or a larger pool producing satellite spots. These spatters could be misinterpreted if the entire pattern were not considered.

Figure 2-54 Victim who sustained gunshot wound which entered left bridge of nose near inner canthus of left eye and exited near inner canthus of right eye.

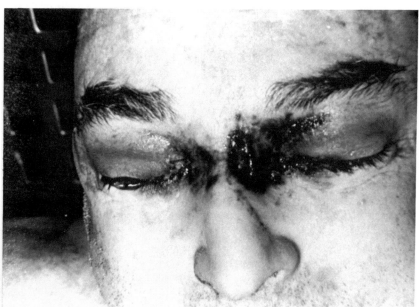

58

Figure 2-55 Victim of gunshot wound described in Figure 2-54 left blood-stains on the wall at the scene and on front of his shirt that were created by the coughing and wheezing of blood due to severe sinus trauma. The cause of death was attributed to a second gunshot which entered the left side of the brain.

Figure 2-56 Closer view of upper left front shirt of victim shown in Figure 2-55 showing detail of bloodstain pattern produced by wheezing and coughing of blood.

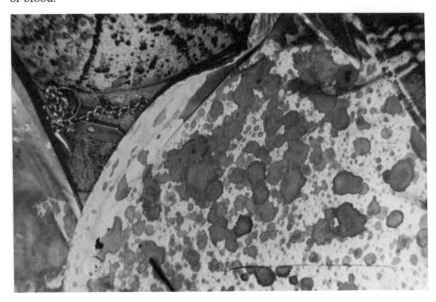

Bloodstain Patterns Produced by High-Velocity Impact

A bloodstain pattern produced by high-velocity impact is characterized by the presence of high-velocity blood spatter. A high-velocity impact is considered to be approximately 100 feet per second or greater. Many of the blood droplets produced by this type of impact are extremely small and create a mistlike dispersion, and because of their low density travel only a short distance (2–3 feet) through the air. Individual bloodstains within a high-velocity pattern are usually 0.1 mm or smaller in diameter but are frequently seen in association with larger bloodstains in the medium-velocity range of size (Figure 2-57). The larger droplets of course will travel a greater distance owing to their higher density. Because of their relatively small size, care must be taken when observing and measuring high-velocity bloodstains for directionality and impact angles. A pocket microscope or other magnifying device with a scale in tenths of millimeters is very useful.

At crime scenes, evidence of high-velocity blood spatter is most frequently associated with gunshot injury but is seen also in cases involving power tool and machinery injuries as well as in some automobile accidents. When a victim has sustained gunshot injury there may be evidence of backspatter from the entrance wound and forward spatter associated with the exit wound if one exits. Backspatter results from blood droplets directed back towards the source of energy, in other words, the weapon. It may be deposited on skin, clothing, or any object or surface near the entrance wound relative to the position of the victim at the time of discharge of the firearm. Backspatter may also be deposited on the firearm and the exposed hand, shirt cuff, or arm of an assailant holding the weapon if it is discharged at contact or close range. If there is an exposed source of blood such as may be the case with multiple gunshot wounds, muzzle to target distances of up to 6 inches may produce significant backspatter. Shooting into exposed blood will increase the quantity of backspatter but the distance it will travel will still be limited to 2–3 feet. In cases of possible self-inflicted gunshot injury, the hands and arms of the victim, and the weapon should be carefully examined for evidence of high-velocity blood spatter that may indicate the position of the hands on the weapon at the time of discharge of the firearm (Figures 2-58 and 2-59).

Forward spatter is produced by blood droplets traveling in the same direction as the source of energy and in gunshot cases is usually associated with the exit wound (Figures 2-60 and 2-61). An exception to this would be a shoring or furrowing projectile path on a peripheral area of the body where a true exit wound is not apparent. The demonstration of the presence of high-velocity forward spatter will assist in the location of the victim at the time of discharge of the weapon. When a projectile has reentered a body after passing through a hand or arm, there will likely be high-velocity forward spatter around the periphery

Figure 2-57 High-velocity blood spatter that has impacted on a vertical smooth cardboard surface at 90 degrees.

Figure 2-58 Self-inflicted gunshot wound of forehead sustained by victim sitting in vehicle. High-velocity backspatter of blood present on dorsal surface of right hand close to muzzle of firearm. Blood flow pattern on right cheek was produced when head was in a more upright position.

of the reentry wound, and its presence will help reconstruct the position of the victim at the time of weapon discharge.

The quantity and distribution of high-velocity blood spatter whether it be forward or backspatter varies considerably depending upon many factors. Usually, when there is an exit wound the amount of forward spatter will exceed that of backspatter. The amount of backspatter is affected by the type of weapon and ammunition, muzzle to target distance, and anatomic features of the wound site. Stephens and Allen in 1983 documented factors affecting amount of backspatter experimentally. They noted that backspatter may be completely absent with considerable muzzle to target distances. With respect to shotguns and high-powered firearms a greater quantity of high-velocity blood spatter would be expected especially when the weapon is discharged at close or contact range. The quantity of back- and forward high-velocity blood spatter is also reduced by the blocking effect of hair and clothing including hats and or other headgear worn by a victim. Pex and Vaughan in 1987 conducted further experiments with backspatter and applied their findings to actual case investigation where backspatter

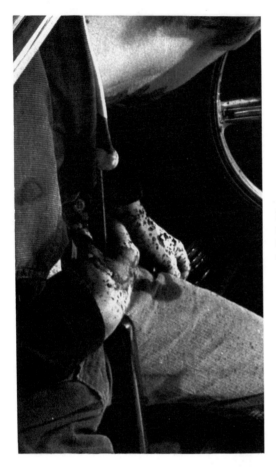

Figure 2-59 Detailed view of backspatter on each hand of gunshot victim in vehicle described in Figure 2-58.

was identified on the sleeve of suspects. Their work also corroborated the work of Stephens and others.

Another phenomenon associated with contact and close-range gunshot injury is the drawback effect. This is the presence in the barrel of a firearm of blood that has been drawn backward due to the effect of the discharged gasses accompanying the projectile. Original research in this area was conducted by MacDonell and Brooks in 1977 and it was demonstrated that the depth of penetration of blood into the muzzle of a firearm was a function of the caliber of the weapon and the discharge distance.

It should be obvious that the examination of firearms for blood both on the outside surface and within the barrel should be conducted prior to handling and test firing of the weapon in question.

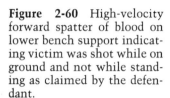 **Figure 2-60** High-velocity forward spatter of blood on lower bench support indicating victim was shot while on ground and not while standing as claimed by the defendant.

Figure 2-61 High-velocity forward spatter of blood on interior roof of van around exit hole produced by shotgun slug which passed through left upper shoulder of suicide victim in driver's seat. The shot was discharged against the lower right abdomen.

Significance of Partially Dried and Clotted Bloodstains

A blood clot is formed by a complex mechanism involving the plasma protein fibrinogen, platelets, and other clotting factors. It is observed visually as a network of fibrous material (fibrin and red blood cells). Subsequently, the blood clot begins to retract causing a separation of the remaining liquid portion which is referred to as serum (Figure 2-62). Blood clots and serum stains surrounding them as well as the degree of observed drying of blood should be recognized as important information at crime scenes. Occasionally, events take place after blood has been shed and has begun the clotting process. Bloodstain patterns produced by partially clotted or clotted blood indicate a time interval between the bloodshed and the activity producing the pattern (Figure 2-63). This interval may be short or extended depending upon the degree of clotting, source and quantity of blood, and environmental conditions existing at the time. An average time of 3–15 minutes for blood to commence clotting outside the body may be used as a guideline for a minimal interval. Examples of the significance of partially clotted or clotted bloodstain patterns are:

1. Clotted blood spatter on victim's clothing and/or surrounding surfaces associated with a beating death may indicate a significant

Figure 2-62 Appearance of clotted blood on wood surface. Note shiny appearance of serum, retraction of central blood clot, and drying of bloodstain around edges.

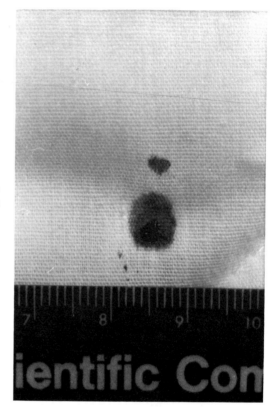

Figure 2-63 Close-up view of spatter of clotted blood on fabric.

interval between blows administered and possibly postmortem infliction of injury.

2. Clotted bloodstain patterns associated with a pedestrian victim on a roadway may indicate an interval between impacts associated with more than a single vehicle.

3. Coughing up of clotted blood by victim may be associated with postinjury survival time.

An estimation of the degree of blood clotting and drying of pools of blood associated with a victim, when used in conjunction with other signs of postmortem change, may be helpful in the determination of the postmortem interval or in substantiating postmortem movement of the victim. Estimations of degree of clotting and drying time of blood at crime scenes must be reproduced experimentally using freshly drawn human blood of similar volume placed on an identical surface with similar environmental conditions existing during the experiment as were observed at the scene. Estimates of this interval should be made with caution.

As bloodstains increase in age, they progress through a series of color changes from red to reddish brown and eventually to dark brown and black. This change of color is attributable to alterations in the hemoglobin of the blood. A particular environment will affect the sequence and duration of color changes in bloodstains. Therefore, estimations of the age of bloodstains based upon their color at the scene should be very conservative.

References

1. Balthazard, V., Piedelievre, R., Desoille, H., and DeRobert, L. 1939. Etude des gouttes de sang projecte. Presented at the 22nd Congress of Forensic Medicine, Paris, France.
2. Bevel, T. 1983. Geometric bloodstain interpretation. *FBI Law Enforcement Bulletin*. Office of Congressional and Public Affairs, Vol. 52, No. 5, pp. 7–10, May.
3. DeForest, P.R., Gaensslen, R.E., and Lee, H.C. 1983. *Forensic Science—An Introduction to Criminalistics*, pp. 295–308. New York: McGraw-Hill.
4. Kirk, P.L. 1967. "Blood—A Neglected Criminalistics Research Area." In *Law Enforcement Science and Technology*. Vol. 1, pp. 267–272. London: Academic Press.
5. ———. 1955. Affidavit regarding state of Ohio vs. Samuel Sheppard. Court of Common Pleas, Criminal Branch. No. 64571, April 26.
6. ———. 1974. *Crime Investigation*. 2nd Edition, pp. 167–181. New York: John Wiley & Sons.
7. Laber, T.L. 1985. Diameter of a bloodstain as a function of origin, distance fallen and volume of drop. *I.A.B.P.A. News*. Vol. 2, No. 1, pp. 12–16.
8. Laber, T.L., and Epstein, B.P. 1983. *Bloodstain Pattern Analysis*. Minneapolis, MN: Callan Publishing Co., Inc.
9. Lee, H.C., Gaensslen, R.E., and Pagliaro, E.M. 1986. Bloodstain volume estimation. *I.A.B.P.A. News*. Vol. 3, No. 2, pp. 47–54.
10. LeRoy, H.A., 1983. Bloodstain pattern interpretation. *Identification Newsletter of the Canadian Identification Society*, January.
11. MacDonell, H.L. 1971. Interpretation of bloodstains: Physical considerations. *Legal Medicine Annual*, Cyril Wecht, Ed., pp. 91–136. New York: Appleton-Century-Crofts.
12. MacDonell, H.L. 1977. Preserving bloodstain evidence at crime scenes. *Law and Order*, Vol. 25, pp. 66–69, April.
13. MacDonell, H.L. 1977. Reconstruction of a homicide. *Law and Order*, Vol. 25, No. 7, pp. 26–31, July.
14. MacDonell, H.L. 1981. Criminalistics—bloodstain examination. *Forensic Sciences*, Vol. 3, Cyril Wecht, Ed., pp. 37-1–37-26. New York: Mathew Bender.
15. MacDonell, H.L. 1982. Bloodstain pattern interpretation. Laboratory of Forensic Science, Corning, New York.
16. MacDonell, H.L., and Bialousz, L. 1971. Flight characteristics and stain patterns of human blood. United States Department of Justice, Law Enforcement Assistance Administration, Washington, D.C.
17. ———. 1973. Laboratory manual on the geometric interpretation of human bloodstain evidence. Laboratory of Forensic Sciences, Corning, New York.

18. MacDonell, H.L., and Brooks, B. 1977. "Detection and Significance of Blood in Firearms." In *Legal Medicine Annual*, Cyril Wecht, Ed., pp. 185–199. New York: Appleton-Century-Crofts.
19. MacDonell, H.L., and Panchou, C. 1979. Bloodstain pattern interpretation. *Identification News*, Vol. 29, pp. 3–5, February.
20. MacDonell, H.L., and Panchou, C. 1979. Bloodstain patterns on human skin. *Journal of the Canadian Society of Forensic Science*, Vol. 12., No. 3, pp. 134–141, September.
21. Pex, J.O., and Vaughan, C.H. 1987. Observations of high velocity blood spatter on adjacent objects. *Journal of Forensic Sciences*, Vol. 32, No. 6, pp. 1587–1594, November.
22. Pizzola, P.A., Roth, S., and DeForest, P.R. 1986. Blood droplet dynamics—I. *Journal of Forensic Sciences*, Vol. 31, No. 1, pp. 36–49, January.
23. ———. 1986. Blood droplet dynamics—II. *Journal of Forensic Sciences*, Vol. 31, No. 1, pp. 50–64, January.
24. Stephens, B.G., and Allen, T.B. 1983. Backspatter of blood from gunshot wounds—observations and experimental simulation. *Journal of Forensic Sciences*, Vol. 28, No. 2, pp. 437–439, April.
25. White, R.B. 1986. Bloodstain patterns on fabrics—The effect of drop volume, dropping height, and impact angle. *Journal of the Canadian Society of Forensic Science*, Vol. 19, No. 1, pp. 3–36.
26. Wilson, F.E., and Schuessler, D. 1985. Automated geometric interpretation of human bloodstain evidence. *I.A.B.P.A. News*, Vol. 2, No. 4, pp. 36–43, December.

Medical and Medicolegal Aspects of Bloodshed at Crime Scenes

3

WILLIAM G. ECKERT, MD

Factors Affecting Volume of Bleeding

Many factors affect the amount of bleeding that will occur after an injury. These factors may be related to human data such as age, size, sex, physical health, condition of the blood vessels, and anatomic location of major vessels in the injured areas. The size of the individual is an important consideration. A very muscular male may be able to absorb impact from a blunt instrument resulting in no more than a hematoma of the soft tissues. Muscle mass may interfere with the penetration of a knife or other sharp object. Projectiles may be slowed in their penetration into muscle mass depending upon their caliber and velocity. In contrast, those with less muscle mass such as women and children may sustain more severe injury in a given situation. The elderly victim may have a thin bone structure, which provides no strong support to prevent serious injury. The presence of natural disease processes (cirrhosis of the liver, hemophilia, malignancy of lungs, vitamin deficiencies, etc.), alcoholism and drug use, or medications required for the treatment of a disease such as anticoagulants may tend to increase the amount of bloodshed due to the delay in coagulation. Bleeding associated with natural disease may be seen in hemophiliacs. The rapidity of death of the victim may be related to inefficient cardiac status that may contribute to death inasmuch as the heart may be in a state of failure and the bleeding may be the final episode and insult to the heart. The failing heart may also produce hypoxia or low oxygen circulation to the brain and, ultimately, failure of the respiratory and cardiovascular centers of the brain. The rapidity of death may also be associated with acute myocardial infarction or a ruptured aortic aneurysm. In these instances there is a relatively short period of bleeding either externally or internally.

Location of the Wound

Another factor relates to the location, nature, and features of the wound itself as well as the body structure or organ involved, including the major vessels that are injured. The severity of the injury is a major consideration. Amputation or destruction of the head by its very nature will produce massive bleeding while lethal puncture wounds may produce minimal bleeding (Figure 3-1). The number of injuries and the increased number of anatomic areas involved increase the number of bleeding opportunities. Thus multiple lacerations or penetrating wounds to any area of the body usually produce massive bleeding.

The susceptibility of the organ or vessel in the body to injury is an important consideration. The brain is in a protected cavity surrounded by the skull and, unless direct blunt or penetrating trauma occurs, it is perhaps the best-protected organ in the body. A recent assault case involved head injuries sustained by the victim as the result of an attack with a roofing ax. The skull resisted severe penetration and the victim survived the injuries (Figures 3-2 and 3-3). The head offers variable amounts of bleeding depending upon the area and type of injury. Scalp lacerations may produce severe bleeding, especially when the temporal arteries are involved. Intoxicated individuals frequently fall and suffer head injuries of this type that, when unattended, may result in a fatal

Figure 3-1   Massive head destruction resulting from self-inflicted shotgun wound.

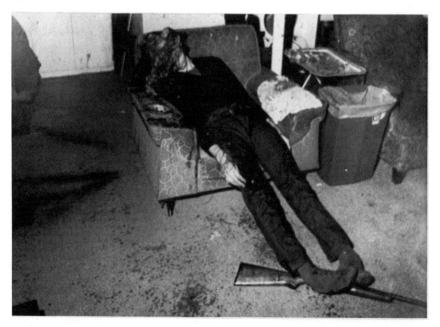

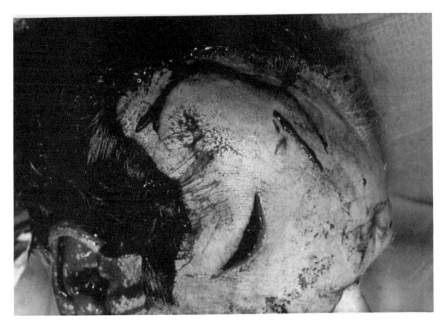

Figure 3-2 Head injuries inflicted with roofing ax from which the victim was able to survive.

Figure 3-3 View of roofing ax used by assailant to inflict victim's head injuries shown in Figure 3-2.

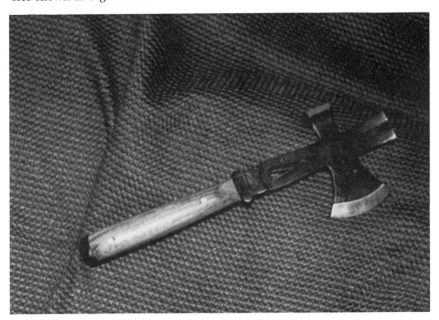

outcome. In a case in New Orleans, an intoxicated person in jail fell and struck his head on the bed frame in his cell. He developed severe shock and died as his head hung over the edge of the bed while bleeding, producing a 1500-ml pool of blood on the floor. He was not discovered until morning. His death was inexcusable and liability was proven. Penetrating bullet wounds of the head may produce minor bleeding with scanty blood flow from the entrance site. This minimal bleeding may indicate a relatively rapid death or minimal intracranial pressure. Often the spinal cord or brain stem is severed by a gunshot wound to the neck or when a gun is discharged in the victim's mouth. In the cranial cavity there may be heavy accumulation of blood in the subdural space. This hematoma may be unilateral or bilateral with a volume of 150–200 ml of blood. There may be bleeding from the ears or the nose associated with basal skull fractures because of the derangement of the skull and vessel injuries that result.

The nose and mouth are prominent structures that are frequently injured because of their location and may produce considerable bleeding due to their vascularity. There may be very heavy bleeding from the nasal cavity associated with trauma resulting in a fractured nose, nasal polyp, sinus infections, or excessive nasal picking. Nasal hemorrhage may also be associated with a marked hypertension. Oral hemorrhages may result from bleeding of varices of the esophagus or as a result of hemoptysis. The mouth and nose are also associated with bleeding from the respiratory tract or larynx due to injury, infections, tumors, or chemical inhalation.

Injuries to the neck produced by penetration of a projectile or by slashing or stabbing with a sharp instrument may produce profuse bleeding from the severance of the jugular vein or the carotid arteries. The major vessels of the neck including the jugular veins and the carotid arteries are located near the surface and have a fixed structure beneath them and are perhaps the most vulnerable vessels in the body. The resulting hemorrhage is massive and disabling. Arterial blood may be projected a considerable distance. The effect of this massive bleeding produces inadequate circulation and reduced oxygen supply to the brain which leads to a state of anoxia, unconsciousness, and ultimate death.

The organs of the chest including the heart, lungs, and aorta are located within the rib cage and are thus protected from all but severe injury to the chest. The amount of bleeding may be minimal to none when the injuries are not severe. Chest wounds of a blunt nature will cause hemothorax formation but often no external bleeding unless there is hemoptysis from an injured lung or crushed chest (Figure 3-4). Penetrating injuries to the chest related to gunshot or stab wounds often produce more internal bleeding than external bleeding unless

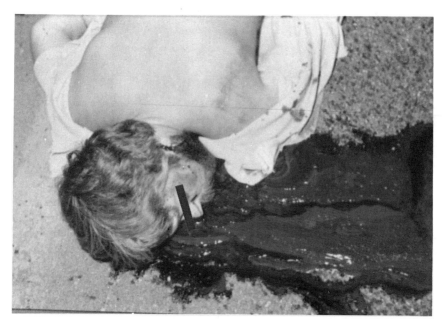

Figure 3-4 Extensive bleeding from the mouth resulting from crushed chest sustained by road traffic victim run over by vehicle.

there is perforation of the heart or aorta or a large, gaping wound of the chest wall. In these situations there may be an unimpaired flow of blood from the external wound site. The blood volume that may accumulate in the pericardial cavity after heart penetration may reach a volume of 100–200 ml. The effect of this blood accumulation in the pericardial sac acts as a hydraulic impediment to the movement of the heart. If there is injury to the coronary artery, there may be further reason for cardiac standstill and death. The amount of bleeding into the chest cavities after lung injury or aortic transection may be in a range of 1000–1500 ml. On one occasion where a robbery victim was stabbed in the anterior chest wall, he collapsed and regained consciousness only to be stabbed again in the back. At autopsy the knife outline produced by the stabbing in the back was clearly visible through the massive blood clot in the chest cavity produced by the initial injury (Figure 3-5).

In the abdominal cavity there is protection of the organs in the upper area where the lower rib cage is still a very significant protective factor. In the pelvic area the bones of the pelvis serve to protect the lower abdominal cavity organs including the bladder, rectosigmoid region, and large vessels below the abdominal aorta bifurcation. Injuries to the abdomen from blunt or penetrating trauma may show bleeding that

Figure 3-5 Evidence of penetration of knife blade into blood clot in chest of stabbing victim.

may occur over a period of time greater than that seen in chest injuries. A large entrance wound produced by shotgun discharge in the abdominal cavity will produce great damage to the abdominal wall as well as the internal organs in that region. The liver is a frequent target for injury because of its size and location and may bleed over an extended period of time unless there are numerous sites of tear or rupture. The spleen is an extremely vascular organ and its rupture is associated with rapid bleeding, shock, and ultimate death in the absence of medical intervention. Trauma to the kidneys may produce very serious bleeding depending upon the extent of injury. Aortic injury or rupture produces severe bleeding in the chest and abdominal cavity that may rapidly produce shock and ultimate death unless rapid surgical intervention is available. Bleeding from mesenteric artery tears or injuries may be relatively slow depending upon the site of injury. In a recent case involving a tear of the superior mesenteric artery of a child, a total of 750 ml of blood was observed in the abdominal cavity. The death occurred hours after injury, which was more of a squeezing injury than a blow. Damage to mesenteric vessels may impede circulation to portions of the intestine and result in delayed intestinal necrosis and perforation in surviving victims. The separation or fracture of the pelvis may produce a slowly forming retroperitoneal hematoma which

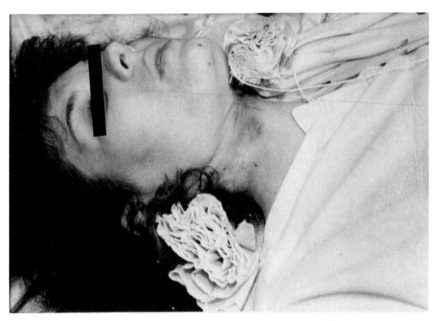

Figure 3-6 Victim of suicidal hanging utilizing bed sheet showing wide compression mark on neck.

may produce shock a day or more after injury. This is common in victims of vehicular accidents and falls.

Bleeding from urethral and anal orifices may be associated with natural disease including tumor formation, polyps, or severe infections that may cause spontaneous as well as voluntary expulsion of blood. During the investigation of a recent suicidal hanging of a female utilizing a bed sheet, a large accumulation of blood was noted on the front of the victim's blue jeans and on the floor below the victim. This was determined to have been due to profuse menstrual blood flow (Figures 3-6 and 3-7). There may also be an unnatural cause for bleeding from these orifices owing to mechanical intrusion into these areas by foreign bodies and objects manually pushed into the orifices by others or by self-abuse acts of the individuals themselves. In the absence of an accurate history these injuries may not be able to be identified as self-inflicted. The forms of bleeding associated with natural disease may stimulate an unnatural problem and thus have to be differentiated from one another.

The femoral arteries and veins are also located in a vulnerable position but they do not have a fixed body behind them so that their injury potential is much less than that of the neck vessels. The vessels of the elbows and wrists are also located in vulnerable areas.

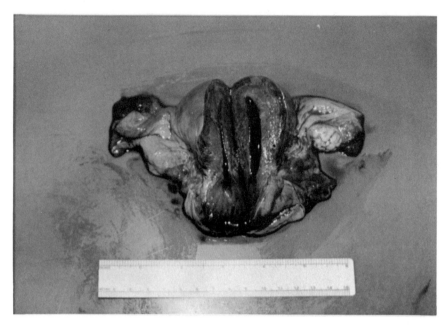

Figure 3-7 View of blood clots in hemorrhagic uterus of hanging victim shown in Figure 3-6 who bled profusely onto floor while suspended.

Large amounts of bleeding by a victim due to major injury can be designated as quantities in excess of 200 ml or 6 ounces, and small amounts as less than that quantity. Large amounts of bleeding are associated with such events as decapitation, crushing of the head by blunt force, explosive destruction of the body, amputation of an extremity, shotgun injuries to various areas of the body, and slashing or stabbing with numerous varieties of sharp instruments (Figures 3-8, 3-9, and 3-10). Denudement of large areas of skin and tissue such as may occur with motor vehicles and other types of machinery may produce massive bleeding. Minimal bleeding may occur in a variety of situations. A short postinjury survival time may reduce bleeding of a victim. The bleeding from a lacerated face, nose, or mouth may be small in volume. In those areas of the body that lack large blood vessels, injury may not produce excessive bleeding. Bleeding from the nose or ear associated with skull fracture may be minimal. There may be some bleeding associated with multiple abrasions from blows or as a result of friction from contact with a surface onto which a victim has been thrown.

The amount of blood flow will vary in different anatomic regions of the body and is an important consideration not only for medicolegal purposes but also for the emergency medical team and emergency

Figure 3-8 Heavy bleeding onto bed produced by victim stabbed several times in neck.

Figure 3-9 View of stab wounds in neck of victim shown in the scene depicted in Figure 3-8.

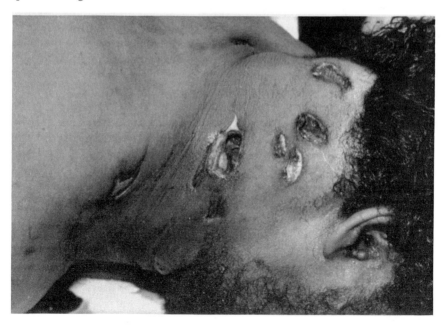

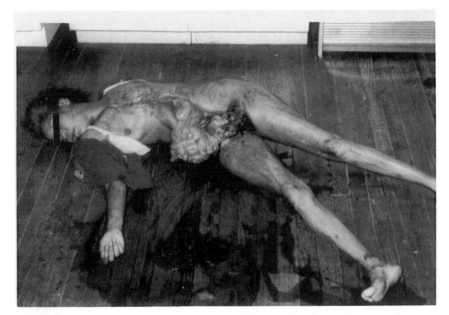

Figure 3-10 Evisceration of intestines and heavy bleeding of victim who sustained severe cutting and stabbing injuries.

room physicians who may treat the victim in a trauma unit. On the body one can observe the close proximity of arteries to the skin by feeling the pulse in the various arterial locations including the wrists, ankles, backs of the knees, groin, sides of the neck, the temple, and the heart in the precordial region of the chest (Figure 3-11). The average rate of arterial blood flow through various anatomic regions during a set period of time is demonstrated in Table 3-1.

Significance of Blood Evidence

Blood evidence provides an important source of information for a case concerning the scene, the victim, and the assailant.

Blood evidence is essential in the following situations:

1. Where the position of the victim at the time of injury is determined.
2. Where the movement of the victim can be observed.
3. Where the removal of the body from the scene is traced.
4. Where storage of the body can be noted.
5. Where evidence remains where the body has bled before removal.
6. Where blood soaking through a mattress, floor, or other surface may provide volume estimation.

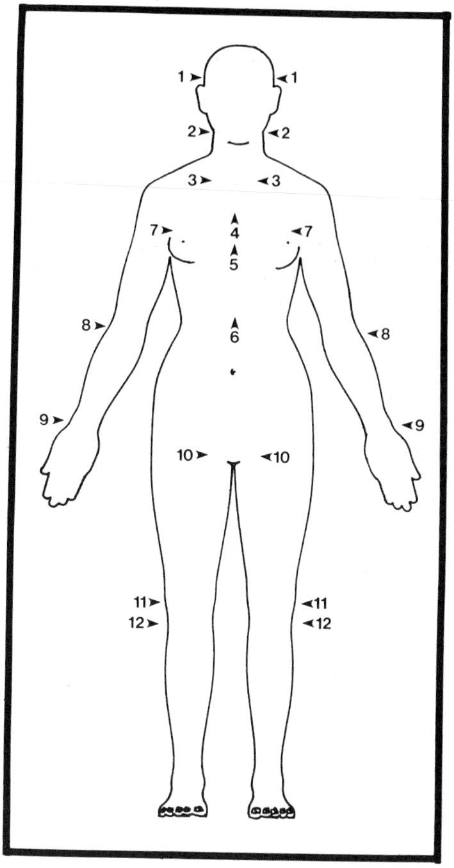

Figure 3-11 Common sources of arterial spurting: *1*, temporal artery; *2*, carotid artery; *3*, subclavian artery; *4*, heart; *5*, thoracic artery; *6*, abdominal artery; *7*, brachial artery; *8*, ulnar artery; *9*, radial artery; *10*, femoral artery; *11*, tibial artery; *12*, popliteal artery.

Table 3-1 Average Rate of Arterial Blood Flow through Various Areas of the Body

Organ or vessel	Rate of flow (liters per minute)
Brain	0.75
Carotid arteries	0.19
Lungs	5.50
Heart	3.50–9.00
Ascending aorta	11.80
Liver	1.30
Spleen	0.24
Kidney	0.60
Abdominal aorta	11.10
Brachial artery	0.09
Femoral artery	0.18
Muscles	1.00
Bone	0.80

7. Where the relationship of the victim to the assailant may be deduced from the blood on the assailant's clothing.
8. Where the amount of blood loss is to be determined.
9. Where aging of the blood accumulation must be determined.
10. Where it is required to determine whose blood is present and whether there are intoxicants present.
11. Where there may be a question of how much blood loss is present and its potential effect on the condition of the victim.
12. When there is any tissue present in the blood evidence such as brain tissue that would make it difficult for the victim to move or be conscious.

The examination of bloodstains on the victim, assailant, weapon, and scene should be a routine procedure. The shooting death of a female was initially thought to have been suicidal in nature. Investigation revealed that the victim had sustained a large-caliber entrance wound in the left cheek which penetrated through the brainstem and exited in the right neck area. Death would have occurred almost immediately. The bloodstain evidence clearly shows that the victim's left cheek initially rested on the bed in contact with the major pool of blood on the bed and she was subsequently moved to her right (Figures 3-12 and 3-13). The weapon was located on the bed near the victim (Figure 3-14). The barrel contained blood spatter traveling toward the

Figure 3-12 View of shooting victim on bed after head was moved to right away from initial contact with blood pool on left side of body.

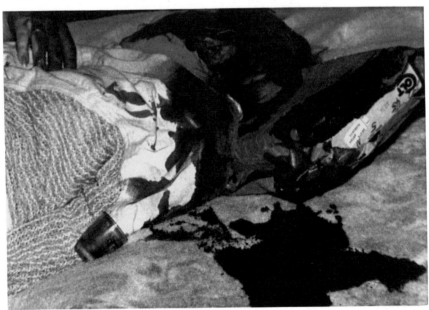

Figure 3-13 Transfer blood-stain on left side of victim's face which resulted from contact with blood pool on bed. Entrance wound is located just forward of the lobe of the left ear.

Figure 3-14 Weapon on bed close to shooting victim showing blood spatter on inside of trigger guard and on barrel traveling towards the muzzle.

Figure 3-15 Large accumulation of blood remaining at scene where the victim was shot and transported to another location.

muzzle and blood spatter was present on the inside of the trigger guard. The locations and directionality of these blood spatters are inconsistent with backspatter's having been produced at the time of discharge of the weapon. The weapon was most likely tossed onto the bed after the shooting and movement of the victim and struck the exposed pool of blood, producing the spatter on the trigger guard and muzzle. The husband was ultimately arrested and convicted of homicide. The development of information derived from careful bloodstain interpretation is invaluable and should not be overlooked.

From a medicolegal perspective there are additional parameters and factors that should be considered in conjunction with blood at the scene and involve the amount or volume of blood that has been shed. There is also a need to relate the quantity of blood with the nature of the bleeding and the anatomic site of bleeding. This may be especially helpful in those cases where the victim has been injured or killed at a scene and removed to another location (Figure 3-15).

The volume of blood loss becomes important for several reasons including the evaluation of the degree of activity of a victim after he or she has received a lethal injury. Estimations of external blood loss should be made at the scene as well as internally during the postmortem examination by measuring the volume of free blood present in the various body cavities. The rapidity of death after the wound has been sustained is an important factor to evaluate plus the possibility that the assailant's clothing received victim's blood during the struggle or attack.

The various situations where blood evidence becomes important do not always involve criminal cases as in the case of the accidental leakage of blood from a surgical patient when intravenous tubing became disconnected and significant blood loss occurred. The questions were how to measure the blood loss in a quantitative manner and to evaluate the significance of the blood loss in relation to the death of the patient. Unexpected internal bleeding may bring up questions as to cause and what measures of medical treatment would have been effective under the proper conditions. The question of activity after a lethal injury is frequently asked during testimony in trials. The degree of external and internal bleeding must be carefully evaluated in these cases.

Blood Volume Estimation

In those cases where there is a scene with substantial quantities of blood present and the absence of a victim, important information may be derived from careful study of the character of the bloodstains and the quantity of blood that was shed. The location of the victim at the time of injury and the site and nature of injury may often be determined as well as movement of the body after injury to include evidence of dragging or carrying the victim from the scene (Figure 3-16). The motion or movement of a body after injury may be established by the blood distribution at the scene such as arterial gushing and transfer of blood indicating movement on a floor or against a wall in a room or corridor. If the victim is located in a closet, under a bed, or in the trunk of a car, the blood accumulation may be measured or weighed and compared to the blood accumulation at the scene where the injury occurred (Figure 3-17).

Dr. Henry Lee has conducted experiments involving the weighing of a bloodstained rug or other surface and comparing this finding to the weight of unstained comparative sizes of the same surface to arrive at an estimation of the weight of blood present on the original surface. The difference in weight is related to the quantity of blood shed on that surface. When the surface is not removable, the dried blood may be scraped up and weighed. This would provide an estimation of blood shed by relating the weight in grams of the blood to volume in cubic centimeters.

Figure 3-16 Bloodstain pattern produced as a result of victim being stabbed multiple times on bed and subsequently dragged from bed across floor to adjoining room.

Figure 3-17 Measurement of the area of a bloodstain produced by a known quantity of blood on a carpet surface by a grid method to be compared with bloodstains found at scene on similar carpet.

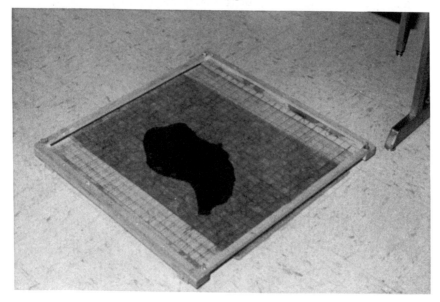

Medicolegal Aspects of Blood Evidence

Examination of the blood at the scene may also be used as a source of information as to the survivability of the victim after injury. The careful examination of the blood accumulation may reveal additional tissue such as hair, skin, and brain tissue whose presence would help establish not only the injury site on the victim but also the capabilities of the victim after injury and an approximation of post injury survival time. The appearance of the blood may also provide information regarding the origin of blood from the body. Lung injuries often result in frothy blood in the mouth associated with respirations of the victim. There may be evidence of the coughing up or vomiting of blood that would be significant. A cut to the sides of the neck may result in the severance of the carotid artery and produce a rapid spurting type of bleeding and rapid disablement of the victim with death occurring very shortly after the injury at the location where the attack took place. This would also apply to accidental or suicidal injuries to areas of the body where arteries are accessible.

Abdominal or chest wounding very often may have little or no extrusion of blood since blood may accumulate within the body cavities. The clothing may become soaked and impede further extrusion of blood from the body. Clothing which is tight against the skin of a victim may impede the outward flow of blood from the body. A prone body may have blood leakage owing to gravity depending upon the position of the body. A chest wound on a victim who is on his back may show little evidence of external bleeding but when the body is turned over considerable blood may leak from the chest cavity. If the circulation is impaired by the rapid drop of blood pressure prior to death, external blood loss may be minimal. Cold temperatures may limit the extent of bleeding in a victim because of the body's reaction to preserve internal heat by peripheral vessel contraction.

The determination of the period of time that the blood has been present may be an issue as well. This may relate to the clotting time of blood as well as the drying time of quantities of blood on a particular surface and may have to be determined by experimental work. The character of the blood at the scene must be described as to the degree of drying and clotting. The blood clots will change after a period of time with visible separation of the serum from the clot. It may be possible to relate the appearance of the blood clot and drying of blood to its approximate time of deposit. Although it is variable, one might expect a considerable amount of dried blood at a scene 24 hours after injury. The environment and type of surface upon which the blood is deposited are important considerations with experiments of this type.

Attempts to evaluate cases in which blood loss evidence is a crucial factor have to be based on the fact that the known volume of blood present in a normal person in the range of 5000–6000 ml or 5–6 liters

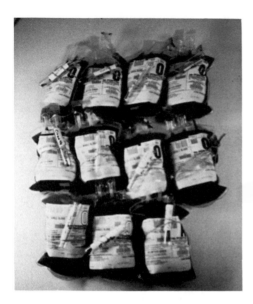

Figure 3-18 Average quantity of blood in the human body represented as units of blood bank collected from blood donors is approximately 5000–6000 ml or 5–6 liters.

(Figure 3-18). When the vascular system of a victim is disrupted so that the blood is able to leak or leave the vessels, the stability of the body will change. Blood may leave the circulatory system externally or accumulate within the cranial, thoracic, pericardial, or peritoneal cavities. When 20–25 percent of the blood volume is lost from the circulation (1000–1500 ml), the first symptoms of shock are forthcoming. This is significant when one also considers this change in conjunction with injuries to a specific organ such as the heart, lungs, or brain whose dysfunction will produce additional changes to impair the victim. The rate of bleeding is also a factor that will vary according to the portion of the vascular system that is injured. An artery, which has a greater pressure than a vein, will produce a more rapid rate of bleeding when severed. The size of the artery determines the relative volume of blood loss, thus the larger the artery the greater volume of blood loss in a given period of time. The presence of arterial spurt patterns at a scene may indicate the severity of injury, as well as disablement of the victim.

The degree of intoxication involving alcohol and/or drug use may have an indirect effect on the amount of bloodshed. After injury, the activities of intoxicated victims may be related to their reduced sense of inhibition and unusual behavior, and increased physical activity may increase bleeding because of the increased action of the heart. Persons may exhibit aggressive behavior which may include attacks on others producing additional injuries, jumping from heights, or attempting to break away from law enforcement officers attempting to assist them.

The Documentation, Collection, and Evaluation of Bloodstain Evidence

4

STUART H. JAMES

Physical evidence is defined as any and all materials or items that may be identified as being associated with a crime scene, which, by scientific evaluation, ultimately establishes the element of the crime and provides a link among the crime scene, the victim, and the assailant. The proper recognition, documentation, collection, preservation, and examination of physical evidence are crucial to the successful reconstruction of a crime scene and litigation in a criminal proceeding. Physical evidence may be present at the crime scene whether it be indoors or outside, on a vehicle, on the victim, on the assailant, and/or his environment. There is frequently transfer of blood and trace evidence between victim and assailant.

It is important to recognize that the study and interpretation of bloodstains at a crime scene should be integrated within the systematic approach to the examination of all types of physical evidence and crime scene reconstruction (Table 4-1). The initial bloodstain evaluation at a crime scene should be able to provide the investigator with the general nature of the activities that took place and relative movements of victim and assailant. A complete analysis of bloodstains at a scene where there exist numerous complex stain patterns may require hours or days of work involving measurements, projections of angles of impact, sketches, diagrams, and extensive photography. Conversely, a crime scene may provide relatively little information with respect to bloodstains that is not already apparent to the investigator. In any event, the bloodstain evaluation should be coordinated with the overall documentation, collection, preservation, and examination of the other types of physical evidence that may be present at the crime scene. The major time-consuming details of bloodstain interpretation can usually be accomplished after the crime scene has been processed

Table 4-1 Outline for Interpretation of Bloodstain Evidence

Scene

Secure scene and exclude unauthorized persons.
Avoid alteration of bloodstains.
Photograph victim and associated bloodstains prior to moving victim.
Photograph weapon if present and secure it.
Note environmental conditions.
Conduct preliminary evaluation of overall bloodstains and patterns.
Move body cautiously.
Collect trace evidence.
Complete search and recognition of bloodstains and patterns.
Photograph bloodstains including close-up views with measuring device.
Take bloodstain measurements including locations, widths, lengths, angles of impact,
    convergences, and origins.
Make preliminary sketches and diagrams.
Perform preliminary blood testing if desired.
Collect, tag, identify, and collect bloodstained items.
Perform string reconstruction if desired.

Assailant	*Autopsy of Victim*
Examine assailant and his environment.	Photograph body, clothed and unclothed, including injuries.
Photograph and document clothing and other physical evidence.	Secure clothing, physical evidence, and blood samples.
Obtain appropriate blood samples.	Obtain autopsy report, x-rays, and medical data.

Laboratory Reports	*Bloodstain Reconstruction*
Blood identification and individualization.	Final diagrams and bloodstain experiments.
Trace evidence, ballistics, and other physical evidence.	Bloodstain interpretation of scene, clothing, and other items.
	Correlation with autopsy and laboratory reports.

Final Conclusions and Report

for other types of physical evidence. In most cases the search and collection of trace evidence such as hairs, fibers, and fingerprints can be given priority over evaluation of the bloodstain patterns. In those instances where trace evidence coexists with bloodstain evidence, consultation and communication between investigators and laboratory personnel at the scene will minimize unnecessary contamination, alteration, or destruction of physical evidence. Initial documentation and photography of bloodstain evidence are essential.

In actual practice the crime scene environment can be indoors, within a room or rooms of a house or other structure, outdoors, or can involve an automobile or other type of transportation vehicle. Not infrequently all these environments may be involved in the commission of the same crime and all may be sources of physical evidence, especially in cases where a victim has been killed in one location and transported to another. The subsequent actions of the assailant may produce additional sources of physical evidence involving disposition of a weapon or other incriminating materials. The assailant's clothing is a valuable source of bloodstain evidence as well as trace evidence, especially when it is acquired within a reasonable time and has not been subjected to extensive washing.

The indoor crime scene is for the most part protected from the elements and easily preserved for extended periods of time. Usually there should be no need to hasten the processing of the scene. Occasionally, complications arise with the examination of a victim and crime scene in public places such as restaurants, stores, and airports because there is pressure to clean up the scene as quickly as possible. In all situations unauthorized persons should be denied access to the scene. Those entering the scene should be cautious in order to minimize the unnecessary tracking of wet blood thereby altering significant bloodstain patterns and produce artifacts.

The crime scene including bloodstain evidence should be documented with high-quality color photographs including close-up views with a scale of reference prior to moving the body or otherwise altering the scene. The use of a video camera is very useful to document the undisturbed scene as well. The bloodstains on the body and clothing should be photographed from above and from all sides. Close-up photographs of small bloodstains on the body should be taken with a measuring device in view. Turning the body for further examination should be done cautiously to minimize alteration of adjacent bloodstains and to avoid the creation of additional bloodstain patterns on the floor or clothing of the victim. Consistency of blood clots and degree of drying of the blood on the body and surrounding area should be documented with the ambient temperature. After the body has been removed, any remaining wet pools of blood should not be disturbed in order to avoid the production of artifacts.

In most circumstances there is no pressing need to remove a deceased victim from the scene. The body should remain undisturbed until the necessary observations and evaluations are completed by the investigators. In those cases where medical attention is given to a surviving victim the scene may be subject to unavoidable alteration. Often it is necessary for a victim to be moved to a more suitable position or location for the administration of medical treatment and emergency procedures. Alteration of bloodstains and creation of new bloodstains and other artifacts may be produced as a result. It is important to recognize these alterations at the crime scene; the activities at the scene during medical intervention should be documented by the investigator. In those cases where the activities of the emergency medical team (EMT) personnel and removal of the victim to the hospital precede the arrival of the investigator, it is important to consult with the medical personnel regarding the original position of the body and the undisturbed condition of the scene upon their arrival. Many EMTs make observations and take notes regarding the environment of the victim as well as movement and treatment rendered at the scene. They should be able to produce records of their procedures utilized on a particular victim that may have produced bloodstains or altered those already present.

When a victim has been transported to a hospital it is important to retrieve physical evidence, including victim's clothing, projectiles, and so forth, from the emergency room before they are grossly altered or lost. The sheets or blankets used on the victim during transport in an ambulance should be collected for these items may contain valuable trace evidence that became dislodged from the victim.

Small bloodstains, spatters, and thin smears of blood will dry rapidly at the scene and will usually remain intact on a surface. There are, however, instances where flaking and ultimate alteration of bloodstains will occur after relatively short periods of time. This phenomenon may occur when there is excessive air movement as created by a fan and when the target surface is warm owing to various heating devices including heated waterbeds. Certain surfaces such as waxed floors may not hold bloodstains very well. In these circumstances slight disturbances can cause bloodstains to become dislodged.

Preliminary testing of blood may be made on dried stains after they have been properly documented and photographed. This may be accomplished with the use of leucomalachite green or an equivalent reagent. This technique is especially helpful when the stains are suspect in nature. In many household crime scenes, reddish brown stains may be easily mistaken for blood and elimination of these stains permits concentration on the actual bloodstains present.

A diligent search for inconspicuous bloodstains at a crime scene should be made using a good light source such as photo floodlights. Many surfaces may be dirty and discolored or the patterns or texture of the surface may blend in with the bloodstains that are present. There also may be areas of the crime scene where there has been an attempt to wipe up the blood or otherwise clean the surface. Blood may still be present especially in cracks in floors and walls. Luminol spray is sometimes used to locate inconspicuous bloodstains.

It cannot be overemphasized that the location of all bloodstains and patterns at a scene should be adequately photographed including a close up with a measuring device. Documentation of bloodstains must be accurate with respect to their size, shape, and distance from a common locus for incorporation into graphs and diagrams. Directionality, points of convergence, angles of impact, and origins should be determined on all surfaces for graphic representation or reconstruction with the use of strings at the scene. It is important to study bloodstain patterns to determine the object or objects that may have produced them. There are instances where the sequence of activities may be determined. For example, the presence of medium-velocity blood spatter impacted over a bloodstain transfer shoe- or handprint may indicate the presence of a certain individual prior to or during the physical activity producing the spatter and not at a subsequent time.

It is important to keep in mind the possible activities of an assailant at the scene not only during the assault but also after the incident has taken place. Assailants may produce bloodstain patterns with the victim's blood or in some instances with their own blood if they have sustained an injury during the altercation with the victim. A bloody knife, for example, may be wiped on a surface leaving a visible pattern. Various items may be used to wipe blood from the assailant's hands including towels, tissues, furniture, rugs, drapes, and the like. Partial blood transfer prints may be deposited on door edges, knobs, handles, and light switches. Bathrooms should be examined thoroughly for bloodstain evidence. Assailants may deposit or transfer blood on sinks, toilets, shower stalls, or tubs during their attempt to clean up prior to leaving the scene. Sink traps and tub traps should be examined and water samples taken to be tested for the presence of blood. A thorough search should be conducted for discarded weapons and bloodstained clothing. An assailant may leave bloodstained cigarette butts or other personal articles such as glasses at the scene. As previously discussed, the clothing of the assailant may provide valuable bloodstain evidence. Evaluation of the transfer of bloodstains and patterns of victim's blood on the assailant's clothing will in many cases indicate the type of physical activity necessary to produce them. Correct interpretation of bloodstains on assailant's clothing can help to establish the probability of his presence at the scene and involvement with the assault on the victim. Often the reason offered by the assailant for his bloodstained clothing can be refuted.

The same principles of recognition, documentation, collection, preservation, and examination of physical evidence that are utilized for crime scenes indoors apply to crime scenes outdoors. Exterior scenes are not as likely to be altered or cleaned by the assailant but the nature of the terrain and environment including weather conditions may significantly alter the appearance of such physical evidence as bloodstains and cause difficulty in their recognition. Bloodstains and patterns may be absorbed into soil or otherwise altered by wind, rain, snow, or ice. It is important to consider the existing weather conditions and their effect on existing bloodstains and their interpretation. Outside target surfaces are more likely to consist of rougher textures than those inside. The interpretation of bloodstains on rock, concrete, and grassy areas may be more difficult with respect to directionality and angle of impact. Bloodstains that have been subjected to moisture may undergo alterations in appearance and appear diffuse and diluted. Blood flow patterns will spread on wet surfaces like ice and appear to be of greater volume as the blood is diluted. In freezing temperatures bloodstains and spatters have been observed to retain their characteristics fairly well and remain quite suitable for interpretation.

Photography and documentation of outdoor crime scenes should be accomplished as soon as possible and practical for the obvious reason that unexpected weather changes may alter the scene considerably and obliterate physical evidence. Bloodstained items should be processed and removed before these changes occur. It may be necessary to videotape and/or photograph the scene at night with the use of strong light sources. The use of a ladder or truck with a boom is useful for overall photographs of the outdoor scene. The weather may not hinder additional photography the following day but if weather change becomes a detrimental factor the night photography is crucial.

It may be necessary to collect soil samples for the demonstration of bloodstain locations. Bushes, leaves, and various outdoor debris should be examined closely for evidence of bloodstains. In certain cases the absence of significant bloodstain evidence may be associated with the dumping of a victim subsequent to the fatal injury's having occurred elsewhere. If sufficient time has elapsed for blood on the body to dry, the existing flow patterns may not be consistent with the present position of the victim.

Prompt examination of road surfaces for evidence of bloodstain patterns during the investigation of pedestrian–vehicular accidents may reveal impact sites and directionality of blood spatter that can assist in the repositioning of the victim and reconstruction of the accident. In addition to examination of road surfaces for bloodstain patterns in pedestrian–vehicular accidents, the vehicle exterior often provides substantial bloodstain evidence in the area of impacting surfaces and undercarriage of the vehicle. The undercarriage of the vehicle should be examined while the vehicle is on a hydraulic lift in a garage.

The examination of vehicles for bloodstain evidence may provide valuable physical evidence in various types of investigations. The interior of vehicles should be examined in a systematic manner and be divided into sections including the trunk. Each area should be photographed and examined separately. The trunk or interior of a vehicle may reveal bloodstain evidence relating to transportation of a victim, bloody clothing, or objects. The assailant may have transferred his own or victim's blood onto door and window handles, steering column, gear shift or dashboard controls, seats, or floor pedals.

In cases of motor vehicle accidents involving injury to driver and/or occupants, the evaluation of bloodstain evidence may help to resolve the issue as to the actual driver of the vehicle and the seat location of passengers. This may be accomplished by characterization of blood-stain patterns and impact sites relative to specific types of injuries in addition to blood grouping and testing of genetic markers.

Methods for Conducting Extensive Crime Scene Searches

In order that bloodstains and other physical evidence are not overlooked it may be necessary to employ an extensive, systematic plan, especially in cases in which the scene encompasses a large area. The scene should be surveyed initially and a search plan formulated that will be suitable for the individual case. Any proximal and obvious physical evidence should be photographed, documented, and collected prior to the initiation of an extensive search in order to avoid alteration or destruction of physical evidence by numerous searchers in an area. The initial survey and evaluation of the scene may suggest the nature of items sought and the method of search most desirable for the particular case. The use of search patterns may be useful. There are several types of search patterns commonly used depending upon the scene environment and the preference of the investigators (Figure 4-1). Zone or quadrant search patterns are usually more applicable to indoor scenes and vehicles. Strip, grid, spiral, and wheel search patterns are more commonly utilized for large areas and outdoor scenes. The particular method chosen is not as critical as the manner in which the search is conducted.

1. Zone: The area is divided into quadrants that may be further subdivided to allow examination of small sections of an area in a systematic manner.
2. Strip: The area is visualized as a rectangle and is searched along paths parallel to one side with each succeeding path parallel and adjacent to the preceding one until the entire area has been traversed.
3. Grid: The area is visualized as a rectangle subdivided into squares. The squares or grids are examined systematically in two directions perpendicular to each other.
4. Spiral: The area is searched in a clockwise manner forming a spiral beginning at the center of the area and spiraling outward until the entire scene has been examined.

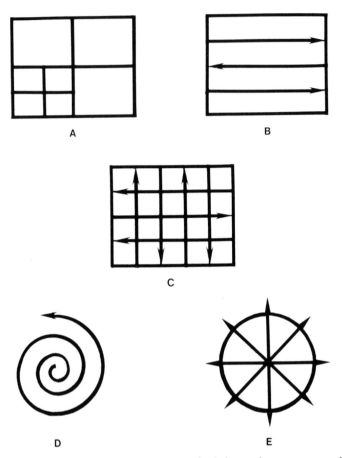

Figure 4-1 Methods of crime scene search. (**A**) Quadrant zone method. (**B**) Strip method. (**C**) Grid method. (**D**) Spiral method. (**E**) Wheel method.

5. Wheel: The area is considered to be roughly circular. The search begins at the center of the circle and progresses outward along a radius of the circle as in following the spoke of a wheel. A return can be made along the same radius back to the center of the circle. Successive radial paths are searched in a similar manner until the entire 360 degrees of the circle have been examined.

Crime Scene Sketching

Good photography is essential for the proper documentation of the crime scene but photographs may not always depict relative distances between objects and other details that are best demonstrated with drawing or sketching. Sketching is the graphic illustration of the crime scene and items within the scene that are pertinent to the investigation. The primary purpose is good orientation to the scene. A sketch will contain only essential items whereas photographs may be over-crowded with detail. A sketch should show overall view, geographic location, size, and position of objects at the crime scene. A good sketch of a crime scene should complement the photographs and together provide the investigator, and eventually a jury, a clear picture of the scene. Some good general rules for crime scene sketching are as follows:

1. Get a general, visual idea of the layout before collecting data and measurements. Use photographs for reference if available.
2. The person reading the tape measure should record the measurements.
3. Measure from finished wall to finished wall and record dimensions of the room.
4. Note that "all measurements are approximate."
5. Note direction in which doors swing.
6. Note position of doors, windows, and light fixtures.
7. Include only essential items of furniture, fixtures, and so forth to avoid clutter in sketch.
8. Measurements of the location of movable objects should be noted in reference to at least two fixed objects so they may be relocated to their original position at a later time.
9. Note position of magnetic north.
10. Note the position from which photographs are taken.
11. Sketch outline of area first and then record objects.
12. If there is more than one body at the scene, number them.

There are two types of sketches. The first is considered to be rough and is usually completed at the scene. The second is the finished or final sketch which is to be used in court. The rough sketch should be retained with the notes of the crime scene. The two-dimensional sketching system utilizing length and width is the most widely used (Figure 4-2). The three-dimensional system shows four walls, ceiling, and floor and is useful for construction of a scale model of the scene (Figure 4-3). Whether a two- or a three-dimensional sketching system is utilized, a diagram should contain essential information and not be cluttered with too much detail and thus be difficult to interpret. Multiple diagrams and overlays of a crime scene can be constructed from the basic sketch to minimize this problem. Diagrams of bloodstain locations and convergences should show the location of the victim and only relevant nearby objects in order to demonstrate effective graphical representation.

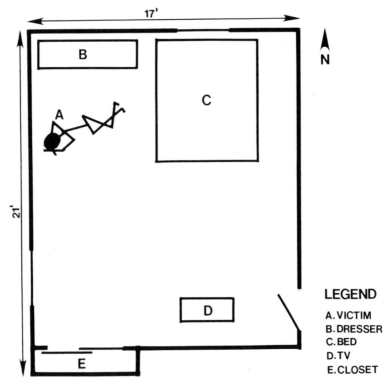

Figure 4-2 Two-dimensional crime scene sketch.

LEGEND

A. VICTIM
B. DRESSER
C. BED
D. TV
E. CLOSET

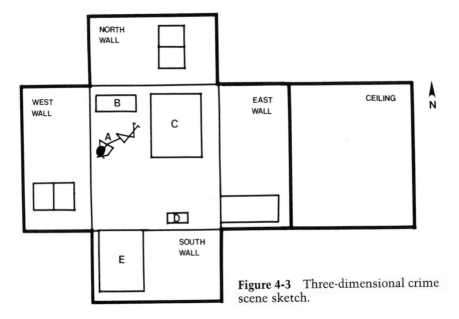

Figure 4-3 Three-dimensional crime scene sketch.

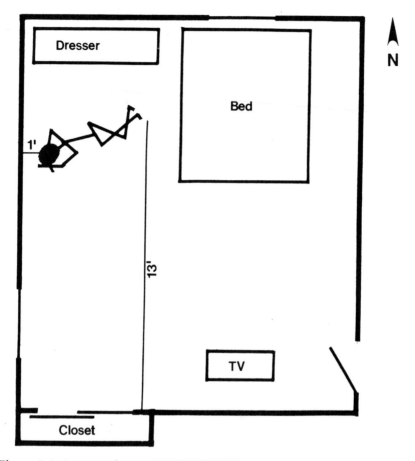

Figure 4-4   Rectangular method of plotting.

There are three basic types of plotting methods:

1. Rectangular—the objects are located by right-angle measurements from fixed baselines such as walls (Figure 4-4).
2. Triangulation—measurements are taken from two or more points to locate objects (Figure 4-5).
3. Transecting baseline—baseline is established through center of area and objects are located from baseline. *AB* is the baseline which is equidistant along *x* and *y* and parallel to *ab*. Point *C* is located by measuring along *AB* to *C* and then at a right angle perpendicular to *C* (Figure 4-6).

The scale of scene sketches and diagrams depends upon the size of the area to be measured. Small rooms can be scaled to the order of ½ inch equals 1 foot. Larger rooms may be scaled to the order of ¼ inch

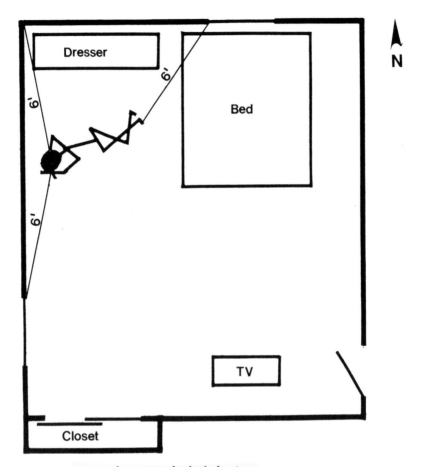

Figure 4-5   Triangulation method of plotting.

equals 1 foot. Outside locations may be scaled to the order of ⅛ inch equals 1 foot or ½ inch equals 10 feet.

The basic materials needed for sketching at crime scenes are as follows:

1. Tape measures (100 feet, 10–20 feet)
2. Assorted rulers and triangles
3. Graph paper and sketching paper
4. Appropriate pencils, pens, and eraser
5. Templates (building interiors, body, etc.)
6. Compass
7. Press on or touch letters, numbers, and arrows (excellent for use with finished sketches)

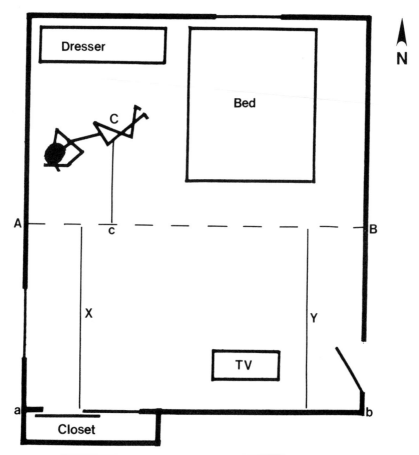

Figure 4-6 Transecting baseline method of plotting.

Collection and Preservation of Bloodstain Evidence

The identification of blood and forensic serological studies for species determination, grouping, and genetic marker individualization are utilized in conjunction with bloodstain interpretation and are often mutually beneficial to the reconstruction of a crime scene. Both disciplines are important sources of physical evidence. In some cases the bloodstain interpretation may provide more valuable information, whereas in others the serological studies may be more revealing and informative. The value of each should be considered when the investigator is preparing to remove bloodstained objects and individual stains from the crime scene for submission to the laboratory. It is of ultimate importance to photograph and document adequately the location, size, and shape of bloodstains prior to their collection and removal from the crime scene.

The extent of grouping and testing of genetic markers in bloodstains that is possible in a given case depends on many factors including the age of the blood, the quantity of blood available, the environmental conditions to which the blood has been exposed, and the degree of contamination that has occurred. Generally, with a limited sample available and with older samples, fewer systems can be tested. Exposure of the blood to extreme heat is detrimental. Also, it should be recognized that laboratories differ in their abilities and techniques to individualize dried bloodstains. Hospital and clinical laboratories are generally better equipped to individualize fresh blood in blood banks for transfusion and in cases involving paternal disputes. Many forensic laboratories have developed sophisticated techniques for the individualization of dried bloodstains. Occasionally, the surface upon which the blood has been deposited may provide a source of contamination and limit the extent of blood individualization, for example, on soiled clothing, floors, and vehicle exteriors where large deposits of crushed insects have accumulated. In all cases it is mandatory to collect, for comparative purposes, a negative control sample from an unstained area on the same surface from which the bloodstain is to be collected.

Putrefied blood presents many problems for the serologist because of the contaminating effect of bacteria, fungi, and the enzymatic breakdown of blood components and often produces misleading or inconclusive testing results. Blood may decompose if not packaged properly. For this reason bloodstained articles should not be packaged wet nor be sealed in airtight plastic bags which may accumulate moisture. Individual packaging of completely dry bloodstained articles in clean paper bags is most desirable. Crusts and scrapings of bloodstains may be packaged in clean folded paper or clean plastic containers. It is important during the collection process not to handle bloodstains or control areas with hands or fingers which may contaminate the samples with the blood group substances of the collector if that person is a secretor. All items should be properly labeled and identified for chain of custody purposes.

The following guidelines generally are recommended to help insure optimal results in the proper collection and preservation of bloodstain evidence. Investigators should consult with the specific forensic laboratory in order to follow particular protocols and to resolve the issues that may arise.

1. If there is a sufficient quantity of wet, pooled blood at a scene, approximately 5–10 ml should be collected with a pipette or medicine dropper and placed into a glass tube containing preservative

and anticoagulant. Appropriate tubes containing sodium fluoride and potassium oxalate to preserve blood samples are available commercially or may be provided by the laboratory. Always check with the laboratory personnel for their preference of blood preservative for specific procedures. The wet blood samples should be refrigerated prior to submission to the laboratory.

2. A moist bloodstain on a nonabsorbent surface such as glass or metal may be collected by adding a small amount of sterile physiological (0.9%) saline to the stain and mixing it thoroughly with an applicator stick and retrieving it with a pipette or medicine dropper. A control sample should be collected in a similar fashion. Both should be refrigerated.

3. Water or other liquids to be tested for blood should be placed into clean jars or other leakproof containers and refrigerated.

4. When feasible, the entire bloodstained article or object should be collected as evidence after the bloodstains have thoroughly dried and their locations have been photographed and properly documented.

5. Do not fold wet clothing or bedding and do not package in a wet condition. When bloodstained sheets, blankets, or pillow cases are removed from a bed or other location, it is important to document top, bottom, left side, right side, and which surface is up or otherwise folded as it was at the scene. Clothing and bedding items should be suspended in a clean area for drying purposes over clean paper to collect any trace evidence that may become dislodged during the drying process. Do not use a hair dryer or heating element to hasten drying. The papers under the dried items should be folded and submitted with the individual articles. The items should be folded and packaged individually in order not to further disturb the bloodstains.

6. Rugs or carpets may be lifted and removed in their entirety in many cases. If this is not feasible, the bloodstained portions and control areas should be cut and removed after photography and proper documentation, and then packaged in clean paper.

7. If it is not feasible or practical to submit the entire bloodstained surface or object, the bloodstains may be scraped with a clean scalpel or razor blade onto clean paper. To avoid cross-contamination, individual disposable blades should be used. Be sure to scrape control surfaces as well. The papers may then be folded, taped and properly identified or transferred to clean plastic containers for submission to the laboratory.

8. If collection of a bloodstain by scraping is not desirable, as with a thin smear on a surface or a bloodstain absorbed into a rough surface such as concrete, it may be best removed by wetting the

stain with physiological (0.9%) saline and collecting it with a pipette or medicine dropper and placing into a clean glass tube and refrigerating. Control samples should be collected in a similar fashion.

9. An alternative method for the removal and collection of dried bloodstains from smooth surfaces is to moisten a sterile cotton swab with physiological (0.9%) saline and rub the stain from the surface with the swab. A control sample should be collected in a similar fashion and refrigerated.

10. Collection of blood samples from the victim at the time of postmortem examination is within the protocol of the medical examiner or forensic pathologist. Consultation with the pathologist will help insure that sufficient blood is obtained for all procedures necessary including toxicological and serological studies. The blood should be collected in separate tubes for each purpose with the appropriate preservatives and anticoagulants.

11. Authority for collection of blood samples from suspects or defendants is obtained through appropriate legal procedures. The forensic laboratory that will test the samples should be consulted to insure that proper samples are collected by a physician, registered nurse, or licensed medical technologist with the proper rules of chain of custody observed in each case.

Examination of Bloodstained Clothing

The careful examination of bloodstained clothing and footwear often provides valuable information for accurate reconstruction of a violent crime. Bloodstain patterns on the clothing of a victim and assailant may represent the activity, position, and movement of each during and subsequent to an attack or struggle after blood has been shed (see Figures 4-7–4-21). Examination of bloodstained garments may be difficult and stain patterns may be complex and sometimes partially obscured on blood-soaked material but a diligent examination is often quite rewarding. Blood found on the clothing of a victim is usually that of the victim, but do not assume this always to be so. Difficult-to-explain features of bloodstain patterns and inconsistent directionalities of individual bloodstains on the victim's clothing may represent blood of the assailant rather than that of the victim. Bloodstain interpretation of patterns on a suspect's clothing will help confirm or refute explanations offered by the suspect concerning the reason for his bloodstained clothing. For optimal results certain procedures and precautions should be observed:

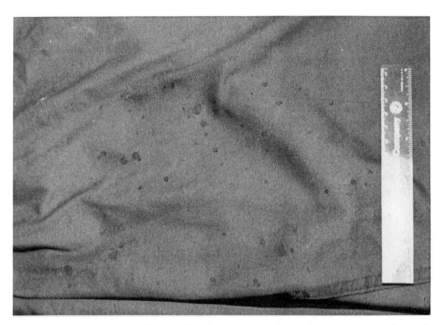

Figure 4-7 Medium-velocity blood spatter on upper front leg area of assailant's trousers produced by beating of victim on bed.

Figure 4-8 Medium-velocity blood spatter on front lower leg area of assailant's trousers produced by beating of victim on floor.

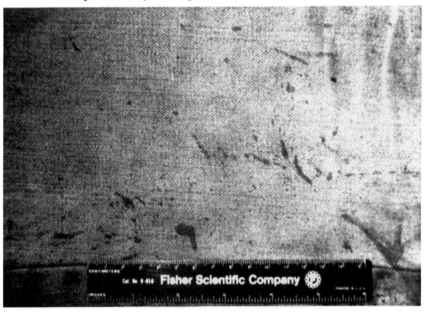

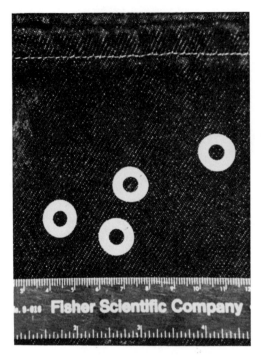

Figure 4-9 Close up of cluster of medium-velocity blood spatters on denim material with location enhanced with the use of white circular ring binders.

Figure 4-10 Transfer of victim's blood to right front pocket area of assailant's blue jeans produced by assailant placing bloody hand in pocket.

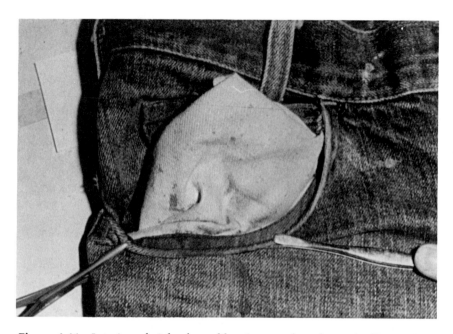

Figure 4-11 Interior of right front blue jean pocket shown in Figure 4-10 showing depth of penetration of bloodstain.

Figure 4-12 Contact bloodstain on knee area of assailant's blue jeans resulting from kneeling in blood pool on floor near victim.

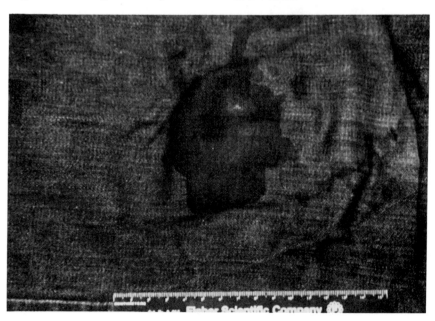

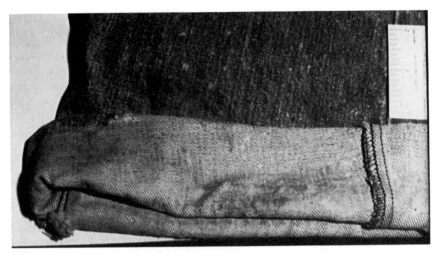

Figure 4-13 Blood transfer on cuff area of assailant's blue jeans which resulted from contact with blood on floor near victim.

Figure 4-14 The placing of bloodstained clothing on a manikin assists with the location and evaluation of the bloodstains.

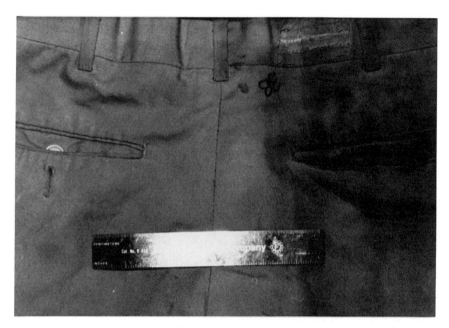

Figure 4-15 Appearance of diluted bloodstain on trousers produced by wetting of garment with water after receiving blood.

Figure 4-16 Appearance of diluted bloodstains on towels in bathroom produced by cleanup attempt by assailant.

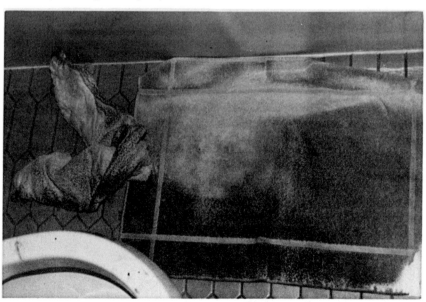

Figure 4-17 Bloodstains on boot of assailant produced by stepping in blood at scene.

Figure 4-18 Close up of cluster of medium-velocity blood spatters on boot with the location enhanced with the use of white circular ring binders.

Figure 4-19   Swabbing of shoe showing positive catalytic color test for blood.

Figure 4-20   Bloodstains on the inside of hat of assailant identified as victim's blood. Hat was worn by suspect at time of questioning by detectives.

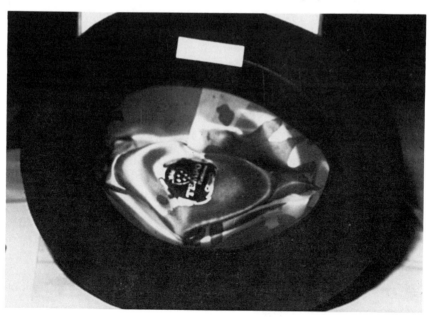

Figure 4-21   Bloodstains on watch of assailant that were identified as victim's blood. Watch was worn by suspect at time of questioning by detectives.

1. The bloodstained clothing of a victim should be carefully removed after initial photography and preserved to avoid contamination and the production of artifacts.

2. Clothing that is haphazardly cut from a victim causes many problems for bloodstain reconstruction. If clothing must be cut from the victim, it should be done in an orderly fashion avoiding bloodstain patterns if possible. Perforations, tears, and other defects in the fabric should not be altered during the removal process.

3. Wet garments should not be folded together nor packaged in a damp condition. Blood transfers may occur as well as possible bacterial contamination of the bloodstains which may hinder blood grouping procedures. It is best to hang and air-dry bloodstained clothing over clean paper in a secure location prior to packaging in paper bags.

4. Trace evidence collection and other special tests and procedures such as examinations for gunshot powder patterns and residue testing should be conducted before extensive bloodstain pattern examination is undertaken.

5. Bloodstain interpretation and serological studies on clothing should be coordinated and appropriate sites chosen for blood

grouping tests. If certain bloodstains must be removed they should be carefully photographed and their exact location documented. One experienced in bloodstain interpretation can suggest grouping and individualization of bloodstains in specific areas that will assist the reconstruction. Remember that the source of all blood on victim's clothing may not be that of the victim.

6. If the clothing of the victim was cut prior to removal at autopsy it can be extremely helpful to restore it by sewing or taping to conform to its original configuration before bloodstain pattern study is begun.

7. The use of a manikin is helpful in orienting the location of bloodstains as they were while the victim or assailant wore the garments.

8. The investigator should study the original scene photographs of the victim at the time the clothing examination is being conducted. This will alert him to the possibility of artifacts being produced during removal and subsequent handling of the garments prior to examination.

9. Clothing should be adequately described in conjunction with the observed bloodstain patterns. Significant bloodstains should be measured and sketched showing their directionalities, relative sizes, shapes, and appearances. Be cautious with the interpretation of physical appearance and directionality of bloodstains on fabrics. Overall and close-up photographs should be taken with a measuring device in place.

10. A good light source is essential especially when small spatters are being examined on dark clothing and denim materials.

11. For photographic and demonstrative purposes the location of small blood spatters may be better visualized by encirclement with white ring binder reinforcements.

12. Mirror images of bloodstains may be created when wet, bloody clothing is folded.

13. Alternate clean areas on bloodstained clothing may indicate folds in the clothing during bloodshed.

14. Search carefully for bloody weapon transfer patterns especially in association with stabbing and blunt force injuries.

15. If blood has soaked through clothing be sure to determine upon which side of the fabric the blood initially made contact.

16. Always check the pockets of assailant's garments for blood transferred from the assailant's hands.

17. An assailant frequently steps in blood at a scene. Be sure to check the soles of assailant's footwear for bloodstain evidence.

18. When prone victims are beaten with a blunt object or kicked, medium-velocity blood spatters are usually found in the region of

the assailant's lower trouser legs and shirt sleeves. Be sure to examine the underside of the cuff areas as well as the shoes and socks of suspects in these situations.

19. The rear trouser leg and rear of the shirt of an assailant may receive cast-off bloodstain patterns from a bloody weapon when it is swung over the shoulder while an assailant is on his knees administering the blows to a prone victim.

20. A careful search for bloodstain evidence should be conducted on suspects clothing in those cases where sufficient time has elapsed for the clothing to have been washed. There is always the possibility that some detectable blood may have survived the cleaning procedure. The effect of water on bloodstained clothing including washed areas may show hemolysis and dilution of bloodstains. Evidence of diffusion of blood to areas previously not bloodstained may be recognizable.

21. Bloodstained clothing and footwear of the assailant may be the source of blood transfer fabric patterns and impressions on walls, doors, floors, and other objects at the scene. When duplicating patterns of this type for purposes of comparison always use the same material upon which the original pattern was produced.

22. The use of a stereomicroscope is very useful for the visualization of small bloodstains on dark fabrics and thick-knitted materials.

23. Leucomalachite green reagent or its equivalent will distinguish blood from spots of foreign substances, (paint, tar, etc.). This type of presumptive testing may prove useful during bloodstain examination of clothing, especially in the case of small spatters and areas not previously tested by a serologist that are important for the final interpretation.

References

1. Adelson, L. 1974. *The Pathology of Homicide*. Ch. 2. Springfield, IL: Charles C. Thomas Co.
2. Califana, A., and Lekov, J. 1978. *Criminalistics for the Law Enforcement Officer*. Chs. 2, 7. New York: McGraw-Hill Co.
3. Cunliffe, F., and Piazza, P. 1980. *Criminalistics and Scientific Investigation*. Ch. 5. Englewood Cliffs, NJ: Prentice-Hall, Inc.
4. Curran, W., McGarry, L., and Petty, C. 1980. *Modern Legal Medicine, Psychiatry, and Forensic Science*. Chs. 3, 5, 6. Philadelphia: F.A. Davis Co.
5. DeForest, P., Gaensslen, R., and Lee, H. 1983. *Forensic Science—An Introduction to Criminalistics*, Appendix Two. New York: McGraw-Hill Co.
6. Department of the Treasury. 1975. *Forensic Handbook*. United States Government Printing Office, Washington, D.C.
7. Eckert, W., Ed. 1980. *Introduction to Forensic Sciences*. Ch. 4. St. Louis, MO: C.V. Mosby Co.

8. Eckert, W. 1987. "Investigation of Deaths and Injuries." Medicolegal and Forensic Investigation Series. Ch. 1. The International Reference Organization in Forensic Medicine, Wichita, Kansas.

9. Fatteh, A. 1973. *Handbook of Forensic Pathology*. Ch. 1. Philadelphia: J.B. Lippincott.

10. Federal Bureau of Investigation. 1974. *Handbook of Forensic Science*. United States Government Printing Office, Washington, D.C.

11. Fisher, R., and Petty, C., Eds. 1977. *Forensic Pathology—A Handbook for Pathologists*. Ch. 5. National Institute of Law Enforcement and Criminal Justice. Law Enforcement Assistance Administration, United States Department of Justice, Washington, D.C.

12. Fox, R., and Cunningham, C. 1973. *Crime Scene Search and Physical Evidence Handbook*. United States Department of Justice, National Institute of Law Enforcement and Criminal Justice, Washington, D.C.

13. Harris, R. 1973. *Outline of Death Investigation*. Ch. 10. Springfield, IL: Charles C. Thomas Co.

14. Hughes, D. 1974. *Homicide Investigation Techniques*. Ch. 2. Springfield, IL: Charles C. Thomas Co.

15. Jones, L. 1959. Scientific Investigation and Physical Evidence, Chs. 1, 10–11. Springfield, IL: Charles C. Thomas Co.

16. Kirk, P. 1974. *Crime Investigation*, 2nd Edition. Ch. 3. New York: John Wiley & Sons.

17. MacDonell, H.L. 1983. Crime scene procedures. *Forensic Sciences*, Vol. 2, Cyril Wecht, Ed., pp. 35-5–35-23. New York: Matthew Bender.

18. Merkeley, D. 1957. *The Investigation of Death*. Chs. 10–11. Springfield, IL: Charles C. Thomas Co.

19. O'Brien, K., and Sullivan, R. 1972. *Criminalistics—Theory and Practice*, 2nd Edition. Ch. 3. Boston: Holbrook Press Inc.

20. O'Hara, C. 1970. *Fundamentals of Criminal Investigation*, 2nd Edition. Ch. 4. Springfield, IL: Charles C. Thomas Co.

21. O'Hara, C., and Osterburg, J. 1974. *An Introduction to Criminalistics— The Application of the Physical Sciences to the Detection of Crime*. Chs. 3–4. Bloomington, IN: Indiana University Press.

22. Osterburg, J. 1968. *The Crime Laboratory—Case Studies of Scientific Criminal Investigation*. Bloomington, IN: Indiana University Press.

23. Polson, C. 1967. *The Essentials of Forensic Medicine*, 2nd Edition. Springfield, IL: Charles C. Thomas Co.

24. Saferstein, R. 1981. *Criminalistics—An Introduction to Forensic Science*, 2nd Edition. Chs. 2–3. Englewood Cliffs, NJ: Prentice-Hall, Inc.

25. Snyder, L. 1977. *Homicide Investigation*, 3rd Edition. Chs. 1–2, 4. Springfield, IL: Charles C. Thomas Co.

26. Spitz, W., and Fisher, R. 1980. *Medicolegal Investigation of Death*, 2nd Edition. Chs. 15, 25. Springfield, IL: Charles C. Thomas Co.

27. Svensson, A., and Wendell, O. 1965. *Techniques of Crime Scene Investigation*, 2nd Edition. New York: Elsevier Science Publishing Co.

28. Swanson, C., Chamelin, N., and Territo, L. 1977. *Criminal Investigation*. Santa Monica, CA: Goodyear Publishing Co.

29. Turner, R. 1949. *Forensic Science and Laboratory Techniques*, Chs. 2–3. Springfield, IL: Charles C. Thomas Co.

30. Weston, P., and Wells, K. 1980. *Criminal Investigation*, 3rd Edition. Englewood Cliffs, NJ: Prentice-Hall, Inc.

The Identification and Individualization of Blood

5

STUART H. JAMES

The study of the physical, chemical, and serological aspects of blood and bloodstains has broad applications in forensic science. In conjunction with the interpretation of bloodstain patterns for crime scene reconstruction, blood evidence must be tested to (1) establish that the substance or stain is in fact blood, (2) determine whether it is of human or animal origin, and (3) establish an association with a particular individual by blood grouping and characterization of genetic markers. The methods utilized for the identification and individualization of blood are based upon the composition of the cellular and fluid components of the blood. The cellular components of the blood consist of red blood cells containing hemoglobin and cellular proteins, white blood cells or leukocytes, which are involved in functions of immune responses, and platelets or thrombocytes, which are an integral part of the blood clotting mechanism. The plasma or fluid portion is the transport medium for the cellular components of the blood as well as numerous, complex plasma proteins and biochemicals (Figure 5-1).

Preliminary Tests for Blood

The verification that a substance or suspected stain is blood is the initial step in the identification process. On the one hand, blood at crime scenes and on the clothing and body of victims is generally recognized without difficulty but verification is necessary for the ultimate reconstruction of a case and as an element of proof in a legal proceeding. On the other hand, the presence of blood at a crime scene may not be apparent to the investigator as in the case of small spots and smears. Food stains, paint, rust, cosmetics, and other reddish-

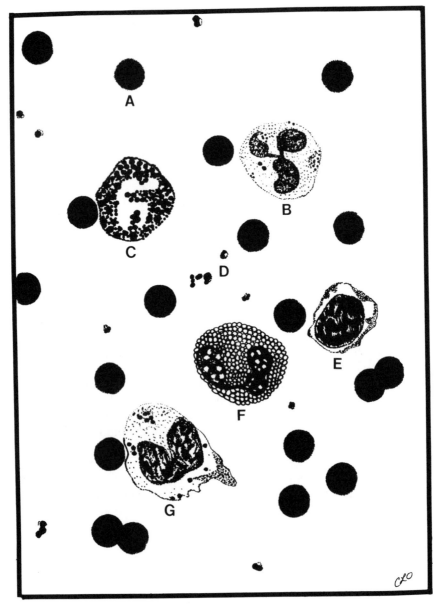

Figure 5-1 Normal cellular components of human blood as viewed micro-scopically. **(A)** Red cell (erythrocyte). **(B)** White cell (leukocyte—neutrophil). **(C)** White cell (leukocyte—basophil). **(D)** Platelet (thrombocyte). **(E)** White cell (leukocyte—lymphocyte). **(F)** White cell (leukocyte—eosinophil). **(G)** White cell (leukocyte—monocyte).

brown-colored materials may have the appearance of dried bloodstains and chemical testing is necessary to make the distinction.

When blood at a crime scene is in a fresh or wet state, the identification of blood can be established by microscopic examination. A sample drop of blood is smeared on a glass slide forming a thin film and allowed to air dry. The slide is then stained with a histological stain known as Wright's stain to permit microscopic visualization of the blood cells and characterization of their morphology. This technique is universally used in hospitals and clinical laboratories for evaluation of blood disorders and other disease conditions. By evaluation of nucleated red blood cells, the forensic microscopist can often distinguish animal from human blood in fresh bloodstain samples. The reconstitution of dried bloodstains for microscopic study is often difficult. Methods have been devised to restore the distorted morphology of blood cells in dried stains and crusts of blood by immersing the fragments in solutions containing physiological (0.9%) saline, albumin and glycerol prior to the histological staining procedure.

The chemical tests employed for the detection of blood are based upon the presence of hemoglobin and its derivatives. The tests are of two types, catalytic and crystal, which are frequently used in conjunction with one another in the laboratory. The catalytic tests for blood are presumptive in nature and employ an oxidation reaction and the catalytic peroxidase activity of the heme portion of the hemoglobin molecule. Positive results are characterized by production of a color or luminescence. Crystal tests are confirmatory for the presence of blood and based upon the formation of hemoglobin derivative crystals which are examined and identified through the microscope.

The catalytic color and luminescence tests for blood are utilized as presumptive or screening tests. They are highly sensitive to minute traces of hemoglobin but are subject to interference or false-positive reactions owing to the presence of a variety of nonblood substances and therefore not considered specific for the detection of blood. Preliminary testing of blood by these methods is a routine procedure in the laboratory but it is often desirable and productive to utilize them for testing suspected bloodstains at the crime scene. Although a negative test result may exclude a suspect stain as blood, all positive tests require confirmation to prove the presence of blood.

At the crime scene it is important to evaluate suspected bloodstains before attempts are made to dislodge or collect them for preliminary testing. Care should be exercised to minimize alteration of the stains. Prior to collection each bloodstain should be well documented, measured, and photographed. In most circumstances the blood-testing reagent should not be directly applied to the stain in that this may interfere with subsequent serological testing procedures. An exception to this rule is the use of the luminol test which will be described subsequently.

A convenient method of sample collection for preliminary blood testing at the scene is to gently rub a sterile cotton swab moistened with physiological (0.9%) saline or distilled water over an edge or portion of the suspected stain. An alternative method is to similarly moisten a corner of a piece of clean filter paper and touch the edge of the stain and allow the material to diffuse or absorb onto the filter paper. If the suspected stain is on cloth or other absorbent surface, a small thread or fiber may be removed with forceps and placed on a moistened section of filter paper. The blood-testing reagent is then applied to the swab or filter paper and the color reaction observed and recorded. It is imperative to perform the same procedure and test on an unstained area of the same surface to serve as a negative control. Additionally, it is recommended to perform a positive control test using known human blood. This will insure that the blood-testing reagent is working properly. Sections of filter paper containing small stains of human blood can be prepared, stored, and used for this purpose as needed. The type of test utilized will depend upon the preference of the investigator, the nature of the sample, and the degree of sensitivity desired. The common reagents that have been utilized as presumptive catalytic tests for blood are benzidine, o-tolidine, leucomalachite green, phenolphthalein, and luminol. Benzidine and o-tolidine are excellent, sensitive reagents for the detection of blood. However, each is considered potentially carcinogenic and their production and availability is restricted and no longer officially used in many laboratories. Leucomalachite green reagent, phenolphthalein, and luminol are widely used. Blood-testing reagents are available commercially in kit form and the manufacturer's directions should be followed for their use. The preparation of reagents and methods for these tests are not difficult and should be utilized by the crime scene investigator.

Benzidine Test

Preparation of Reagents

Reagent I (single stage). Add sufficient benzidine base to 2 ml of glacial acetic acid to make a saturated solution. Then add 2 ml of 3 percent hydrogen peroxide. This reagent should be prepared fresh for use in a dropper bottle.

Reagent II (two stage). An alternative method of preparation is to dissolve 0.25 g of benzidine base in 175 ml of absolute ethanol. Add 5–10 drops of glacial acetic acid. This mixture should be stored in a dropper bottle and refrigerated when not in use. A 3 percent solution of hydrogen peroxide should be stored in a separate dropper bottle.

Methods of Use

If reagent I is used, 1–2 drops is applied to the swabs or filter paper containing the unknown samples and controls. If reagent II is used, 1–2 drops is applied to the swab or filter paper containing unknown sample and controls followed by 1–2 drops of the 3 percent hydrogen peroxide. A rapidly developing deep blue color indicates a positive test. This color should develop within 10 seconds. The sensitivity of benzidine test is approximately 1 part in 300,000–500,000.

O-Tolidine Test

Preparation of Reagents

Add 1.6 g of o-tolidine base to 40 ml of absolute ethanol. To this are added 30 ml of glacial acid and 30 ml of distilled water. This solution should be stored in a dropper bottle and refrigerated when not in use. A 3 percent solution of hydrogen peroxide should be stored in a separate dropper bottle.

Method of Use

Apply 1–2 drops of reagent to the swabs or filter paper containing the unknown samples and controls followed by 1–2 drops of 3 percent hydrogen peroxide. A rapidly developing deep blue color indicates a positive test. This color should develop within 10 seconds. The sensitivity of the o-tolidine test is similar to that of benzidine.

Leucomalachite Green Test

Preparation of Reagents

Reagent I (single stage). Mix 0.32 g of sodium perborate thoroughly in a mortar and pestle with 0.1 g of leucomalachite green. Any multiple of this ratio may be used. This reagent should be stored at room temperature. Prepare a dilution of glacial acetic acid with distilled water using 8 ml of acetic acid to 4 ml of distilled water. Any multiple of this ratio may be used. At time of use add the reagent to the acetic acid solution. Individual quantities of preference may be prepared and stored for this purpose. A convenient quantity of test reagent is 0.14 g of the leucomalachite green/perborate mixture added to 4 ml of the acetic acid/water mixture. The test reagent mixture must be prepared fresh daily in a dropper bottle.

Reagent II (two stage). An alternative method of preparation is to mix 10 mg of leucomalachite green into 10 ml of the 8 ml of acetic acid/4 ml of distilled water solution. This reagent mixture must be prepared fresh daily in a dropper bottle. A 3 percent solution of hydrogen peroxide should be stored separately in a dropper bottle.

Methods of Use

If reagent I is used, apply 1–2 drops of reagent mixture to the swabs or filter paper containing the unknown samples and controls. If reagent I is used, apply 1–2 drops of reagent mixture to the swabs or filter paper containing the unknown samples and controls followed by 1–2 drops of the 3 percent hydrogen peroxide solution. A rapidly developing, deep blue-green color indicates a positive test. This color should develop within 10 seconds. The sensitivity of the leucomalachite test is approximately 1 part in 100,000.

Phenolphthalein Test

Preparation of Reagent

Mix 2.0 g of phenolphthalein, 20 g of potassium hydroxide, and 100 ml of distilled water. This mixture is refluxed with 20 g of powdered zinc until the solution becomes colorless (2–3 hours). This stock solution should be stored in a dark bottle under refrigeration with some powdered zinc added to maintain the reduced form.

The working solution is prepared by adding 20 ml of phenolphthalein stock solution to 80 ml of absolute ethanol and kept refrigerated when not in use. A solution of 3 percent hydrogen peroxide should be stored separately in a dropper bottle.

Method of Use

Apply 1–2 drops of the working reagent to the swabs or filter paper containing the unknown samples and controls followed by 1–2 drops of the 3 percent hydrogen peroxide solution. The rapid development of a bright pink color is a positive test. The sensitivity of the phenolphthalein test is approximately 1 part in 5 million.

Luminol Test

Luminol is a well-known chemiluminescent compound and is used as a presumptive, catalytic test for the presence of blood utilizing the peroxidase-like activity of heme for the production of light as an end product rather than a true color reaction.

Preparation of Reagents

A mixture of 0.5 g of luminol (3-aminophthalhydrazide) and 25 g of sodium carbonate is prepared and stored. A mixture of 3.5 g of sodium perborate in 500 ml of distilled water is prepared fresh as needed. At the time of use the luminol/sodium carbonate mixture and sodium perborate solution are mixed together for the working solution.

Method of Use

With the use of a spraying device, luminol reagent is applied on objects or areas containing traces of suspected bloodstains. A bluish-white luminescence or light production on the suspected area is a positive test. The luminescence must be observed in the dark. Luminol reagent is best utilized for the detection of traces of blood that are not readily observable at crime scenes such as light tracking of blood on dark surfaces, cracks and crevices in floors, washed areas, and plumbing traps. The patterns of blood traces resolved by the luminol test may be as important as the detection of the blood itself. The patterns of luminescence can be photographed or videotaped for permanent documentation. Successful photography and videotaping have been accomplished with the attachment of night vision devices to the cameras. The luminol test is nondestructive and does not interfere with confirmatory or subsequent serological tests of the blood.

The sensitivity of the luminol test is approximately as high as 1 part in 5 million. Aged and decomposed blood reacts better with luminol than do fresher bloodstains. Sensitivity of the luminol test to trace quantities of fresher blood may be enhanced by prior spraying of the suspect area with 2 percent hydrochloric acid.

The advantages of the above-described preliminary tests for blood are (1) the reagents are extremely sensitive to small quantities of blood, (2) the tests are relatively easy to perform and adaptable to crime scene work, (3) the results are rapidly obtained, and (4) reagents and supplies are relatively inexpensive and can often be obtained from a laboratory. Commercial kits for blood testing are more expensive but are packaged in vials for individual test use and reagent preparation is simplified.

Generally, a negative result with a catalytic color or luminscence test is accepted as proof of the absence of detectable quantities of blood in that sample. It should be noted, however, that the presence of strong reducing agents such as ascorbic acid may inhibit catalytic tests and false negatives may be obtained. Bloodstained objects that are improperly cleaned leaving blood residue and then subjected to heat or sterilization may render a falsely negative test result.

The major concern with the catalytic tests for blood is their lack of specificity or the obtaining of falsely positive results because of interfering substances of nonblood origin. The major sources of false-positive reactions with the catalytic tests include chemical oxidants, catalysts, and salts of heavy metals such as copper and nickel. Some examples of common substances that may produce false-positive reactions include iodine, household bleaches, rust, and formalin as well as plant peroxidases as found in horseradish, citrus fruits, bananas, watermelon, and numerous vegetables.

Many chemical oxidants will show a positive test result prior to the addition of hydrogen peroxide. If no color is produced until after the addition of hydrogen peroxide the sample more likely contains blood. A two-stage test would have to be employed to make the distinction between the plant peroxidases. Plant peroxidases may be destroyed by heating of the sample at 100 degrees centigrade for 5 minutes prior to testing which will not appreciably affect the heme portion of the hemoglobin if present.

The described catalytic tests for blood vary in their reactivity with interfering substances and specificity can be enhanced by application of the above procedures. Suspect stains tested with benzidine, o-tolidine, leucomalachite green, or phenolphthalein should be considered doubtful for the presence of blood when (1) the reaction is very faint in color, (2) the color is slow to develop (more than 10 seconds), (3) the color is concentrated at a small spot rather than diffused on the swab or filter paper, and (4) the color is abnormal. The luminol test is not exempt from interferences especially on metal surfaces. Experience with the reading of the color and luminescence reactions aids with the interpretation of doubtful stains. However, catalytic tests should be generally characterized as nonspecific for blood and each requires confirmatory testing to meet a rigorous standard of proof for the presence of blood. Catalytic tests do not differentiate between human and animal blood.

Confirmatory testing, species differentiation, and individualization of blood are performed in the laboratory. From a practical perspective the investigator should concentrate on the proper performance of the catalytic color or luminescence tests as a guide and aid to the investigation of the crime scene. When proper controls are utilized and good procedure followed, the preliminary positive test for blood will usually be proven correct by confirmatory testing. At many crime scenes, experienced observations and negative results with preliminary screening of suspect stains can also be of great assistance to the investigation and the overall crime scene reconstruction process.

Confirmatory Tests for Blood

The crystal tests for blood identification are considered to be more specific for the presence of blood than the catalytic tests and are generally considered to be a confirmatory test for suspected bloodstains. The crystal tests are based upon the formation of hemoglobin derivative crystals such as hematin, hemin, and hemochromogen. These crystals are developed by chemical conversion of the hemoglobin to characteristically shaped crystals which are identified by microscopy. When there is a sufficient quantity of blood available, crystal tests may be performed in the laboratory as a confirmation procedure for the presence of blood. The two popular crystal tests for blood identification are the Teichmann (hematin) test and the Takayama (hemochromogen) test.

Teichmann Crystal Test

Preparation of Reagent

A mixture of 0.1 g of potassium bromide, 0.1 g of potassium chloride, and 0.1 g of potassium iodide is dissolved in 100 ml of glacial acetic acid.

Method of Use

A small quantity of suspected bloodstain is placed on a clean glass slide and covered with a coverslip. A drop or two of the reagent is allowed to flow under the coverslip and make contact with the material. Air bubbles should be avoided. The slide should be gently heated with a flame until bubbles begin to form. A positive test is the formation of prismatic, yellow-brown hemin crystals observed through the microscope (Figure 5-2).

Takayama Crystal Test

Preparation of Reagent

A mixture is prepared containing 1.0 ml of 10 percent by volume sodium hydroxide, 1.0 ml of pyridine, 1.0 ml of saturated glucose (100 g/ 100 ml), and 2.0 ml of distilled water. Saturated glucose may be prepared by mixing 100 g of glucose in 100 ml of distilled water and heating to dissolve. The reagent should be prepared fresh prior to use.

Method of Use

A small portion of the suspected bloodstain is placed on a clean glass slide and covered with a coverslip. A drop or two of the reagent is

Figure 5-2 Teichmann test —hemin crystals.

allowed to flow under the coverslip and make contact with the material. The slide should be gently heated with a flame until bubbles begin to form. A positive test is the formation of pink-to-red hemochromogen crystals observed through the microscope (Figure 5-3).

The sensitivities of the Teichmann and Takayama tests are comparable and can detect as little as 0.001 ml of blood. The sensitivities are considerably lower than the catalytic tests. False positives are considered less of a problem with the Takayama test, which provides better results with samples taken from wood and leather surfaces and is generally preferred over the Teichmann crystal test for the confirmation of suspected bloodstains. Performance of the crystal tests tends to be time-consuming and an experienced microscopist is required to observe the results. The pyridine reagent is noxious and good ventilation is required when it is used. These tests are not generally suitable as crime scene procedures and are usually performed in a laboratory in conjunction with species of origin and other serological evaluations of bloodstain evidence.

In the laboratory, additional methods may be utilized for the identification of blood based upon the identification of hemoglobin and its derivatives. Absorption spectroscopy measures hemoglobin and its derivatives through their specific absorption spectra in the near-ultraviolet and visible light ranges. The separation and identification of hemoglobin may be achieved by electrophoretic separation on paper or cellulose acetate gel. Electrically charged hemoglobin molecules are moved by electrophoresis through the support medium towards the

Figure 5-3   Takayama test—
hemochromogen crystals.

electrode of opposite charge and the individual bands are visualized by means of catalytic color reagent. Paper chromatography, column chromatography, and thin-layer chromatography techniques have been developed for the identification of hemoglobin and its derivatives. All employ a separation procedure and visualization via a catalytic color reagent.

Species Differentiation of Blood

Once a suspected substance or stain has been identified as blood, it is important to establish whether it is of human or animal origin, and in some cases, the particular species of animal. Occasionally, blood at a crime scene may be animal blood for a variety of reasons and it is not uncommon for a suspect to claim that bloodstained clothing is the result of hunting or meat preparation. Proof of violations of fish and game regulations or domestic animal theft may require the determination of species of origin of a variety of animals. Sometimes fragments of flesh are discovered and it is imperative to make a distinction between animal and human remains.

The determination of species of origin of bloodstains is accomplished in forensic laboratories by an immunological procedure referred to as a precipitin test. Immunological tests involve reactions between antigens and antibodies. Generally defined, antibodies are proteins in the blood produced in response to a foreign substance, or antigen, introduced into a human or animal. Specific antibodies are produced in the blood in response to infectious diseases. Similarly, when human serum is injected into a rabbit or other animal, the foreign substance will cause an immunological response in the animal to produce antibodies to human serum. Rabbits are frequently used for this purpose. When blood is removed from the rabbit the serum, which now contains anti-human antibodies, is processed and is referred to as anti-human serum. It will react with human proteins in vitro and form a flocculent, white precipitate which is the basis for the precipitin test. In a similar manner antisera may also be produced that will react specifically with human hemoglobin and human seminal fluid. Each species of animal has specific proteins in its blood from which the corresponding antibody may be produced by injection into an animal of another species. Many laboratories maintain supplies of antisera of a variety of domestic and wild animals for species determination utilizing the precipitin test. Certain related species of animals may not be well differentiated such as horse/mule, goat/sheep, or dog/wolf. Anti-human serum exhibits cross-reactivity with the blood of apes and monkeys. However, in most parts of the world this does not pose a great problem. Immunological tests are universally used for species determination of bloodstains.

The precipitin test for species determination is quite sensitive and may be applied to small bloodstains. Any stain that is visible and imparts some color to the stain extract should be sufficient in size. The classic procedure and simple method is the interfacial or ring precipitin test. The stain is extracted and diluted with physiological (0.9%) saline. This extract is carefully layered over the antiserum in equal amounts in a small test tube or capillary tube without mixing. A positive test is the formation of a ring of white, opaque precipitate at the juncture of the two layers. A positive and negative control should be run in a similar manner.

Gel diffusion and electrophoretic techniques have been developed for antigen–antibody precipitin reactions. A double-diffusion technique in two dimensions, with the use of agarose plates as a medium with punched-out wells for stain extract and antiserum, is preferred by many forensic laboratories. This was first developed by Ouchterlony in 1949. Agarose gel is prepared in small plastic plates or dishes. Equidistant holes are punched in the gel around the periphery of the dish and one in the center. Individual stain extracts including positive and negative controls are placed in the outer wells and a specific antiserum in the center well. Antigen and antibody will diffuse outward from their respective well into the agarose gel medium. A thin line of white precipitate will form at the point of equivalence or contact of the reactants. Diffusion through this gel is slow and may require 24–48 hours for a visible precipitin line to form. Concentration of antibody and antigen is not as critical as some other techniques and small quantities of material may be tested with this procedure. This type of gel diffusion is commonly utilized for anti-human serum, anti-human hemoglobin, and anti-human seminal fluid reactions as well as a variety of animal species differentiation. When anti-human hemoglobin is utilized in the precipitin test it provides a single operation for the identification of blood and origin of species. This is especially useful when a limited quantity of stain is available.

Immunoelectrophoresis is a newer, more refined technique allowing the individual proteins to be defined by their electrophoretic mobility and their antigenic specificity. Procedures such as crossed-over electrophoresis and other related sophisticated techniques permit both qualitative and quantitative assays to be performed, require less time, and are capable of analyzing multiple samples.

The sensitivity of precipitin reactions to blood and tissue is decreased by aging, decomposition, washing, and excess exposure to heat. Positive results have been obtained on samples several years old. Samples that are contaminated with certain chemicals such as alcohol, formalin, acids, and alkalis may not react well. Leather and wood surfaces may contain tannins, which are protein precipitants and may cross-react with antisera. The proper use of positive and negative control samples is essential.

In 1973, Cayzer and Whitehead developed a sensitized latex particle technique for species determination of blood stains. It is a rapid slide-agglutination technique which in the future may have application within the range of potential crime scene investigative techniques.

Identification of the Sex and Race of Blood

Examination of bloodstains for sex and race determination has been successful with fresh blood. Nuclear bodies in leukocytes have been studied and chromatin masses corresponding to the XX chromosomes of the female referred to as Barr bodies have been demonstrated. These appear microscopically as a "drumstick" projection from the nucleus of neutrophilic leukocytes. Methods of identifying the male Y chromosomes have been developed using fluorescent techniques with fresh blood.

Radioimmunoassay procedures have been applied to bloodstains to establish sex by means of sex hormone quantitation. Associated with sex determination, the identification of menstrual blood has application in certain cases. Fresh menstrual blood may be examined microscopically for specific cellular composition. Electrophoretic separation of lactic dehydrogenase isoenzymes and studies of the clot-inhibiting substances in menstrual blood show promise as identification techniques. Application of these techniques with older dried bloodstains is complex and these tests are not routinely performed.

Differentiation between adult and fetal bloodstains is possible by electrophoretic separation of hemoglobin F or fetal hemoglobin. Electrophoresis is also utilized for the separation and identification of abnormal hemoglobins in bloodstains which can assist with the determination of race. Certain abnormal hemoglobins are associated with race-related blood disorders such as sickle cell anemia. Carriers of the sickle cell trait characterized by hemoglobin type A/S are normally confined to black populations or persons of black ancestry.

Bloodstain Grouping and Genetic Marker Individualization

When blood or dried bloodstains related to a crime scene have been identified as human in origin, the forensic serologist attempts to further characterize this blood in order to relate it to a particular individual, or, of equal importance, to prove that a particular individual could not have produced the bloodstain in question. This is important information for the evaluation of specific bloodstains found at crime scenes on relevant clothing, weapons, or other objects inasmuch as they relate to the blood of the victim or the assailant and the reconstruction of the scene. Blood grouping and individualization assist with the association of a victim with an assailant when there has been transfer of blood from victim to assailant's clothing, vehicle, or other environment. Sometimes during the course of a struggle or violent activity, an assailant may bleed and deposit bloodstains at the scene or on the clothing of the victim. The blood groups and genetic markers found in bloodstains must be compared to the blood of one or more persons in order to provide an association or exclusion.

The individuality of fresh human blood depends upon genetic factors and their population distribution. These genetic factors are inherited and do not change throughout life. The genetic individualizing features of human blood are a complex system of blood groups and biochemical markers and can be classified into the following major groups:

1. Blood group or red cell antigens
2. Red cell isoenzymes
3. Serum or plasma proteins
4. Hemoglobin variants
5. HLA system antigens
6. DNA polymorphisms

An increasing number of blood group systems and biochemical markers are being discovered and there is a vast amount of scientific literature on the subject. Full comprehension of the significance of blood individuality requires a complete knowledge and understanding of genetics, statistics, and sophisticated serological techniques. It is important to recognize that the highest degree of individuality is achieved with fresh, whole-blood samples. The degree of individuality that is possible with a corresponding dried bloodstain depends upon the amount of sample available and the persistence of the antigenic and biochemical substances over time and under varied and often unpredictable environmental conditions. Small and or aged stains will permit characterization of fewer systems. Dried bloodstains may be subject to excessive heat and desiccation as well as deterioration and contamination. None of these conditions are conducive to good results. Other than the ABO antigenic group, few systems persist more than a year in dried stains. It is also significant that laboratories involved with the grouping and individualization of dried bloodstains may choose to type different combinations and numbers of antigenic systems and genetic markers for a variety of reasons and preferences. It is not possible to completely individualize a person's blood to the exclusion of all others. However, with sufficient sample size, timely collection, absence of sample contamination, and good system selection, significant individualization of dried bloodstains is frequently achieved.

Blood Group Antigens

The initial effort to further individualize human bloodstains is the determination of the blood group within the ABO system. Landsteiner is credited with the discovery of the ABO system in 1901. He observed that the red cells of some co-workers would agglutinate or clump when mixed with the serum of some other co-workers but not all. This led to the division of all individuals into four main blood groups based upon the fact that A and B antigen can be present individually, together, or may be absent from the blood. Anti-A and anti-B antibodies occur naturally in the serum of individuals not possessing the corresponding antigen (Table 5-1). The designated blood groups were classified as A, B, AB, and O. The observations and studies of Landsteiner provided a scientific basis for the individualization of human blood and the com-

Table 5-1 Antigens and Naturally Occurring Antibodies in ABO Groups

Group	Antigen on red cell	Antibody in serum
A	A	Anti-B
B	B	Anti-A
AB	A and B	None
O	None	Anti-A and anti-B

patibility or noncompatibility of human blood for transfusion. Subsequent studies of immune reactions after transfusion and immunizations acquired after pregnancy led to the discovery of additional red cell antigenic systems. An important milestone in medicine was the discovery of the Rh system in 1941 by Landsteiner and Weiner which further reduced the incidence of transfusion reactions that previously were unexplained. The principles of red cell antigen and serum antibody systems are applied in all present studies of blood group systems in medicine and forensic science.

The ABO grouping of fresh, whole blood is easily accomplished and is a routine procedure in blood banks, hospitals, and forensic laboratories. The grouping is established by the detection of antigenic substance on the red cells and the natural antibodies in the plasma or serum of the blood. Group A blood possesses A antigen and anti-B antibody. Group B blood possesses B antigen and anti-A antibody. Group AB blood possesses A and B antigen but neither anti-A nor anti-B antibodies. Group O blood possesses neither A nor B antigen but does possess both anti-A and anti-B antibodies.

Almost all human red cells contain a quantity of H substance protein. Group O blood contains the highest quantity of H substance. This is detected by reaction and agglutination with anti-H lectin which is extracted from the seeds of the plant *Ulex europaeus*. The reactivity of anti-H lectin varies with the ABO group decreasing in strength as follows:

$$O > A_2 > A_2B > B > A_1 > A_1B$$

Most group A individuals are classified as (A1) or A. The designation A2 is a weaker subgroup of A which may not react with anti-A serum and is sometimes misclassified as group O. The protein substance anti-A lectin is extracted from the seeds of the plant *Dolichos biflorus* and produces a specific and potent agglutination with A1 and A1B red cells and is routinely used to make this differentiation.

With fresh, whole blood, ABO grouping may be accomplished by procedures referred to as forward and reverse grouping performed on glass slides or in test tubes. Forward grouping of blood (Table 5-2) is performed by placing a drop of anti-A, anti-B, and anti-H antisera in

Table 5-2 Agglutination of Red Cells with Forward ABO Grouping of Blood

Blood group	Anti-A serum	Anti-B serum	Anti-H serum
A	+	−	+/−
B	−	+	−
AB	+	+	+/−
O	−	−	+

separate locations on glass slides or in individual marked test tubes. To each is added a drop of whole blood which is mixed with the antisera. The glass slides are gently rotated to achieve proper mixing and observed for agglutination. If the test tube method is used, the tubes are centrifuged after mixing and gently shaken and observed for agglutination.

Reverse grouping or confirmation of the results of forward grouping is performed by placing 2 drops of plasma or serum into each of three test tubes which are identified and labeled A and B. Two drops of a 2 percent suspension of known A red cells is added to test tube A and 2 drops of known B red cells is added to tube B. Each is mixed, centrifuged appropriately, and observed for agglutination.

The ABO grouping of dried bloodstains is more complex than with fresh blood and different techniques are employed to test them. The red blood cells rupture and hemolyze when the bloodstains dry, and there is no way to restore them to their original condition in order to observe the agglutination process. Therefore, indirect methods are usually employed for the grouping of dried bloodstains.

The Lattes crust test is sometimes utilized when the bloodstain is of sufficient quantity and is not too old. This test is actually a version of reverse grouping of fresh blood in that it detects serum antibodies on the dried bloodstain (Table 5-3). Known red cell suspensions of group A and group B are allowed to mix with small crusts or fragments of the bloodstain on separate sections of a glass slide beneath a coverslip. If the corresponding antibody is still present on the fragments, agglutination of the red cells will occur as it would in the reverse grouping of fresh blood. The presence of agglutination is observed microscopically. Negative results with A and B cells may be considered inconclusive. The results with O cells must be negative or the test cannot be interpreted. This test does not work well with bloodstains more than a few weeks old and contamination may produce cross-agglutination of the red cells. The use of good controls is essential.

Despite the fact that the red cells are ruptured in dried bloodstains, the ABO group antigenic substances persist in the stain for a considerably longer period of time and are far more stable than the natural

Table 5-3 Reaction of Serum with Known Red Cells in Reverse ABO Grouping

Blood group	Reaction with A red cells	Reaction with B red cells
A	−	+
B	+	−
AB	−	−
O	+	+

antibodies that are detected with the Lattes crust test. There are three types of indirect methods for the detection of ABO antigenic substances in dried bloodstains: (1) absorption-inhibition, (2) absorption-elution, and (3) mixed agglutination. These methods correspond in a sense to the forward grouping of fresh blood.

Absorption-elution is the most popular technique utilized in forensic laboratories for ABO grouping as well as for MN and Rh typing and thus will be described in some detail. Depending upon the nature of the sample to be tested, different methods of sample preparation may be employed for the absorption-elution procedure. The Howard-Martin technique is often utilized for bloodstained clothing and fibers. Individual bloodstained threads are removed from the sample and affixed to glass plates, cellulose acetate sheets, or other suitable medium with glue or clear nail polish. The Kind-Cleeveley technique involves the extraction of the bloodstain with a few drops of 5 percent ammonium hydroxide and applying the extract to glass slides and fixing the stain with gentle heat. With each technique it is imperative to run simultaneous controls of known A, B, AB, and O group bloodstains in addition to negative control samples. The absorption-elution procedure that follows is similar with respect to each technique of sample preparation.

The principle of the absorption-elution technique for ABO grouping is that blood group antigens persisting in dried bloodstains will specifically bind to corresponding antibodies when mixed and incubated with the specific antiserums, anti-A, anti-B, and anti-H on the glass plates or cellulose acetate sheets at 4 degrees centigrade (Table 5-4). Unbound antibodies and the excess antisera are removed from the antigen—antibody complex by multiple washings with ice-cold saline and air dried. A drop of each of the indicator cells, 0.5 percent suspensions of known A, B, and O cells, is added to the appropriate area on the glass plates or cellulose acetate sheets which are then incubated for 15 minutes at 56 degrees centigrade. The plates or sheets are then rotated gently for 20 minutes at room temperature. Agglutination is observed microscopically.

Anti-H serum will give a strong agglutination with group O blood

Table 5-4 Absorption-Elution Technique for ABO Grouping: Reactions of Dried Bloodstains on Plate or Sheet

Blood group	Anti-A serum and A cells	Anti-B serum and B cells	Anti-H serum and O cells
A	+	−	+/−
B	−	+	−
AB	+	+	+/−
O	−	−	+

Table 5-5 The Average White Population Frequency of the ABO System

Group	Percentage	Group	Percentage
O	43	B	12
A	42	AB	3

and with the subgroup A_2 and A_2B. As described previously reaction with B, A_1, and A_1B in that order is relative to the amount of H substance present on the red cells.

Nonspecific absorption may occur with absorption-elution techniques owing to bacterial contamination or other interfering substances which may interfere with the interpretation of the test results. Blood group antigen proteins are secreted into body fluids by approximately 80 percent of the population. It would follow that contamination of the bloodstain sample with saliva, urine, and perspiration of another individual can cause problems in interpretation. For this reason it is important that the sample area of a dried bloodstain to be tested not be touched with the hands to avoid transfer of antigenic substance to the bloodstain or surrounding area of the surface upon which it has been deposited. Again it is emphasized always to utilize negative as well as positive controls during the testing procedures. A major advantage of the absorption-elution technique is its sensitivity. Quantities of blood in the range of 0.01–0.02 mg may be grouped in the ABO system. Modifications to the absorption-elution technique can increase the sensitivity to 0.001 mg of blood.

The population distribution of the ABO blood groups throughout the world has been shown to vary within certain races and localities (Table 5-5). Marked differences may persist in populations with a varied ethnic composition (Table 5-6).

Table 5-6 The Ethnic Variation of the ABO System

Race	O	A	B	AB
Whites—New York	45.6	36.4	13.5	4.5
Blacks—New York	44.2	30.3	21.8	3.7
Sioux Indians—South Dakota	91.0	7.0	2.0	0.0
Chinese—Peking	30.7	25.1	34.2	10.0
English—London	44.4	42.8	9.6	3.2
Welsh—Wales	47.9	32.8	16.2	3.1
Japanese (Ainu)—Okinawa	63.9	17.3	13.6	4.9
Germans—Berlin	40.0	39.5	15.1	5.4
Filipinos	41.6	23.1	30.3	5.0
Italians	46.7	40.8	8.9	3.6

(Blood group percent)

Source: Tedeschi, Eckert, and Tedeschi, *Forensic Medicine,* Vol. 2, Chapter 26, W.B. Saunders Company, 1977.

Table 5-7 Comparative Nomenclature of the Common Rh
Classification Systems

	Fisher-Race	Weiner
	D	Rh
	C	rh'
	E	rh''
	c	hr'
	e	hr''

The Rh system (Table 5-7) bears no genetic relationship to the ABO
system. The Rh type is determined in fresh and dried blood samples
with the use of specific antisera such as anti-Rh(D). The characterization of the Rh system in dried bloodstains may be performed by absorption-elution techniques. However, relatively large sample sizes are required than for ABO grouping and bloodstains older than 6 weeks may
not react. Rh typing of dried bloodstains is not yet a routine procedure
in all forensic laboratories. The Rh(D) antigen is most frequently characterized. Approximately 85 percent of the population possess this
antigen and are considered Rh positive with the remaining 15 percent
characterized as Rh negative (Table 5-8). Different Rh types have been
identified.

A third group of red cell antigens that has received attention in
forensic laboratories is the MNS system (Table 5-9). In this system the
MN group is closely linked to the S group. However, this system is not
utilized routinely for the characterization of dried bloodstains. Three
blood groups belong to the MN system.

When the genetically linked Ss group is included with the MN
group, the approximate population frequency may be further subdivided (Table 5-10).

Table 5-8 The Approximate Relative Population Frequency of the Common
Rh Types in the United States

System	Type	White percent	Black percent
Rh	Rho	2	48
	Rh_1rh	34	20
	Rh_1Rh_1	18	2
	Rh_2rh	12	14
	Rh_2Rh_2	3	1
	Rh_1Rh_2	13	3
	rh	14	6
	Rarer types	4	6

Source: DeForest, Gaensslen, and Lee, *Forensic Science—An Introduction to Criminalistics,*
McGraw-Hill, 1983.

Table 5-9 The Average White Population Frequency of the MN System

Group	Percent frequency
MN	50
M	28
N	22

Table 5-10 Approximate Population Frequency of the MNSs Blood Group System in the United States

System	Type	White percent	Black percent
MNSs	MS	6	2
	MSs	14	6
	Ms	9	15
	MNS	3	3
	MNSs	24	12
	MNs	24	35
	NS	1	2
	NSs	5	5
	Ns	14	20

Source: DeForest, Gaensslen, and Lee, *Forensic Science—An Introduction to Criminalistics,* McGraw-Hill, 1983.

A number of other red cell antigen systems have been discovered such as the Kell, Duffy, Lewis, Kidd, Lutheran, Diego systems (Table 5-11), which have significant application in cross-matching fresh blood for transfusion and blood testing in cases of disputed parentage. Their forensic application to the typing of dried bloodstains is limited to highly specialized forensic serology laboratories.

Table 5-11 Approximate Population Frequencies of the Kell, Duffy, and Kidd Systems in the United States

System	Type	White percent	Black percent
Kell	KK	<1	<1
	Kk	9	2
	kk	91	98
Duffy	Fy(a$^+$b$^-$)	17	9
	Fy(a$^+$b$^+$)	51	4
	Fy(a$^-$b$^+$)	32	23
	Fy(a$^-$b$^-$)	—	64
Kidd	Jk(a$^+$b$^-$)	27	55
	Jk(a$^+$b$^+$)	52	38
	Jk(a$^-$b$^+$)	21	7

Source: DeForest, Gaensslen, and Lee, *Forensic Science—An Introduction to Criminalistics,* McGraw-Hill, 1983.

The Red Cell Isoenzymes

The red blood cells contain numerous and varied protein enzymes or catalysts for very specific biochemical reactions. Methods of electrophoresis and isoelectric focusing using various support mediums are utilized for the separation and characterization of these isoenzymes (Table 5-12). Many of the isoenzymes are polymorphic in nature in that different individuals will possess different forms of a particular enzyme. Those associated with glucose metabolism are particularly useful for forensic individualization. Laboratories develop their own protocols for characterization of particular isoenzymes. Of important consideration are size and age of sample, stability of the isoenzyme, and the useful population frequency of the polymorphs of the isoenzyme system. For example, the phosphoglucomutase (PGM) system is very stable and possesses three phenotypes within the population.

Table 5-12 Approximate Population Frequencies of the Red Cell Isoenzyme Systems in the United States

System	Type	White percent	Black percent
Phosphoglucomutase (PGM)	1	59	66
	2-1	35	29
	2	6	5
Adenylate kinase (AK)	1	93	99
	2-1	7	1
	2	<1	<1
Erythrocytic acid phosphatase (EAP)	A	12	7
	BA	42	32
	B	40	58
	CA	2	1
	CB	4	2
	C	<1	<1
Glyoxalase I (GLO)	1	18	14
	2-1	52	41
	2	30	45
Esterase D (ESD)	1	79	84
	2-1	20	15
	2	1	1
Adenosine deaminase (ADA)	1	90	97
	2-1	10	3
	2	<1	<1
6-Phosphogluconate dehydrogenase (6PGD)	A	96	93
	AC	4	7
	C	<1	<1

Source: DeForest, Gaensslen, and Lee, *Forensic Science—An Introduction to Criminalistics,* McGraw-Hill, 1983.

Table 5-13 Approximate Population Frequencies of the Serum Group Systems in the United States

System	Type	White percent	Black percent
Haptoglobin (Hp)	1	17	29
	2-1	48	39
	2	35	19
	2-1M	<1	10
	0	<1	3
Group-specific component (Gc)	1	50	76
	2-1	42	22
	2	8	2
Transferrin (Tf)	C	99	95
	CB	1	0
	CD	<1	5
Gm and Km	Many		

Source: DeForest, Gaensslen, and Lee, *Forensic Science—An Introduction to Criminalistics*, McGraw-Hill, 1983.

Serum and Plasma Proteins

Some of the proteins in serum and plasma exhibit several variants similar to the red cell isoenzymes. The most significant ones are the immunoglobulin genetic markers, Gm and Km, which are typed serologically and have been found to be quite stable. The most important serum group systems are haptoglobin (Hp), group-specific component (Gc), and transferrin (Tf). These are usually determined by electrophoresis or isoelectric focusing techniques (Table 5-13).

DNA and Additional Individualization Systems and Parameters

The human leukocyte antigen (HLA) system consists of numerous antigens located on the lymphocytic white cells and various tissues and is used primarily for the investigation of disputed parentage and may be applied to the individualization of dried bloodstains in the future.

There is also current interest in DNA coding for the identification of bloodstains, postmortem tissue analysis, and individualization of seminal stains. DNA fingerprinting is a term applied to the isolation of portions of the DNA chain which have a wide application of uses. In each person's DNA chain, there are breaks referred to as "Stutters" which appear in a repetitive pattern throughout the DNA molecule. Dr. Alec Jeffries, a British researcher, has developed a procedure in which DNA is extracted and purified from a sample of blood, semen, or other DNA bearing tissue. The DNA is then cut apart with a restriction enzyme that fragments the DNA double strands at specific DNA sequences. After further separation, the DNA fragments are transferred to a nylon membrane where the DNA probes are added. The probes attach themselves to specific invisible bands of repetitive DNA in such a manner that they fit like the teeth of a zipper. The membrane is then exposed to an x-ray film which results in a "DNA fingerprint." The bands of the fingerprints are analyzed and compared to establish a positive identification. The bar code that results from this procedure is unique to every individual except identical twins. In forensic investigations, a direct comparison would be made between the sample of blood, semen or other tissue obtained from the crime scene or victim with a sample obtained from a suspect. There will either be a direct match or virtually no similarity between the two samples. Small quantities of sample will suffice for analysis. The procedure can be accom-

Table 5-14 Outline of Bloodstain Identification

Documentation and Photography of Bloodstain

Collection of Sample

Presumptive Catalytic Color Tests	*Confirmatory Crystal Tests*
Benzidine	Teichmann
O-tolidine	Takayama
Leucomalachite green	
Phenolphthalein	
Luminol	

Origin of Species
Anti-human serum
Anti-human hemoglobin

Individualization

Red Cell Antigen Systems	*Red Cell Isoenzymes*
ABO	Phosphoglucomutase (PGM)
Rh	Adenylate kinase (AK)
MNS	Erythrocytic acid phosphatase (EAP)
	Glyoxalase I (GLO)
	Esterase D (ESD)
	Adenosine deaminase (ADA)
	6-Phosphogluconate dehydrogenase (6PGD)

Serum Genetic Markers
Gm
Km
Transferrin (Tf)
Group-specific component (Gc)
Haptoglobin (Hp)
Hemoglobin variants

plished on 1 to 2 drops of blood, trace seminal stains, and as few as ten hair roots. The DNA molecule is very stable and may persist in samples weeks, months, and even years old. However, as is the case with the more traditional methods of blood groupings and genetic marker profiles, the older the sample the more likely the results will be not as reliable.

Current research is also being conducted on dried bloodstains to investigate individualization through specific biochemical profiling, specific antibody profiling produced by allergic or disease states, and the detection of trace quantities of various drugs.

Summary

An outline of bloodstain identification, as provided point by point in this chapter, is given in Table 5-14.

References

1. American Association of Blood Banks. 1970. *Technical Methods and Procedures,* 5th Edition. Chicago, Illinois.
2. BNA Criminal Practice Manual. 1987. Trial Practice Series, Vol. 1, No. 19. Cellmark Diagnostics, Germantown, Maryland.
3. Boyd, W.C. 1966. *Fundamentals of Immunology,* 4th Edition. New York: Interscience Publishers.
4. Camps, F.E., Ed. 1968. *Gradwohl's Legal Medicine.* Baltimore, MD: Williams and Wilkins Co.
5. Chisum, W.J. 1971. A rapid method for grouping dried bloodstains. *Journal of the Forensic Science Society* 11, 205–206.
6. Culliford, B.J. 1971. "The Examination and Typing of Bloodstains in the Crime Laboratory." United States Government Printing Office, Washington, D.C.
7. Culliford, B.J., and Nickolls, L.C. 1964. The benzidine test—critical review. *Journal of Forensic Sciences* 9, 175.
8. DeForest, P.R., Gaensslen, R.E., and Lee, H.C. 1983. *Forensic Science—An Introduction to Criminalistics.* Ch. 9. New York: McGraw-Hill Co.
9. FBI Laboratory. 1972. Examination of biological fluids. *Federal Bureau of Investigation Law Enforcement Bulletin,* Washington, DC, 1972.
10. Fiori, A. 1962. "Detection and Identification of Bloodstains." In *Methods of Forensic Science,* Vol. 1, pp. 243–290. New York: Interscience Publishers.
11. Gaensslen, R.E., and Camp, F. 1983. Forensic serology: Analysis of bloodstains and body fluid stains. *Forensic Sciences,* Vol. 2, Cyril Wecht, Ed., pp. 29-3, 29-93. Matthew Bender Co., New York, New York.
12. Gaensslen, R.E., Desio, P., and Lee, H.C. 1986. Genetic marker systems: Individualization of blood and body fluids. *Forensic Science,* 2nd Edition, Geoffrey Davies, Ed. American Chemical Society, Washington, DC.
13. Gonzales, T.A., Vance, M., Helpern, M., and Umberger, C. 1954. *Legal Medicine, Pathology, and Toxicology,* 2nd Edition. New York: Appleton-Century-Crofts Co.
14. Grodsky, M., Wright, K., Kirk, P.L. 1951. Simplified preliminary blood

testing—An improved technique and comparative study of methods. *Journal of Criminal Law and Criminal Police Science* 42, 15.

15. Harris, H. 1970. *The Principles of Human Biochemical Genetics.* New York: Elsevier Science Publishing Co.
16. Hyland Laboratories. 1964. *Reference Manual of Immunohematology,* 2nd Edition. Los Angeles, California.
17. Jones, L.V. 1959. *Scientific Investigation and Physical Evidence.* Ch. 11. Springfield, IL: Charles C. Thomas Co.
18. Kanter, E., Baird, M., Shaler, R., and Balazs, I. 1986. Analysis of restriction fragment length polymorphisms in deoxyribonucleic acid (DNA) recovered from dried bloodstains. *Journal of Forensic Sciences,* Vol. 31, No. 2, pp. 403–408, April.
19. Kind, S.S. 1962. The ABO grouping of bloodstains. *Journal of Criminal Law, and Criminal and Police Science* 53, 367–374.
20. Kirk, P.L. 1974. *Crime Investigation,* Ch. 15. New York: John Wiley & Sons.
21. Kirk, P.L., Grunbaum, B. 1969. Individuality of blood and its forensic significance. *Legal Medicine Annual,* Cyril Wecht, Ed. New York: Appleton-Century-Crofts Co.
22. Knight, B. 1977. "Blood Identification." In *Forensic Medicine,* Vol. II, edited by Tedeschi, C.G., Eckert, W.G., and Tedeschi, L.G. Philadelphia: W.B. Saunders Co.
23. Landsteiner, K., and Levine, P. 1927. Further observations on individual differences of human blood. Proceedings of the Society of Experimental Biology and Medicine 24, 941.
24. Lee, H.C. 1982. "Identification and Grouping of Bloodstains." In *Forensic Science Handbook,* edited by Saferstein, R. Englewood Cliffs, NJ: Prentice-Hall, Inc.
25. Marsters, R., and Schlein, F. 1958. Factors affecting the deterioration of dried bloodstains. *Journal of Forensic Sciences* 3, 288–302.
26. Moenssens, A.A., Inbau, F.E. 1978. *Scientific Evidence in Criminal Cases,* 2nd Edition. Mineola, NY: The Foundation Press, Inc.
27. Moureau, P. 1963. *Determination of Blood Groups in Bloodstains Methods of Forensic Science,* Vol. 2. New York: Interscience Publishing Co.
28. Nelson, M., Turner, L., and Reisner, E. 1980. A feasibility study of human leucocyte antigen (HLA) typing from dried bloodstains. *Journal of Forensic Sciences,* Vol. 25, No. 3, pp. 479–498.
29. Nickolls, L.C., and Pereira, M. 1962. A study of modern methods of grouping dried bloodstains. *Medicine, Science, and the Law* 2, 172–179.
30. Ortho Diagnostics. *The ABO and Rh Systems.* Raritan, NJ: Ortho Diagnostics and Pharmaceutical Co.
31. Race, R.R., and Sanger, R. 1968. *Blood Groups in Man,* 5th Edition. Philadelphia: F.A. Davis Co.
32. Schleyer, R. 1962. "Investigation of Biological Stains with Regard to Species Origin." In *Methods of Forensic Science,* Vol. 1. New York: Interscience Publishing Co.
33. Sensabaugh, G.F. 1982. "Biochemical Markers of Individuality." In *Forensic Science Handbook,* edited by Saferstein, R. Englewood Cliffs, NJ: Prentice-Hall, Inc.
34. Stuver, W.C., et al. 1975. "Forensic bloodstains and physiological fluid analysis." In *Forensic Science,* Geoffrey Davies, Ed. American Chemical Society, Washington, DC.
35. Weiner, A.S. 1961. *Advances in Blood Grouping,* vols. 1 and 2, p. 965. New York: Grune and Stratton Co.

Experimentation, Special Procedures, and Research

6

Construction of a Simulated Head for High-Velocity Blood Spatter Experiments with Firearms
Stuart H. James

A basic course in bloodstain interpretation includes laboratory exercises to create bloodstains of various patterns that are studied in relation to actual bloodstains found at crime scenes. For detailed descriptions of fundamental bloodstain experiments, reference should be made to *Laboratory Manual for the Geometric Interpretation of Human Bloodstain Evidence* by MacDonell or *Experiments and Practical Exercises in Bloodstain Pattern Analysis* by Laber and Epstein.

During the reconstruction of crime scenes utilizing bloodstain interpretation, it is often desirable to conduct experiments under known conditions for comparison to and verification of conclusions drawn from the actual bloodstain patterns at the scene.

The investigation of gunshot injuries of the head often produces significant bloodstain patterns of high-velocity blood spatter usually more prevalent in the form of forward spatter from the exit wound. In conjunction with the angle of entry and exit of the projectile and wound characteristics, the quantity and distribution of this blood spatter can assist with the reconstruction of the shooting and the distinction between homicide, suicide, or accident. Laboratory experiments in basic bloodstain courses have utilized the principle of shooting through blood-soaked polyurethane sponges to demonstrate forward and backspatter. This creates an amount of high-velocity blood spatter in excess of that produced at many crime scenes since the blood source is fully exposed and not covered by hair, skin, tissue, or bone. Head gear is occasionally encountered on some victims of shootings which provides an additional barrier to distribution of high-velocity blood

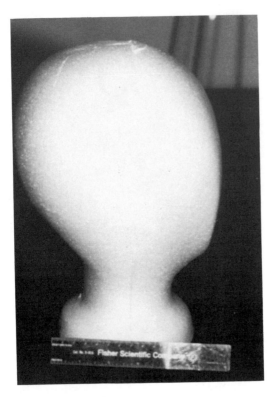

Figure 6-1 Styrofoam wig head prior to head construction.

spatter. The following described construction of simulated human heads was devised to study experimentally the distribution of high-velocity forward blood spatter and has been related effectively to actual case work.

The procedure for construction of the heads was a modification of a technique developed by MacDonell and Brooks for their research of the drawback effect of blood into the muzzle of firearms, which is described later in this chapter. Styrofoam wig supports were chosen for the head structures (Figure 6-1) and were sawed longitudinally into left and right halves. A propane torch was utilized to hollow out a "brain cavity" (Figure 6-2). The halves were then reunited and taped together (Figure 6-3). Gelatin was prepared to simulate brain material and the liquid was poured into the head cavities through the existing opening in the necks. The heads were then refrigerated overnight to allow the gelatin to solidify.

With the use of a heated putty knife $3\frac{1}{2} \times 3\frac{1}{2} \times \frac{1}{2}$-inch depressions were created in the styrofoam surface in areas approximating the entrance and exit wounds that existed on the victim (Figure 6-4, a and b). Within these depressions were placed cut sections of skull that were available for this purpose (Figure 6-5, a and b). For comparative pur-

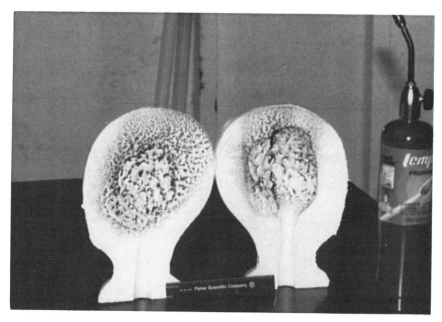

Figure 6-2 Styrofoam head halved with saw and cavities hollowed out with propane torch.

Figure 6-3 Styrofoam head reassembled and cavity filled with gelatin to simulate brain tissue.

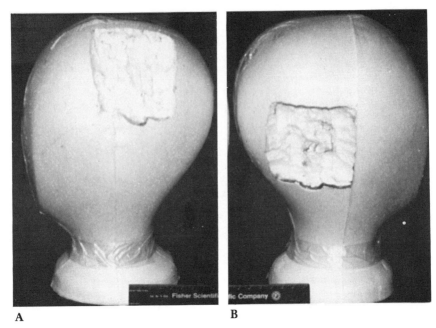

A B

Figure 6-4 (A) Entrance wound area formed with hot putty knife. (B) Exit wound area formed with hot putty knife.

Figure 6-5 (A) Bone or plastic inserted into entrance wound site. (B) Bone or plastic inserted into exit wound site.

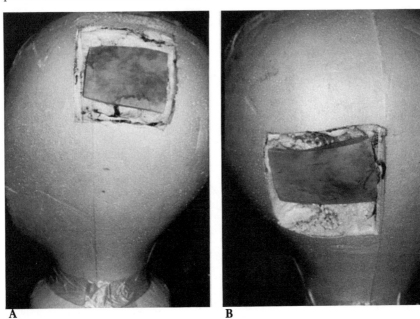

A B

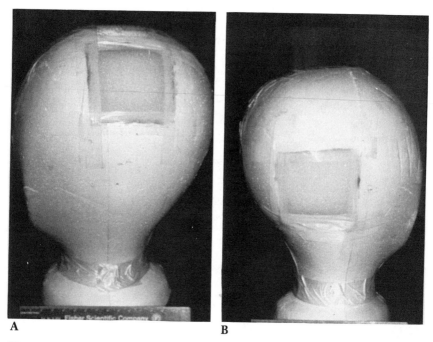

Figure 6-6 (A) Polyurethane sponge inserted into entrance wound site. (B) Polyurethane sponge inserted into exit wound site.

poses hard plastic sections were substituted for bone in some of the heads.

Sections of polyurethane sponge were then placed in the depressions over the bone or plastic previously inserted to act as a matrix for blood (Figure 6-6, a and b). Fresh pigskin was obtained from a local slaughterhouse. This was cleaned, shaved, and cut into sections. The pigskin sections were then taped over the depressions containing the bone or plastic and polyurethane sponge to simulate human skin. Fresh, anticoagulated human blood was obtained and approximately 20 ml was injected into the polyurethane sponges through the pig skin to simulate the blood supply in the wound areas (Figure 6-7). Finally, wig hair was placed over the exit wound site and the completed prepared styrofoam head was then positioned in the appropriate location and held with clamps (Figure 6-8).

The areas expected to receive the blood spatter were covered with white sheets to enhance visibility of the bloodstains (Figure 6-9). The identical weapon and similar ammunition was utilized for test firings through the simulated heads approximating the angle of entry and exit wounds of the victim. Another application of firing through pigskin in

Figure 6-7 Human blood injected into entrance wound site through pigskin covering.

experiments of this type is the determination of estimations of the distance from muzzle to target based upon distribution and amount of observed gunpowder tatooing (Figure 6-10).

This form of head simulation has been used with success and the quantities and distribution of high-velocity blood spatter were found to be more realistic than those seen when uncovered blood-soaked polyurethane sponge is fired through. Figure 6-11 a, b, and c, shows a diagrammatic representation of the sequence of simulated head construction. Quantities of forward and backspatter are decreased owing to the blocking effect of the hair, skin, simulated tissue, and bone. To date, this experimental head simulation has been utilized in gunshot cases where the distances from muzzle to target have been within 6 inches and the emphasis has been on the distribution of the quantity and location of the forward high-velocity blood spatter. However, it is anticipated that this type of head simulation will be useful in studying further the extent of backspatter especially related to increased distances from muzzle to target as described by Stevens.

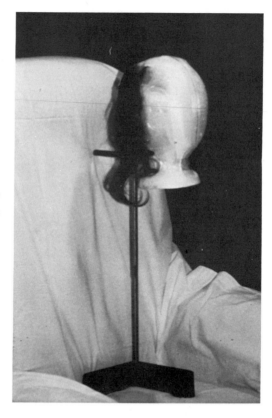

Figure 6-8 Hair placed over exit wound site and head placed into target area.

Figure 6-9 Documentation of high-velocity forward blood spatter from exit wound on white sheet covering chair.

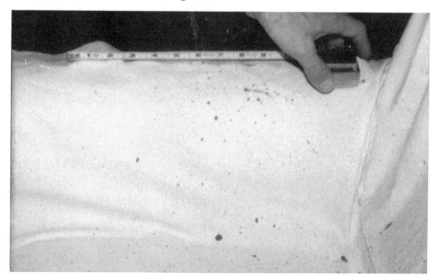

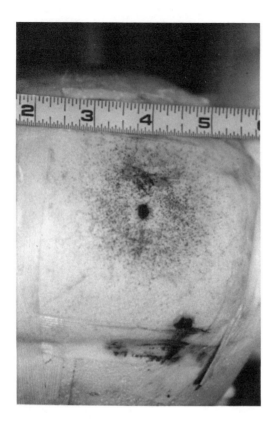

Figure 6-10 View of entrance wound site of simulated head after discharge of weapon at muzzle to target distance of approximately 4 inches.

Figure 6-11 (**A, B,** and **C**) Diagrammatic representation of simulated head preparation.

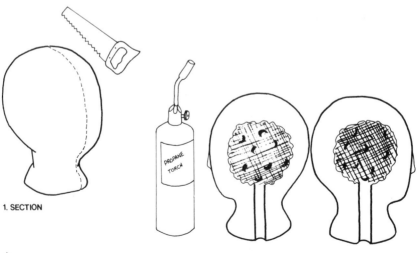

1. SECTION

A

2. FORM CAVITY

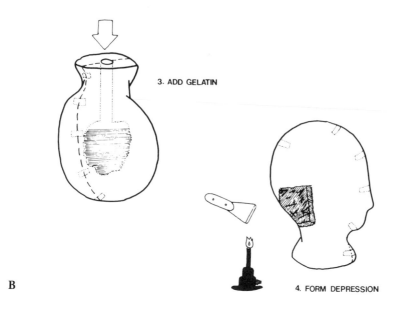

3. ADD GELATIN

4. FORM DEPRESSION

B

C

5. INSERT BONE AND SPONGE

   COVER WITH PIG SKIN

   INJECT BLOOD

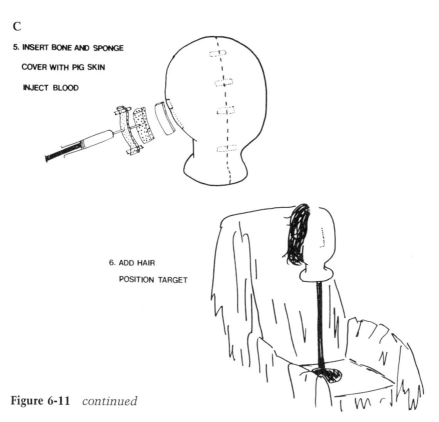

6. ADD HAIR

   POSITION TARGET

Figure 6-11 *continued*

Detection of Blood in the Barrels of Firearms
Herbert Leon MacDonell and Brian Brooks

In 1977, MacDonell and Brooks published in the *Legal Medicine Annual* an article entitled "Detection and Significance of Blood in Firearms." Their research determined that a relationship existed between discharge distance and the distance to which blood is drawn back into the barrel of firearms. The heavier concentrations of blood were found nearer the muzzle. Maximum discharge distances at which traces of blood were detected to a depth of 5 mm or greater inside the weapon's muzzle ranged from 1–1½ inches for .22 caliber revolvers to 5 inches for 12-, 16-, or 20-gauge standard shotguns. Several general observations were made as a result of their research:

1. The larger the caliber or gauge, the greater the depth of penetration into the barrel.
2. Recoil-operated autoloading weapons will produce less depth of blood penetration than a weapon whose barrel does not recoil.
3. The use of magnum or similar, higher-energy loads will produce more depth of blood penetration than standard ammunition in the barrel of a given firearm.
4. When a double-barreled shotgun is discharged at contact, considerable backspatter occurs (up to 12 cm) in the dormant barrel.

The MacDonell and Brooks procedure for detection of blood in the barrel of handguns is detailed in Figure 6-12.

1. A straw is cut about 1 inch longer than the barrel of the weapon. A piece of pipe cleaner is cut about 2 inches longer than the straw.
2. The pipe cleaner is first saturated with water and then inserted into the straw until it is flush on one end. The flush end is inserted into the barrel of the weapon until it extends about ½ inch from both breech and muzzle. If possible, insertion should be made from the breech end. This is not possible with solid-frame revolvers. It is important that the insertion of the straw be accomplished without scraping the inside of the barrel. Such contact could result in possible contamination farther down the barrel and would suggest greater depth of blood penetration. Naturally, this applies only when the straw has been inserted from the muzzle end.
3. The plastic straw is pulled back flush with the breech by holding the pipe cleaner about 1 inch from the muzzle and sliding the straw over the pipe cleaner.
4. The exposed pipe cleaner in the breech is bent over and firmly held while the straw is withdrawn from the muzzle end.
5. A "crank" is formed by making two right-angle bends in the pipe cleaner at the muzzle end. This crank is rotated to wipe the internal surface of the barrel.

STRAW

PIPE CLEANER

WEAPON

PRIOR TO TESTING.

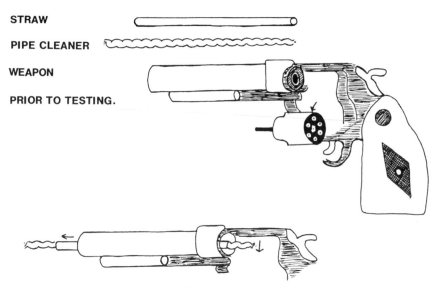

INSERT STRAW AND PIPE CLEANER
INTO BARREL FROM BREECH END.

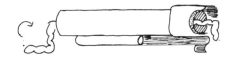

ROTATE CRANK TO WIPE INTERNAL SURFACE.

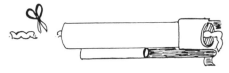

STRAIGHTEN CRANK AND CUT
FLUSH TO MUZZLE.
REMOVE STRAW FROM MUZZLE.

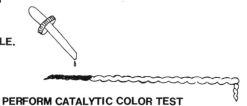

PERFORM CATALYTIC COLOR TEST
FOR PRESENCE OF BLOOD.

Figure 6-12   Procedure for the detection of blood in the barrels of firearms.

6. The crank is straightened out and cut flush with the muzzle.
7. The pipe cleaner is withdrawn from the breech end and tested with a catalytic color test for the presence of blood.

The procedure for rifles is similar to that for handguns with the exception that the length of the straws and pipe cleaners must be extended by splicing the straws and attaching pipe cleaners together.

The procedure for shotguns is modified to accommodate barrel size with the use of 3/8-inch wooden dowels of appropriate length. The wooden dowels are securely wrapped with moist filter paper both with double-sided Scotch tape and spiral wrapping with thread. The dowel is then inserted into the breech end of the shotgun barrel avoiding contact with the sides of the barrel. The use of wooden blocks is suggested to guide the dowel in order to avoid accidental contact and contamination. The barrel is then wiped in a fashion similar to handguns, removed, and tested.

Geometric Bloodstain Pattern Interpretation Using a Computer Program

Donald R. Schuessler and Frederick E. Wilson

Geometric interpretation of human bloodstain evidence has been the subject of much investigation and experimentation. Contemporary was first presented in 1939 with Balthazard's study of the influence of trajectory on resulting bloodstain shape. Of particular interest to those charged with crime scene reconstruction has been the development of empirical formulae relating to a bloodstain's width, length, and orientation to its point of origin. Using methods described by MacDonell and Bialousz, DeForest et al., and Balthazard, a computer program has been developed that greatly simplifies the data handling and computations necessary to apply the formulas. Further, this program can be used to represent schematically, the position of a victim in a room at the instant of bloodshed, thus making the task of manual reconstruction of the point of origin unnecessary.

The program is primarily applicable to medium- and high-velocity impact patterns, as found in shootings and beatings. The program by its nature treats the crime scene as a cube with six possible horizontal and six possible vertical surfaces. Therefore, the analysis of bloodstain patterns on walls and floors is the primary focus of this program. Bloodstain patterns on flat surfaces of oblique orientation can be analyzed for point of convergence with the program. However, the feature of the program that places the point of origin in three dimensions can not be used in this circumstance.

Bloodstains may be found to lie in a radially distributed pattern with their long axes aligned parallel to the radials. If radials from all the bloodstains are traced back to a common point on the same surface, such a point is called the point of convergence. If the impact angles of several bloodstains are known, this information can be combined with the distances at which these bloodstains lie from the point of convergence, to yield the distances from the bloodstained surface at which the drops of blood originated. Then, statistical interpretation can indicate the probable locations of the points of origin of the drops of blood. In general, victim location can be estimated from the results.

If a great number of bloodstains are to be examined, data handling quickly becomes a burden. The burden increases if the analyst wishes to sort out bloodstains caused by multiple impacts to the victim. If the analyst wishes to obtain an averaged distance of the point of origin from the point of convergence based on several bloodstains, or a distribution of impact angles in order to eliminate questionable data points, the process again becomes unwieldy.

To facilitate a more accessible application of the above technique, the authors have developed a BASIC language program to build a database, perform the necessary calculations, and display the results both numerically and graphically. At this time, the program is not a sophisticated package, rather an automated approach to the same task performed manually. Planned future improvements include the capability to rotate the viewpoint of the graphics, to place a human figure in the product, to provide automatic statistics, and to remove questionable data points from the database. The program runs on a Tektronix 4052 Graphic Computing System, but could easily be rewritten for many other microcomputers. It is included in its entirety in Appendix C.

To use the program, the analyst must first collect bloodstain widths, bloodstain lengths, and distances from the various points of convergence found at the crime scene. Methods for accomplishing this task are fully described in this book as well as the accompanying references. Further, the locations of the points of convergence, as measured from one corner of the room, must be noted. These locations will enable the program to display the origins of the bloodstains on a perspective drawing. The analyst then enters the collected data into the program, and may optionally save it on a floppy disk. Bloodstain measurements collected from six separate vertical surfaces and six separate horizontal surfaces may be entered into the program. Table 6-1 demonstrates a representative display of bloodstain data. At present, the program can be used to place four points of origin in three dimensions, using the information from 360 bloodstains to place the points at the moment of impact. Independently derived confidence levels generally indicate a very small probability of error when numerous bloodstains are mea-

Table 6-1 Program Analysis of Bloodstain

When done entering bloodstains to surface F1, enter 0 under bloodstain width. You can return to F1 to enter more stains at any time.

Width (mm)	Length (mm)	Distance (mm)
2.8	9.8	1390

Angle	Tangent	Height
16.601549599	0.298142397	414.41793183

Hit ⟨RETURN⟩ to continue.

sured, which indicates that the points of origin should be placed with as many stains as possible.

This computer program was utilized in a homicide investigation which originated from a missing persons report. In July 1986 a local businessman was reported missing by his daughter. While looking around the residence of the missing person for clues to the reason for this disappearance, investigators noticed several small bloodstains on the floor of the victim's garage.

Forensic analysts were called to the scene (Figure 6-13) to look for physical evidence. The analysts located numerous radially distributed medium-velocity impact spatters on the garage floor. All of the stains were at least 4 feet from an area of convergence. When luminol was applied to the floor, wipe marks appeared in an area approximately 10–11 feet in diameter. A handprint flanked by two large circles, believed to represent bucket marks, were also visible.

Approximately twenty bloodstains were located, measured, and utilized in the bloodstain analysis for the case. Seven well-defined bloodstains were utilized for geometric computer interpretation. The computer analysis indicated a point of origin 15–16 inches above the garage floor (Figure 6-14). Determination of the area of convergence of the remaining bloodstains indicated several different points of origin also close to the garage floor. The radially distributed bloodstain pattern was consistent with the type found at other crime scenes where beatings had occurred.

Approximately one year after the crime scene was discovered, a suspect led investigators to a roadside grave in a remote wilderness area of Oregon. The skeletal remains found in the grave were identified as those of the missing businessman. Although no soft tissue was left for examination of physical injuries, the skull had fractures in two different areas. Pathological examination indicated that the fractures could have been caused by blows inflicted to the victim's head.

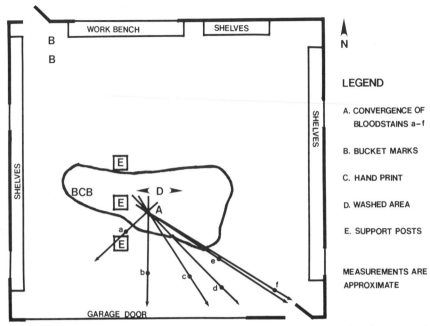

Figure 6-13 Diagram of garage floor showing convergence of bloodstains and additional areas of bloodstains including washed area.

Figure 6-14 Computer analysis displaying determined point of origin of bloodstains on garage floor.

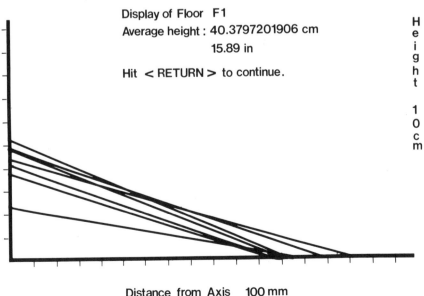

The suspect in this case gave several versions of his activities immediately prior to the victim's death. None of the suspect's stories were consistent with the bloodstain patterns found at the scene. The bloodstain pattern evidence combined with pathological findings indicated that the victim had been struck on the head five or six times with sufficient force to fracture the skull in two locations.

The prosecutor assigned to the case utilized the bloodstain pattern evidence in his opening statement at trial. He indicated that bloodstain pattern evidence would be utilized to disprove the defendant's version of the victim's death and summarized this evidence for the court. The night after the opening statements were given, the suspect committed suicide in his jail cell.

The use of the computer program allows the analyst to devote more time to the examination of individual bloodstains and eliminates the necessity of manual reconstruction of the points of origin. By examining additional bloodstains, more data points can be included in the bloodstain pattern analysis. Statistical interpretation can then indicate a more precise point or points of origin of the bloodstains. This information combined with autopsy findings allowed the placement of the victim at the moment of bloodshed in the described case. The automated bloodstain analysis program is just one of a spectrum of methods that may be utilized in the reconstruction of crime scene events.

Recognition and Identification of Bloodstains at Fire Scenes
David R. Redsicker

Fire scenes by their nature are probably the most destructive in altering physical evidence. Fires, either accelerated with criminal intent or created by accidental means, progress normally from a low level such as a floor, top of a bed, or top of a couch. From that point they generally spread upward in a vertical direction. At crime scenes many bloodstains are usually located at the lower levels of a structure such as on the floors and furniture as well as walls and ceilings. When these areas are spared complete destruction, which is often the case at fire scenes, bloodstains and patterns can be recognized. The effects on bloodstains in these situations are due to heat from the fire and to combustion by-products, smoke, soot, and various gasses.

David R. Redsicker of Peter Vallas Associates in Hackensack, New Jersey, has studied bloodstains at fire scenes and conducted research and performed experiments relating to the effect of fire on bloodstains using various surfaces. He has found that exposure to fire does not necessarily alter the geometric shape or pattern of many bloodstains. Therefore, once a bloodstain can be identified, its value as a reconstruction tool may be the same as in any crime scene. Identification of

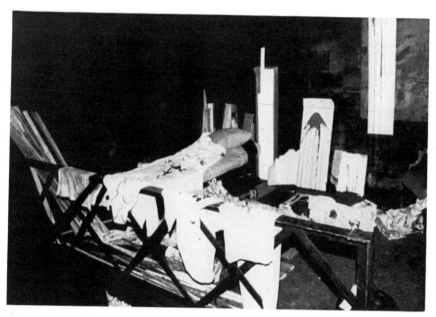

Figure 6-15 Bloodstained items arranged in room prior to ignition of fire.

blood after exposure to fire has been accomplished on different types of floor surfaces including hardwood, floor tiles, carpets, and concrete. Even in the presence of such accelerants as gasoline, the most characteristic alteration of bloodstains is discoloration. Fresh and old blood become discolored in a similar manner which is described as a dark brown to black. Recognizable patterns may be discerned by careful examination in areas of soot accumulation. Redsicker has also observed that many absorbent surfaces such as carpets, carpet pads, upholstery, and clothing retain wet blood even after exposure to a fire in the room. This may lead to the possibility of the further value of species determination and possible grouping of the intact blood.

Tests were conducted over a period of one year using a variety of seasonal conditions. The variety of floor surfaces, walls, ceilings, furniture, and weapons were stained with human blood in a room of a reburnable structure (Figures 6-15 and 6-16). The room was doused with a gallon of gasoline and ignited (Figure 6-17). Burning continued for approximately 1 hour (Figure 6-18). There did not appear to be any variation of results when bloodstains were recovered from the various target surfaces for preliminary testing of blood at the scene. Leucomalachite green was utilized as the blood-testing reagent and was positive in all cases. Bloodstained weapons were also found to be positive for blood after exposure to fire. The bloodstains were collected with saline

Figure 6-16 Closer view of bloodstain pattern on Sheetrock.

Figure 6-17 Fire in progress in room with bloodstained items.

Figure 6-18   Appearance of bloodstained items in room after 1-hour exposure to fire.

swabs and positive and negative controls were utilized. As with any crime scene the importance of good photographic documentation is stressed at fire scenes.

The Effects of Rotational Acceleration and Other Observations on Human Blood and Stain Patterns
William C. Fischer

Is there a predictable relationship between the size of a bloodstain and the velocity of the object causing bloodshed? If so, could we determine the revolutions per minute (RPM) of an industrial machine by examining the bloodstains from an accident or the speed at which a car struck a pedestrian? Are the atomized bloodstains associated with gunshot the result of explosion from the wound or the blood being sucked from the wound behind the vacuum created by the bullet?

It has been demonstrated by MacDonell that although perpendicular impacts result in circular bloodstains, blood impacting targets at other than 90 degrees will result in elliptical stains. Previous experiments have also shown that when different levels of force are applied to blood-soaked objects, different bloodstain patterns result on targets in proximity to the point of impact. Although these phenomena have been observed, a direct and continuous relationship between bloodstain size and velocity has not been established.

Hypothesis

The diameter of a bloodstain (as measured perpendicular to its line of flight) will vary inversely to the velocity of the mechanism that accelerates it.

Corollary

The quantity (number per unit area) of spots produced by a given volume of blood will vary directly with the velocity of the mechanism that projects it.

Operationalization

Accelerate known quantities of human blood through an incremental range of velocities. Then project the accelerated blood onto a suitable target while controlling for:

1. Blood volume
2. Exit velocity
3. Blood temperature
4. Distance from accelerator to target
5. Angular orientation of target to accelerator
6. Surface texture of target
7. Capillary index (porosity of target)

Methodology

Using a three-way vacuum bulb, heparinized human blood warmed to approximately 34.4 degrees centigrade was released from a pipette 1 drop (0.043 ml) at a time above the center of a horizontally rotating disk (Figure 6-19). The rotation forced the blood to the edge of the disk where it was dispersed into small droplets and projected onto a vertical target concentrically arranged around and about 4 inches away from the edge of the disk. This target was a curved tin sheeting guard mounted on the machine around the drive shaft. This permitted a fixed distance from edge to target. From the perimeter of the guard a 2-inch by 8-inch slot was cut. White cardboard targets were taped over the slot to the outside of the guard. As the blood flecks spun off the disk, they would fly through the slot and strike the target. The rotation of the disk produced a random distribution of bloodstains. The machine is

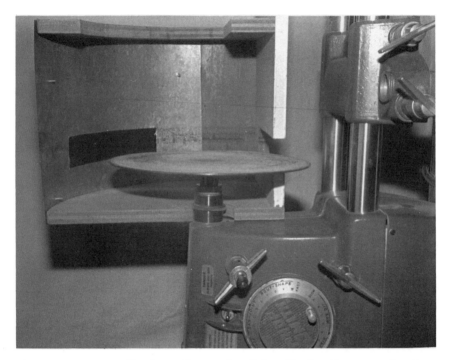

Figure 6-19   View of horizontally rotating disk utilized to disperse and project blood onto vertical targets.

designed so that the speed can be continuously increased from about 700 through 5000 RPM. The edge speed of the disk was calibrated in miles per hour at intervals of 100 RPM over the range of 700–3600 RPM. Edge speed of the disk was calibrated with a Tractest model 5101 electric speedometer manufactured by the Weston Equipment Company. This device is an electrically monitored rubber tire and wheel assembly commonly used to test police car speedometers. It has a digital readout to the nearest ½ MPH. The unit was grounded to dissipate static. At each RPM setting the rubber tire of the Tractest was butted to the edge of the disk until both disk and tire reached equilibrium. The overall accuracy with the Tractest unit according to literature provided by the Weston Equipment Company can be within 0.33 percent.

Test firings were conducted and fresh targets installed at each RPM setting (Figure 6-20). Resulting bloodstain diameters from three populations of 100 stains each were taken from each target. These population samples were then averaged and plotted as a function of the edge speed of the disk (Figure 6-21).

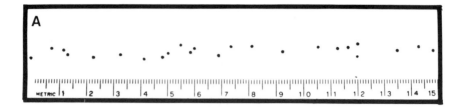

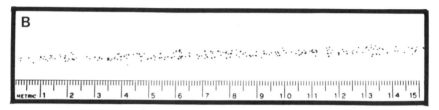

Figure 6-20 (**A**) Bloodstain pattern produced by projection of 2 drops of blood from disk with rotational velocity of 13.0 MPH. (**B**) Bloodstain pattern produced by projection of 2 drops of blood from disk with rotational velocity of 30.5 MPH.

During the initial trials blood was dropped several inches out from center to the back of the disk as the drive shaft occupied the center. The experiment immediately failed because of the unanticipated existence of a phenomenon known as the boundary layer. At 700 RPM the great majority of blood flew off the disk en masse after about 90 degrees of rotation. Two drops were required to produce forty small spots. These bloodstains were round indicating an angle of impact of 90 degrees. Increasing the RPM required a dramatic increase in the volume necessary to get a visible target pattern. At 2600 RPM, 50 drops were required to produce seventeen very fine spots of blood on the target.

Because of its internal friction, air or any other fluid has a resistance to flow smoothly which is referred to as viscosity. Flow of air immediately adjacent to a surface possesses peculiar properties of its own, in that it never actually flows over the surface at all. The concept of the boundary layer assumes that however smooth a surface may be, the molecules of air that are in actual contact with the surface remain motionless and do not move over it. At some distance above the surface the air moves smoothly and at full speed but sandwiched in between this main flow is the boundary layer where the velocity of the air molecules increases outward from the surface. This velocity gradient is confined to an extremely shallow layer of air which is usually about 0.01 inch thick. No matter how rapidly the object is moving, whether it is a bullet or a supersonic fighter, the relative velocity of the air at its surface is exactly zero (Dalton, 1977).

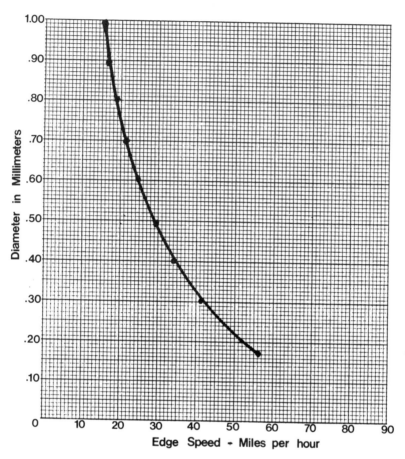

Figure 6-21   Bloodstain diameter as a function of edge speed.

When the drive unit was inverted on the machine, the blood could be released directly over the center of an unobstructed disk. A second series of tests was run and the anticipated results appeared on the targets. After each firing, observation of the disk when stopped showed that narrow spokes or trails of blood had broken away from the impact area in the center and led radially to the edge. The higher the RPM, the narrower and more numerous were the spokes. The number of spokes was always lower than the number of bloodstains on the target. This indicated that many small blood droplets would follow the path of least resistance and exit the disk via an established spoke. It can be inferred from this that the coefficient of friction (cohesion) between the blood molecules is less than the drag (adhesion) between blood molecules and disk surface.

With the disk at low RPM, much of the blood remained at the center even after having been spun. At 3200 RPM and above nearly all the blood had left the disk. The removal of blood from the center at high RPM was attributed not so much to an increase in centrifugal force which would remain small at the center even at high RPM, but rather to the tremendous rush of air directed at the axis. This inrush of air at the center replaces the air being pulled from the disk by the vacuum created at the edge. This is expected on physical grounds, for in the absence of a radial pressure gradient, the fluid near the disk moves outward under the influence of centrifugal force, and therefore an axial inflow at infinity is required for continuity (MacDonell, 1971).

When examining bloodstains, investigators are faced with a bivariant analysis of blood drop volume and height from which a drop has fallen. In this type of experiment for the results to be useful in interpreting stains on any surface other than the target material, a comparative index of the porosity of the target material had to be established. Capillarity of liquids depends both upon adhesion and surface tension. Adhesion is the force of attraction between molecules of different kinds. Cohesion is the force of attraction between molecules of the same kind. Cohesion produces surface tension which causes drops to form. Viscosity, orifice diameter, and barometric pressure will affect the volume of the blood drops released from a pipette. Accordingly, a capillary index was established by defining the ratio of the area of a stain produced from a drop of blood on a particular surface material to the stain area produced by the same volume of blood dropped on a glass surface from a height of twelve inches. Window glass was used as a standard since it is relatively smooth and nonabsorbent and commonly found at accident and crime scenes. To determine the capillary index value of the target cardboard, three samples with a population of 20 drops each were allowed to fall 12 inches onto clean dry glass and target cardboard. Glass and cardboard temperature was 21.1 degrees centigrade (70 degrees Fahrenheit); blood temperature was 34.4 degrees centigrade (94 degrees Fahrenheit). The average area for bloodstains on glass was 1.111 cm². The average area for bloodstains on the target cardboard was 0.785 cm². The capillary index value for the cardboard targets is then: 0.785/1.111 = 0.707. Note that it is the ratio of stain areas on different materials that is sought, not the absolute value. Therefore, any drop volume may be used as long as it is kept constant.

Surface texture and porosity were controlled during the experiments by using sheets from the same production of target cardboard. Stain size produced by a given volume of blood will vary with absorbency and surface texture of the target. Significant temperature differences will affect the volume of a fluid and the resultant area of the stain produced by the droplet and were controlled as closely as possible throughout the experiments.

Conclusions

Even though there exists a significant correlation between the size of the bloodstain and edge speed, droplet volume will be determined by other forces operating at the surface of the disk such as vacuum pressure and viscosity. Edge speed will determine the magnitude of the centrifugal force, bound vortex, and shear stress. The final volume of the droplets is determined as the blood travels through the boundary layer and bound vortex at the disk edge. We should be able to predict that fluids of higher viscosity and adhesion will resist breakup in the boundary level and result in larger droplet volumes at equivalent RPM.

The results of this study may be of value when interpreting bloodstains caused by rotational acceleration, for example, the swing of an axe, rotary saws, fans, planers, and so on. They will not necessarily be consistent with bloodstains produced by linear impact, for example, vehicular accidents, falling from heights, and the like or stains involving bursting pressures.

Gunshot will produce several different kinds of recognizable patterns. A very fine atomized dispersion pattern will often be found around a bullet hole in a wall or other surface in proximity to an exit wound. The distance from the point of impact to bloodstained surface may be considerably greater than we would expect such small droplets capable of traversing in free flight due to air resistance.

Based on this study, it is suggested that high-velocity bloodstain patterns are not only the result of blood explosively leaving the body, but also that minute volumes are being sucked from the body by the vacuum produced in the trailing vortex of the bullet.

References

1. Balthazard, V., Piedelievre, R., Desoille, H., and Derobert, L. 1939. Etude des gouttes de sang projete. 22nd congres de Medecine legale, Paris, France.
2. Dalton, S. 1977. *The Miracle of Flight.* New York: McGraw-Hill.
3. DeForest, P., Gaensslen, R.E., and Lee, H.C. 1983. *Forensic Science: An Introduction to Criminalistics.* New York: McGraw-Hill.
4. MacDonell, H. 1971. Flight characteristics and stain patterns of human blood. National Institute of Law Enforcement and Criminal Justice, Washington, DC.
5. ———. 1982. *Bloodstain Pattern Interpretation.* Laboratory of Forensic Science, Corning, New York.
6. MacDonell, H.L., and Bialousz, L.F. 1979. *Laboratory Manual for the Geometric Interpretation of Human Bloodstain Evidence.* 2nd edition. Laboratory of Forensic Science, Corning, New York.

Case Investigations in Bloodstain Interpretation

7

The following case investigations have been selected for their value and contribution to the understanding of bloodstain pattern interpretation relating to the activity between victim and assailant and the ultimate crime scene reconstruction. The cases presented will demonstrate injuries and resulting bloodstain patterns and their interpretation in the reconstruction of deaths caused by firearms, cutting and stabbing, and blunt force trauma.

These cases were investigated by one or the other author for the prosecution or defense with court testimony provided in many instances. The bloodstain interpretations are based upon scene examination or photographic review of the cases. It is the position of the authors that bloodstain interpretation from photographs without benefit of actual scene examination should be conservative. Photographs submitted for review do not always depict the entire scene nor entire bloodstain patterns. Photographs may be of varying quality and unfortunately do not always contain a scale of reference or measuring device. Additionally, bloodstain interpretation of a case should be correlated with autopsy findings and all physical evidence including blood groupings and other serological studies of the blood.

Gunshot Trauma

Case 1

A white male serving a sentence for rape escaped from a penitentiary on a Caribbean island. The local police department received a phone call indicating that the escapee had been spotted a few miles from the penitentiary in a thick bushy and wooded area near the center of the island. Several units including K-9 patrols were dispatched to the area to initiate the search for the escaped prisoner. A K-9 officer spotted the escapee running across a road and pursued him into a wooded area a few hundred yards away but visual contact was lost in the dense bush and wooded environment. The police officer and his dog proceeded approximately 100 yards through the wooded area into a cleared area which was partially fenced. At this point the officer encountered a black male carrying a machete who was not the escaped prisoner. Knowing the escapee was likely in the immediate area, the officer ordered the black male to stop and identify himself. The man armed with the machete ignored the command of the officer and ran towards the fence. The dog was unleashed and cornered the black male at the fence. At this point he swung the machete at the dog several times ignoring the officer's commands to drop the weapon. The officer stated that he then drew his revolver and fired once while the individual continued to swing the machete. The officer, thinking he had missed, then fired the remaining five shots which resulted in the death of the black male. Subsequent investigation into the incident resulted in the indictment of the officer for homicide.

Postmortem examination of the victim revealed multiple gunshot wounds of the head, neck, trunk, and extremities with entrance wounds all located on the right side of the body. A gunshot wound of the right upper chest perforated the upper right lung with the projectile passing through the right main stem pulmonary artery, the posterior aspect of the left atrium of the heart, and the left lower lung with ultimate exit through the left lower back which resulted in massive internal hemorrhage. At the initial autopsy it was thought that the entry and exit wounds of the right elbow could be associated with the same projectile that caused the entry wound of the right lower back or right upper chest.

Review of this case was initiated by a call from the federal public defender to determine if there was evidence to substantiate the version of events given by the police officer. An exhumation order was granted and the body of the victim was disinterred approximately nine months after burial for reexamination (Figure 7-1).

The condition of the body permitted visualization of the sites of the multiple gunshot wounds. A forensic pathologist documented these wounds as the following: (1) entrance wound of right anterior chest with exit through left posterior chest wall; (2) entrance wound of right base of skull with no exit; (3) entrance wound of right arm anterior above elbow, through and through; (4) entrance wound of right side of skull at angle of mandible with exit at left side of neck; (5) entrance wound of right leg above heel, through and through, superficial; (6) entrance wound of left thigh through and through, superficial; and (7) entrance wound of upper back, through and through, right to left, su-

Figure 7-1   Exhumed body of victim disinterred approximately nine months after burial in warm climate.

perficial. The entrance wound of the right anterior chest wall was able to be associated with the entrance and exit wounds of the right arm above the elbow and was concluded to be a reentry of the same projectile. In order for the projectile to enter and exit the right arm in that location and reenter the right upper chest, the right arm would have been elevated (Figures 7-2, 7-3, and 7-4). This conclusion was further substantiated by the examination of the clothing of the victim. In the upper right chest area of the shirt of the victim was an apparent bullet entry hole which was surrounded by high-velocity blood spatter that would have originated as forward spatter from the exit wound of the right arm above the elbow (Figure 7-5). This was consistent with the statement of the police officer that the victim was swinging the machete at the time the gun was fired.

Examination of the scene photographs did not reveal evidence of any shots fired while the victim was in a prone position. The bloodstaining on the corrugated fence to the left of the victim was consistent with projected blood most likely from his mouth produced while the head was in motion. The blood flow pattern on the front of the shirt was consistent with blood originating from the mouth as well (Figure 7-6).

The machete was of interest in this case in that the prosecution attempted to prove that this weapon was planted on the victim based

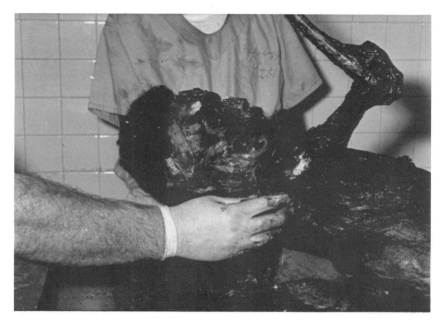

Figure 7-2 Elevation of right arm of victim to demonstrate alignment with gunshot wound, through and through, above elbow and reentry into upper right anterior chest wall.

Figure 7-3 Insertion of probe to demonstrate relationship of exit wound above right elbow and entrance wound in upper right anterior chest wall.

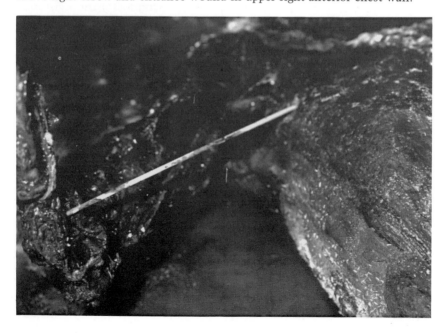

Figure 7-4 Continuation of probe into chest of victim demonstrating exit in left posterior chest wall.

Figure 7-5 High-velocity blood spatter present on upper right front of shirt of victim near projectile reentry hole in fabric.

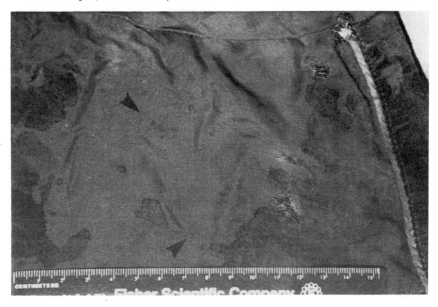

Figure 7-6 Position of victim between tree and corrugated fence showing blood flow pattern on front of shirt and projected bloodstain pattern on fence to the left of victim's head.

Figure 7-7 Machete that was found in the hands of the victim and that prosecutors thought was planted on victim after the shooting.

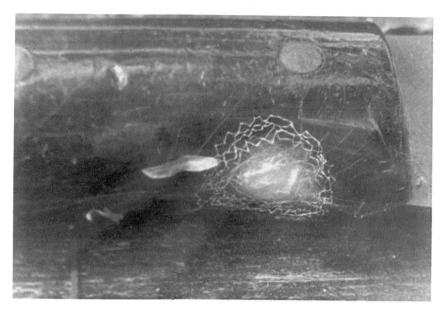

Figure 7-8   Close-up view of spider egg nest attached to handle of machete.

upon the presence of a spider egg nest on the handle (Figures 7-7 and 7-8). During the trial, the defense presented the testimony of an entomologist who demonstrated to the jury the adhesive nature and durability of the egg nest in that it would not become dislodged during violent swinging of the weapon. The wound pathology and bloodstain evidence was also given at trial. The police officer was acquitted of homicide.

The significance of the location and directionality of high-velocity blood spatter associated with gunshot wounds at crime scenes cannot be overemphasized. This is also true of the victim's body, clothing, and other items he or she may have been wearing at the time.

Case 2

A man in his mid-twenties was found unconscious in the rear parking lot of a restaurant in a southern city. Attempts by an emergency medical team (EMT) to revive him did not succeed and he was pronounced dead at the scene as the result of multiple gunshot wounds (Figures 7-9 and 7-10). At the time of postmortem examination these were documented as the following: (1) entrance wound in the face just to the right of the nose surrounded by stippling with the projectile path front to back (Figure 7-11); (2) entrance wound in the neck just to the right of midline, 10 inches below the top of the head surrounded by stippling

Figure 7-9 Victim on ground in rear parking lot of restaurant.

Figure 7-10 Closer view of victim showing position of glasses and gunshot entrance wounds of face, neck, and upper chest.

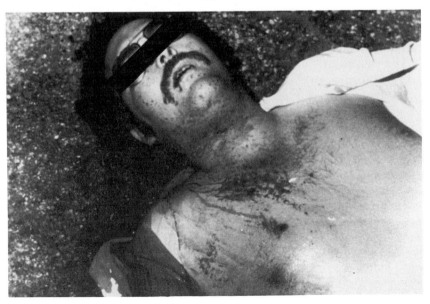

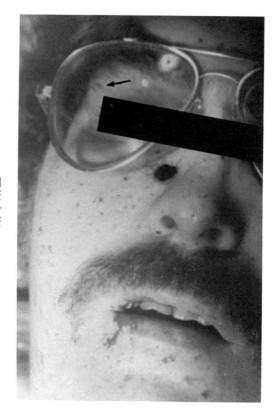

Figure 7-11 Entrance wound of the face just to the right of the nose with high-velocity blood spatter on outer side of right lens of glasses.

with the projectile path front to back; (3) entrance wound in the upper chest located 15 inches below the top of the head with no stippling with the projectile path right to left, front to back, and downward; and (4) entrance wound in the posterior aspect of the right hand with no evidence of soot or stippling with an exit wound on the thumb side of the hand. Associated with this is a reentry wound caused by the same projectile located in the chest about 18 inches below the top of the head. This projectile proceeded from front to back, right to left, and slightly downward (Figures 7-12 and 7-13).

Four projectiles were recovered from the body and determined to be of .38 caliber size. A projectile hole was discovered in the shirt of the victim associated with entrance wound 3. The presence of stippling could not be determined because of the quantity of blood present on the shirt. The shirt had been unbuttoned by the EMT personnel.

The defendant in this case claimed self-defense stating that the larger victim approached him in a menacing manner. The defendant then fired four shots at the victim as he was coming towards him but

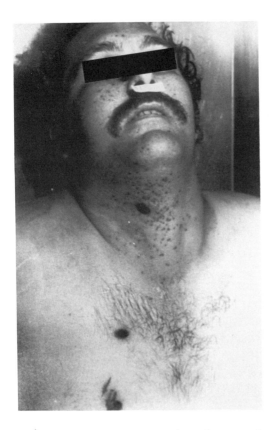

Figure 7-12 Entrance wounds of face, neck, and upper chest showing reentry wound with associated abrasions.

Figure 7-13 Entrance wound on the posterior aspect of the right hand with exit wound at base of right thumb.

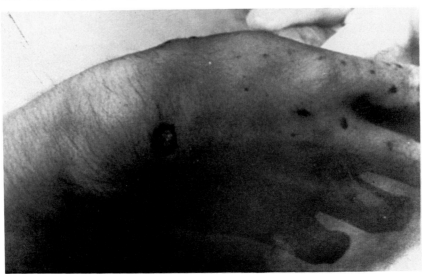

did not fire at the victim as he lay on the ground. The version of events described by the defendant was refuted by the bloodstain evidence. The victim's glasses as seen in the scene photographs are slightly raised on his forehead. The entrance wound to the right of the victim's nose is in an area that would normally be covered by the glasses. Examination of the glasses revealed the presence of high-velocity blood spatter on the outer surface of the right lens whose origin would be the entrance wound close to the lens (Figure 7-11). This backspatter from the entrance wound could not have impacted on the outer surface of the right lens of the glasses if the victim were standing up at the time he received this shot since the backspatter would have traveled in a direction away from the head. However, with the victim lying on the ground at the time he received this gunshot wound, the resulting backspatter traveled upward and then owing to gravity traveled downward and impacted on the outer surface of the right lens of the glasses. The defendant was convicted of homicide.

Case 3

A university coed was found lying on her back on the floor in her rented house with a gaping gunshot wound of the bridge of the nose as the result of a shot from a large-caliber revolver fired by her boyfriend (Figure 7-14). The boyfriend claimed that they had an argument during

Figure 7-14 Victim on floor with rifle near right hand and high-velocity blood spatter on lower wall and baseboard behind her head.

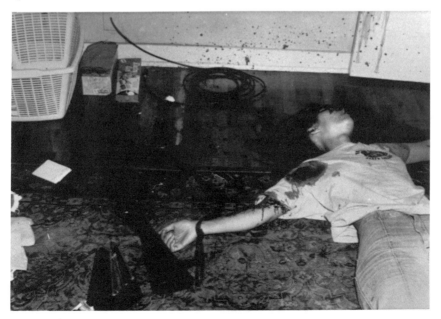

Figure 7-15 Large quantity of pooled blood around head of victim.

which she had threatened him with a rifle. Acting in self-defense, he responded by shooting her in the face while she was standing in front of him. A rifle was noted on the floor near the right hand of the victim.

The victim was immediately disabled by the wound to the head and likely died within minutes as the result of severe damage to the brain. The amount of blood pooling around her head on the floor is a reflection of the length of survival time during which the victim would continue to actively bleed due to the pumping action of the heart (Figure 7-15).

The bloodstain evidence in this case refuted the version of events as described by the boyfriend with respect to the position of the victim at the time the fatal shot was fired. The high-velocity blood spatter present on the wall behind the victim was confined to an area 30 inches above the floor and impacted the wall surface at approximately 90 degrees (Figures 7-16 and 7-17). The source of this blood spatter would be the gunshot injury's producing forward spatter from the exit wound. This would place the head of the victim close to the level of the floor at the time of the fatal shot instead of her being in an upright position as claimed by the boyfriend. This interpretation of bloodstain evidence was given during trial in conjunction with the results of bloodstain experiments to demonstrate the higher location of high-velocity blood spatter that would have resulted if the victim were in a

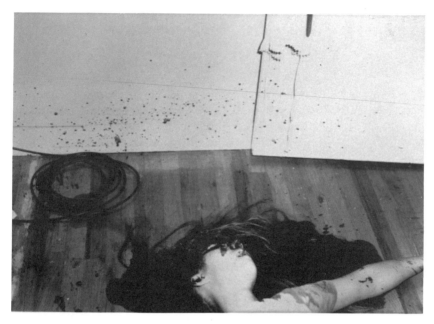

Figure 7-16 High-velocity blood spatter on wall behind victim within 30 inches above floor and impacting at 90 degrees.

Figure 7-17 Another view of high-velocity blood spatter on wall.

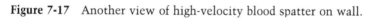

standing position at the time the fatal shot was fired. The boyfriend was convicted of murder in the first degree.

Case 4

The frequency of women who commit suicide with the use of firearms has increased during the past few years. However, this case is unusual in that a shotgun was used as the lethal weapon. In cases of this type it is important to position the firearm correctly in relation to the entrance wound and the resultant high-velocity blood spatter present at the scene.

The victim in this case was found in a seated position in a chair in her living room with the upper portion of her skull missing. The blood flow pattern on her left cheek is consistent with the position of the body in the chair (Figure 7-18). The location of high-velocity blood spatter and tissue fragments on the wall above and behind the chair is consistent with their being produced as the result of the shotgun's being discharged with the victim in the chair at the time (Figures 7-19 and 7-20). Reassembly of the skull fragments to their normal anatomic position clearly demonstrates the location of the entry wound in the

Figure 7-18   Victim with downward blood flow pattern on left cheek in seated position in chair.

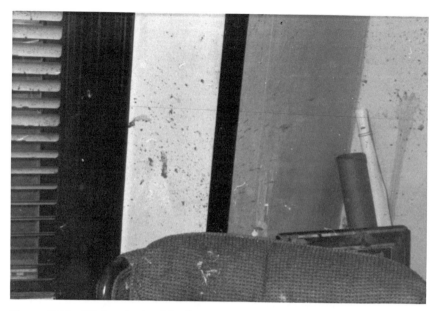

Figure 7-19 High-velocity blood spatter on wall behind and above level of chair in which victim was seated.

Figure 7-20 High-velocity blood spatter on wall to the left and above level of chair in which victim was seated.

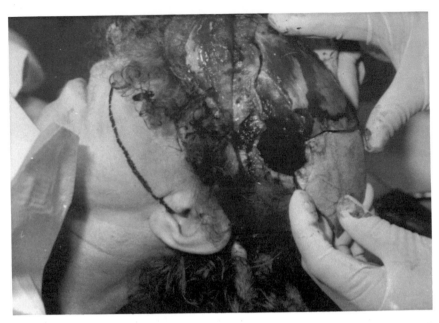

Figure 7-21   Reconstruction of skull fragments demonstrating the location of entrance wound in left side of head of victim.

left side of the head (Figure 7-21). It is consistent that, with the shotgun somewhat vertical to the floor, the victim placed the muzzle against the left side of her head with her head turned to the right. It was also determined that the distance from shoulder to fingertip of the victim's arm would have permitted a finger to reach the trigger mechanism of the weapon. The presence of a suicide note was confirmatory to the conclusions of this reconstruction.

Case 5

A similar case occurred a few years ago in upstate New York. A 21-year-old woman with marital difficulties including a recent abortion returned home to live with her mother and stepfather. She was continually depressed and began therapy at a local clinic. The stepfather returned home for lunch and found his stepdaughter with massive head injury on the floor in her basement bedroom. A high-powered hunting rifle was lying over her abdomen which the stepfather removed and placed on her bed prior to calling the police.

Examination of the scene of this gunshot death revealed the victim to be lying on the floor of her bedroom near the entrance and some-

Figure 7-22 Victim with massive gunshot wound of head on floor of bedroom. Note presence of high-velocity blood spatter on dorsal aspect of right hand.

what parallel to the bed. A blood transfer pattern on the wall behind and above her head indicated that she most likely slumped to the floor from a chair near the foot of the bed. There was high-velocity backspatter present on the dorsal aspect of the right hand of the victim (Figure 7-22). Large fragments of scalp and hair were located on the pillow of the bed and on a wall to the left of the body (Figure 7-23). The ceiling of the bedroom provided additional information necessary to reconstruct this case. There were numerous penetrations in the ceiling that were produced by fragments of the projectile and fragments of skull. There was also a large quantity of high-velocity blood spatter present on the ceiling surrounding these penetrations which exhibited an upward directionality resulting from the exit wound (Figures 7-24 and 7-25). The major portion of projectile was determined to have passed through the ceiling and upper floor and through the roof of the house and was never recovered.

The conclusion in this case was self-inflicted gunshot wound of the head. Despite the massive head injury and fragmentation of the skull, the pathologist estimated the entrance wound to be located on the left side of the head (Figure 7-26). The bloodstain evidence indicated that the victim was most likely seated in the chair with the rifle pointed upward and discharged as she leaned over. It was determined that she

Figure 7-23 Large fragment of scalp and hair including headband from victim on pillow.

Figure 7-24 Pattern of high-velocity blood spatter on ceiling of bedroom above bed.

Figure 7-25 Close-up view of high-velocity blood spatter on ceiling in conjunction with holes produced by projectile and skull fragments.

Figure 7-26 Massive head injury of victim with brain evisceration.

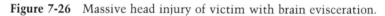

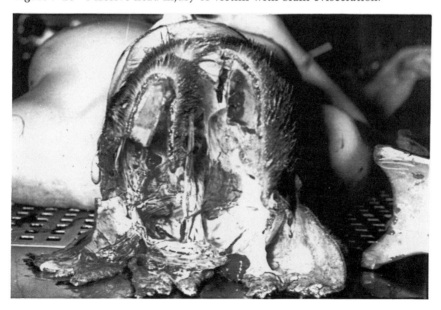

was capable of reaching the trigger with the finger of her left hand. The high-velocity backspatter present on her right hand would place that hand on the muzzle of the firearm at time of discharge. There was no suicide note found in this case but the clinical history of depression was felt to be highly significant. With regard to the use of a high-powered rifle by a young female, it is interesting to note that the victim was quite familiar with the weapon and had in fact hunted with her father on many occasions in the past.

Case 6

A successful businessman was last seen alive by his family leaving for work in the morning in a northeastern state. He was located in his automobile in the early afternoon approximately four miles from his residence in a remote area of the countryside. The absence of fresh tire tracks in the snow other than the victim's vehicle indicated his to have been the only vehicle in the area that day. The engine of the vehicle was running and the tape deck was playing. The windows were up and intact with the exception of the driver's side window which was broken, with glass and brain tissue on the ground beside the vehicle. With massive head destruction the victim was found sitting in the driver's seat (Figure 7-27). A hunting rifle was positioned in the vehicle with

Figure 7-27   Victim with massive head destruction sitting in driver's seat of vehicle.

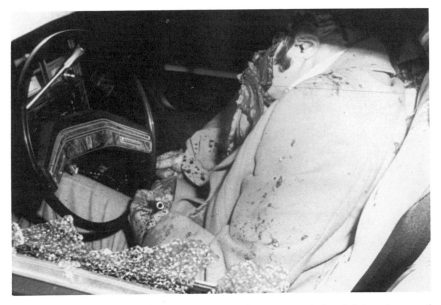

Figure 7-28 Barrel of rifle between legs of victim with his left hand around muzzle.

the stock to the right of the victim and the muzzle pointing upward towards the victim. The left hand of the victim was around the muzzle of the weapon and the right hand near the trigger mechanism (Figure 7-28). High-velocity blood spatter was present on the front of the rifle barrel and on the lateral and dorsal areas of the hands of the victim. Further examination of the vehicle revealed a projectile exit hole in the roof of the automobile above the head of the victim. The front passenger seat, rear seats, and interior windows showed evidence of blood spatter and tissue on their surfaces (Figure 7-29).

Postmortem examination revealed that the firearm was discharged in the mouth of the victim producing massive damage to the head. The presence of the high-velocity backspatter on the hands of the victim was consistent with the left hand's being near the muzzle and the right hand at the trigger mechanism at the time of discharge (Figure 7-30). The locations of bloodstains and spatter on the seats of the vehicle further demonstrated that no other person was in the vehicle at the time the firearm was discharged and that the doors and windows were closed at that time. Subsequent investigation revealed that the victim had been despondent over the recent death of his mother, and that in fact her favorite music was playing on the tape deck in the vehicle at the time the victim was discovered. The manner of death was determined to be suicide although no suicide note was recovered.

Figure 7-29 View of interior of vehicle showing tissue and blood spatter on front passenger seat.

Figure 7-30 High-velocity blood spatter on dorsal and lateral aspect of victim's left hand which was gripped around muzzle of rifle. Note high-velocity blood spatter on lateral aspect of right hand which was used to fire the rifle.

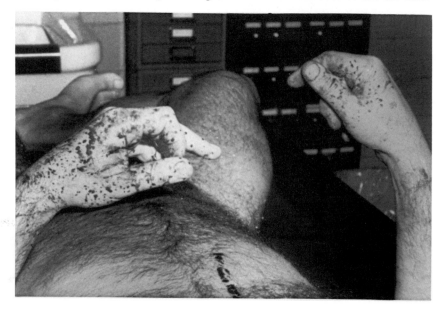

The presence of high-velocity backspatter on the hand or hands of gunshot victims is a strong indication of that hand being in proximity to the source of the blood spatter. In cases of self-inflicted gunshot injury it may be seen on the dorsal and lateral aspects of the hand that is used to steady the muzzle. The absence of this blood spatter does not necessarily indicate that the injury was not self-inflicted. The amount of high-velocity backspatter may be reduced or absent because of the intermediate shielding effect of hair and clothing and by increasing the distance between muzzle and target and through the caliber of the weapon itself.

Case 7

The police in a midwestern city responded to a call that a young man had just shot himself after returning home from a bar with his brother who witnessed the shooting. The victim was found sitting with his legs crossed in a chair at a table in the kitchen of the residence (Figure 7-31). A cocked revolver was in the right hand of the victim (Figure 7-32). Further examination revealed an entrance wound in the left nostril surrounded by powder tatooing. The bloodstain evidence in this case was limited to flow patterns of blood which emerged from the

Figure 7-31   Victim of shooting reclined in chair in kitchen.

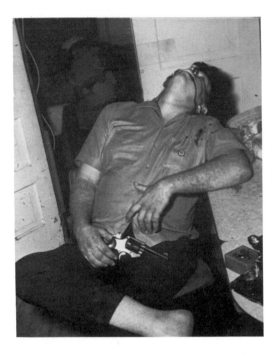

Figure 7-32 Cocked revolver in right hand of victim. Blood flow from mouth is consistent with observed position of victim in chair.

nose and mouth of the victim with some resultant bloodstaining on the left shoulder area and on the floor below the chair (Figure 7-33). There was no apparent high-velocity blood spatter on the hands of the victim. During postmortem examination it was determined by the pathologist that the location and extent of damage to the occipital region of the skull and resultant brain injury sustained by the victim would have produced immediate unconciousness and death and inability to recock the weapon after discharge. It was apparent that this was most likely not a self-inflicted wound, and further questioning of the brother resulted in a confession that he had shot his brother after an argument and had placed the weapon in the hand of the victim.

Case 8

The husband of a 50-year-old woman heard a gunshot in his home and in the bedroom found his wife in bed unconscious and bleeding from a gunshot wound to the head. The victim was pronounced dead at the scene after resuscitative measures failed (Figure 7-34). The victim sustained a through-and-through gunshot wound of the head. The projectile entered at close range in the right temporal region and exited the left temporal region and lodged in a nearby wall. The path of the projectile was approximately parallel to the bed. A pistol was located in the right hand of the victim with high-velocity backspatter visible on the

Figure 7-33 Blood flow pattern on right cheek and neck of victim is consistent with observed position in chair. There is a small amount of bloodstaining on the floor below.

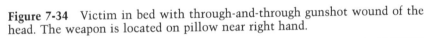
Figure 7-34 Victim in bed with through-and-through gunshot wound of the head. The weapon is located on pillow near right hand.

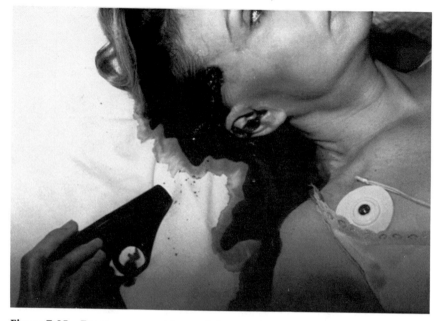

Figure 7-35   Entrance wound located above right ear with heavy blood flow on pillow. Note presence of high-velocity backspatter on pillow between head and weapon.

bed sheet between the weapon and the head near the entrance wound. The victim had bled considerably on the bed and pillow under the head (Figure 7-35). Blood had flowed onto the floor to the right of the bed. On the floor near an area of pooled blood was located an expended cartridge casing which had been ejected from the pistol in the victim's right hand (Figure 7-36).

Prior to the arrival of the medical personnel, the husband stated that he removed a pillow that had been on the bed of the victim and placed it in an adjoining bedroom (Figure 7-37). There was a bullet hole through the pillow surrounded by soot and smoke stains with associated splitting of the fabric that represented contact with the muzzle of a firearm at time of discharge (Figure 7-38).

The husband was arrested and brought to trial for homicide. The prosecution theory in the case was that the husband fired the fatal shot through the pillow using this intermediate barrier to muffle the sound of the shot. However, it was shown at trial that the pillow could not have been placed against the head of the victim and then fired through in that fashion. There was an absence of bloodstaining and spatter on the pillow which would have been expected under those circumstances. Furthermore, had the pillow been in the position at the right

Figure 7-36 Continuation of blood flow pattern on rug to right of bed near expended projectile casing.

Figure 7-37 Pillow on bed in adjoining bedroom with contact projectile hole surrounded by soot and smoke stains and splitting of pillow case fabric.

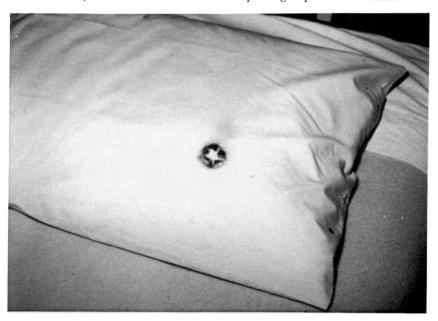

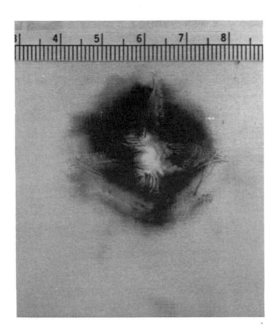

Figure 7-38 Close-up view of contact projectile hole in pillow.

of the victim's head at the time the fatal shot was fired, the high-velocity backspatter would not have been deposited on the sheet near the entrance wound. The husband was acquitted of homicide. It was theorized that the wife had fired the weapon through the pillow at a previous time and placed the pillow on the bed prior to committing suicide perhaps to masquerade the death as a homicide with her husband as the prime suspect.

Cutting and Stabbing Trauma

Case 1

A maximum-security prison was beset with racial problems stemming from encounters between white and black supremacy groups. The victim in this case was attacked while he read at a table in the prison library and suffered two stab wounds to the lower neck inflicted with a sharp instrument (Figure 7-39). The directionality of one was inward, which severed an artery in the neck, and the other traveled a downward course, which resulted in injury to the apex of the left lung and hemothorax (Figure 7-40).

The scene photographs revealed the evidence of the initial confrontation in the area of the library table with overturned chairs, papers, and waste can on the floor and scattered books and papers on the table (Figure 7-41). The bloodstains on the table have resulted from the drip-

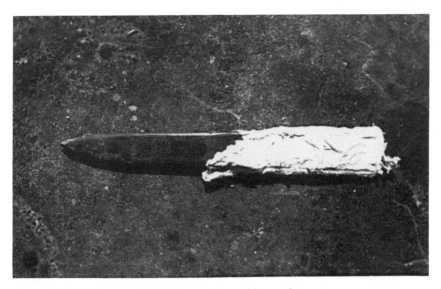

Figure 7-39 Prison-made knife used in stabbing of inmate.

Figure 7-40 Stab wounds in neck of inmate attacked in prison library.

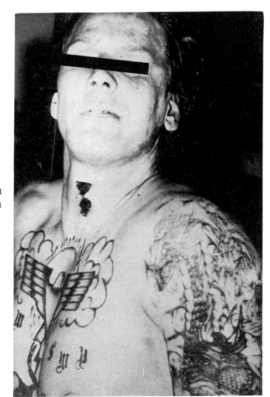

Figure 7-41   Area in prison library where assault occurred.

ping of blood from a source above. These bloodstain patterns are also present on the floor beneath the table in conjunction with larger blood-stain patterns produced by projected blood (Figure 7-42). The trail of bloodstains in the form of projected blood patterns and dripped blood can be traced representing the path of the victim who left the table area after receiving injury (Figures 7-43 and 7-44). In an area near the entrance to the library adjacent to a bookcase is an excellent representation of a projected bloodstain pattern characterized by the narrow, radiating streaks of blood whose origins can be traced back to the central portion of the major bloodstain (Figure 7-45). The source of this blood was moving toward the door of the library. Some drops of blood have fallen from above onto the radiating streaks of blood. Some of these radiating streaks of blood have been smeared. There is a partial transfer shoeprint in blood visible just below the central portion of the stain.

Convicts other than the assailant in this case received considerable bloodstaining on their clothing which resulted from the projected blood from the victim. These bloodstains would be produced by the victim in proximity to these individuals at some point after he received injury (Figure 7-46). The clothing provided a target surface for the arterial spurting from the neck wounds of the victim. This case presents an example of individuals' receiving significant bloodstaining

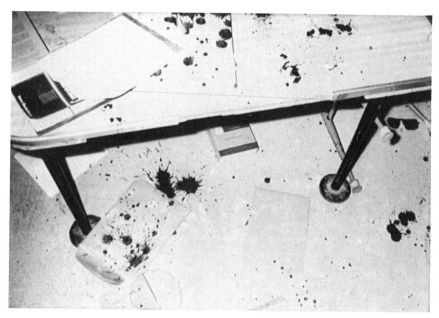

Figure 7-42 Table and floor in prison library showing drips of blood and projected bloodstain patterns.

Figure 7-43 Trail of blood drip patterns from victim leading away from table toward prison library entrance.

Figure 7-44 Blood drip pattern closer to bookcase in library.

Figure 7-45 Projected bloodstain pattern and shoeprint in blood near entrance-way to prison library.

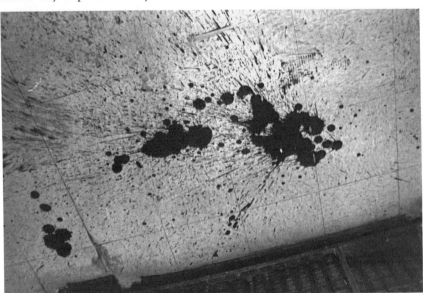

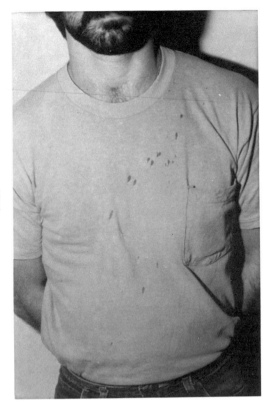

Figure 7-46 Bloodstain on shirt of inmate not involved in assault on victim.

on their clothing after coming to the assistance of a victim which can be explained by the nature of injuries sustained by the victim. Although these individuals were close to the actively bleeding victim, they would not have necessarily been participants in the stabbing to receive bloodstains of that type on their clothing.

This case is also an example of possible survival of a victim of a lethal assault who dies unnecessarily because of his actions after injury that preclude proper medical care. The victim panicked and ran for assistance rather than lying down and applying pressure to the neck. Bleeding from severance of the left subclavian artery can be controlled. The puncture of a lung and the resulting hemothorax is not a fatal process in itself. It may be controlled by surgical intervention, blood replacement, and pulmonary physiological management. The increased cardiac output and blood loss caused by the excited state of the victim as he ran for assistance may have reduced his chances for survival.

Case 2

The body of a man in his early twenties was discovered in the early morning hours near railroad tracks in a northern city by children on their way to school (Figure 7-47). It was first assumed that he was the victim of a pedestrian–train accident because of the severe damage to his neck (Figure 7-48). Closer examination revealed that the victim had suffered a severely slashed throat and multiple stab wounds to the chest, abdomen, and back (Figure 7-49). Autopsy revealed a total of eight stab wounds in addition to the large incised wound of the throat and some minor defensive wounds to the fingers and hands. Death was attributed to massive internal bleeding due to perforation of the heart and liver.

A police officer who had been called to the scene recognized the victim as one of three people in a vehicle that he had stopped the previous evening for speeding. A check of the ticket records led to the identification of the vehicle and two brothers were arrested as a result of this investigation. The three individuals had been drinking together the previous evening at several bars and had decided to continue drinking in a remote area near the railroad tracks where the victim was found. At this point each brother blamed the other for the fatal stabbing which was the result of an argument.

Figure 7-47   Victim on ground near railroad tracks.

Figure 7-48   Victim turned over to show severe slashing of neck.

Figure 7-49   Location of four stab wounds in lower front chest and abdomen of victim.

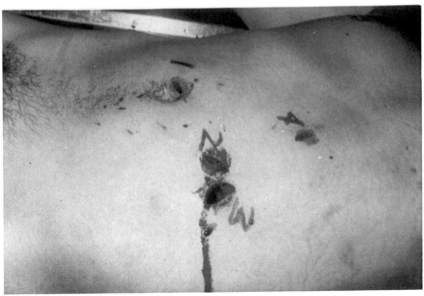

Examination of the scene revealed the presence of some bloodstains and smearing on the railroad track where the altercation most likely began. Only a trace of blood was seen in the snow in the area of drag marks on the ground between the tracks and the final location of the body where a large pooling of blood was present beneath and around the victim.

It was interesting to note in this case that neither defendant showed evidence on their clothing and shoes of the victim's blood which was group O. However, one brother showed blood smearing on the front of his trousers that was consistent with his own blood which was group A. This brother had sustained a moderately severe cut on his right hand which was bandaged when he was apprehended a day after the incident (Figure 7-50). This would explain the blood on his trousers that matched his own group A.

The blue jeans worn by the victim in this case became a key item of evidence linking an assailant to the victim. The victim's blue jeans exhibited moderate bloodstaining in the front midsection and thigh areas some of which was consistent with bleeding by the victim (Figure 7-51). There were additional scattered round and oval-shaped spots of blood present on the right front and rear leg surface of the blue jeans representing dripping of blood and some medium-velocity blood spatter (Figure 7-52). These bloodstains were produced by droplets of blood traveling towards the victim from a source either above, in front of, or

Figure 7-50   Hand of defendant showing cut on dorsal surface.

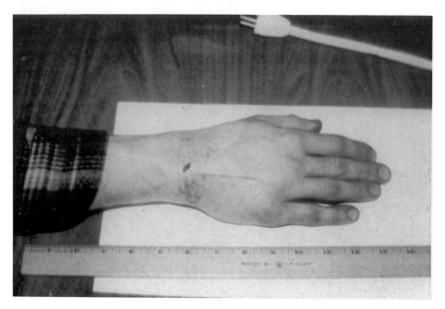

Figure 7-51 Front view of blue jeans worn by victim.

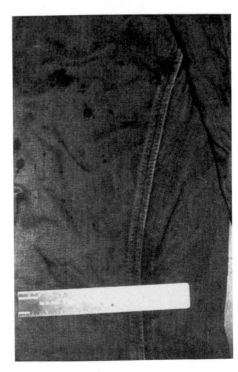

Figure 7-52 Bloodstains on right front leg of victim's blue jeans that were consistent with bleeding by defendant with cut hand.

in back of the victim depending upon his posture at the time. Based upon the location and physical characteristics of the bloodstains, they did not appear consistent with having been produced by blood from the wounds of the victim. Nine of these bloodstains were removed and subjected to blood-grouping tests and were found to be blood group A. Two additional stains were found to be group O. The group A bloodstains were consistent with the blood of the brother with the cut hand who was group A and provided strong evidence of his proximity to the assault at a time when he was bleeding actively from his hand. The second brother possessed group O blood similar to the victim but had no visible injury. The second brother was convicted of homicide despite these findings. The brother with the cut hand later pleaded guilty prior to his trial. Both received life sentences for the homicide.

This case emphasizes the importance of careful examination of the victim's clothing as well as that of a suspect or suspects during an investigation. In this particular case the victim's clothing was bagged after autopsy and was actually examined for the first time by the expert for the defense of the brother whose blood was not on the victim's clothing. Potentially exculpatory evidence was never subjected to any examination or analysis by the medical examiner nor investigating agency. As it turned out the jury did decide that the second brother was at least contributory to the homicide despite the bloodstain evidence.

Another interesting feature of this case is the lack of blood from the victim on both of the suspects despite the multiple stab wounds and throat slashing sustained by the victim. In cutting and stabbing cases the assailant wielding the weapon does not always receive significant bloodstaining from the victim. Often, the most serious bleeding of the victim is internal. Externally, clothing and other apparel worn by the victim will saturate with blood from wounds. Blood spatter may be minimal since it requires impact with an exposed source of blood to be produced. In cutting and stabbing cases, the severance of an artery may produce sizable arterial spurt patterns on assailant and nearby surfaces depending upon their locations. In those cases where the assailant slashes the throat of a victim from a position behind, he may be shielded from impact of the arterial spurting. Sometimes, the severance of a neck artery may occur as a final act or coup de grace subsequent to previous injuries to the victim and arterial pressures may be minimal or absent during the agonal period. In those situations, arterial spurting would not be expected to occur.

Case 3

A young female was found lying wedged between the right side of her bed and the wall, a file cabinet, and a record stand. The left leg of the

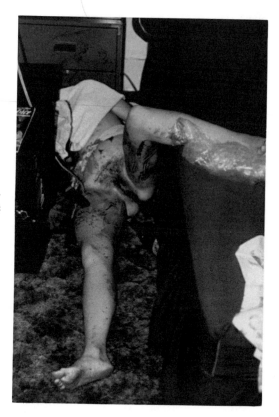

Figure 7-53 Location of victim beside bed with wine bottle between legs.

victim was elevated and rested on the bed. Her throat had been slashed and there was evidence of assault including intrusion of the vagina with a wine bottle which was between her legs (Figure 7-53). Injury to the vaginal tissue was apparent. The hands of the victim were tied behind her back with an insulated type of cord (Figure 7-54). The slashing of the victim's throat severed an artery in the neck which produced an arterial spurt pattern on the wall to the right of her head. Additionally, there was evidence of coughing or wheezing of blood onto the wall (Figures 7-55 and 7-56). Injury to the head area of the victim occurred prior to her observed position as evidenced by the bloody hair swipe patterns above her head on the file cabinet which were most likely produced as she was falling to the floor from the bed (Figure 7-57). The blood smearing on the legs of the victim represents a deliberate act by the assailant and may contribute to the evaluation of his mental state as well as to his character profile. This case remains unsolved.

Figure 7-54 Hands of victim tied behind her back with insulated cord.

Figure 7-55 Arterial spurt pattern on wall to right of victim's head.

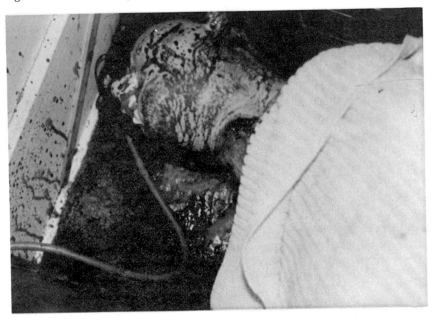

Figure 7-56 Closer view of arterial spurt pattern and evidence of coughing or wheezing of blood on wall.

Figure 7-57 Hair swipe above head of victim on file cabinet.

Case 4

The presence of multiple stab wounds and mutilation of the victim is often an indication of the type of assailant involved. A young man was found on the floor of his living room with more than twenty stab wounds to the chest (Figure 7-58). He was a known homosexual who frequented gay bars. Frequently in cases of this nature the assailant is a lover or former lover of the victim who has acted in a state of rage or jealousy. There may be amputation of the penis to the male victim or mutilation or removal of the breasts to the female victim. A careful search for bite marks inflicted on the victim by the assailant should be conducted.

Case 5

It should be recognized that multiple stab wounds in a victim in an accessible region of the body may be self-inflicted. A middle-aged woman was found on her bed in her apartment. The door was locked and there was no sign of forcible entry. The victim was clad only in her bra and suffered multiple stab wounds of the chest and abdomen (Figure 7-59). The abdominal area also showed a superficial incised wound

Figure 7-58   Victim of multiple stabbing which was determined to have been homosexually related.

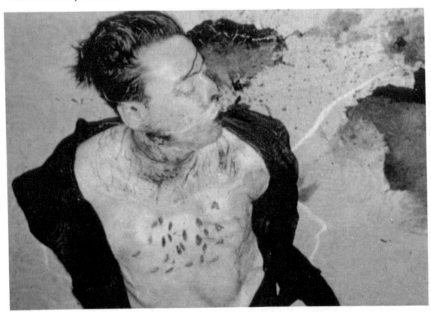

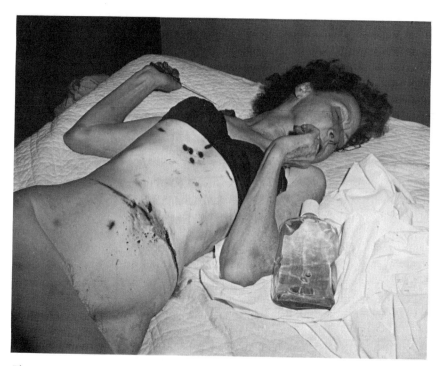

Figure 7-59 Victim with multiple stab wounds that were self-inflicted. Note minimal external bleeding.

and two superficial stab wounds consistent with hesitation injuries. Death in this case was due to massive internal bleeding in the chest and abdominal cavities. The knife in this case was in the right hand of the victim and a partially consumed bottle of rum was near her left elbow on the bed. Toxicology studies revealed a significant blood alcohol content. Most striking in this case is the relative absence of external bleeding and bloodstaining on the bed of the victim. A small flow pattern of blood is seen on the left side of the abdomen with some bloodstaining on the sheet below. This case was ruled a suicide.

Case 6

The owner of a small neighborhood convenience store was discovered in the rear storeroom of his establishment, the victim of multiple stabbing and incised wounds. The wounds were documented as the following: (1) stab wound of right anterior chest (Figure 7-60); (2) stab wound of left lower anterior chest; (3) stab wound of left upper anterior chest; (4) stab wound of midposterior lumbar region; (5) stab wound of

Figure 7-60   Victim of stabbing and throat slashing in convenience store. Stab wound through sweater of right anterior chest.

midposterior thorax; (6) incised wound of anterior neck (Figure 7-61); (7) incised wound of right frontoparietal scalp (Figure 7-62); (8) incised wound of left cheek; and (9) multiple incised wounds of right hand and solitary wound of left hand characterized as defense wounds (Figure 7-63). There were approximately 2000 ml of blood in the right pleural cavity and 1500 ml in the left pleural cavity.

Examination of the scene of this homicide did not reveal any sign of a struggle or altercation having occurred in the main store area. The rear storeroom was cluttered with numerous grocery items including stacks of soft drink cans and other surplus goods. This rear room was also utilized as an area for slicing cold cuts and cheese. The table with the meat slicer showed several areas of circular bloodstains resulting from dripping from above. Several transfer bloodstain patterns were present on the meat slicer. Additional free-falling drops of blood were present on the floor near the table including impact sites on a small metal scale which had been displaced to the floor. This area was determined to be the site of the initial confrontation between victim and assailant. The victim then retreated towards the center of the room in the area of stacked soda cans and subsequently fell to the floor. A bloody hair swipe was noted on the side of a soda carton to the right of the body with a directionality towards the final position of the body

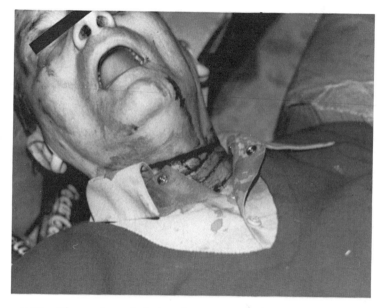

Figure 7-61   Closer view of victim showing incised wound of neck.

Figure 7-62   View of victim showing incised wound of right frontoparietal scalp.

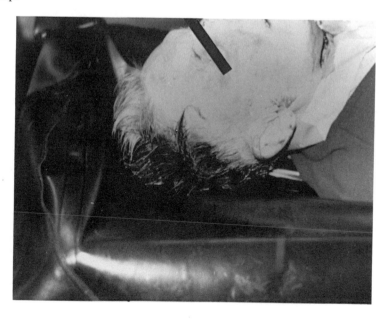

Figure 7-63 Defense wounds on right hand of victim.

Figure 7-64 Bloody hair swipe produced on soda carton by victim showing a directionality from left to right.

Figure 7-65 The clothing of the victim placed on a manikin for bloodstain examination and wound orientation.

(Figure 7-64). There was an additional transfer smearing of blood on a plastic sheet over a box and above the head of the victim which was most likely contacted by his head as he fell to the floor. To the immediate left of the victim's shoulder was a package covered with brown paper which showed some cast-off bloodstaining with a directionality to the left of the victim. The clothing of the victim was placed on a manikin for bloodstain examination and wound orientation (Figure 7-65). The left front collar area of the shirt of the victim showed an area of medium-velocity bloodstaining and a cast-off blood pattern (Figure 7-66). It was concluded that the throat of the victim was slashed from right to left while he was prone in the position in which he was found. In the right upper chest area of the victim's sweater near the penetration of a chest wound was located a 6-inch by 2-inch blood transfer

214

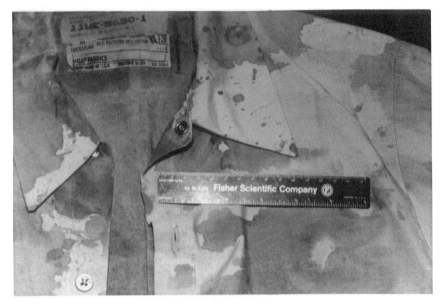

Figure 7-66 Left front collar area of victim's shirt showing medium-velocity blood spatter and cast-off bloodstains.

Figure 7-67 Partial shoeprint in blood on front of sweater worn by victim.

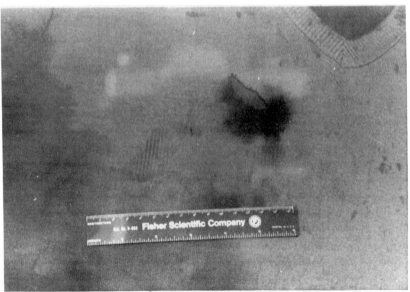

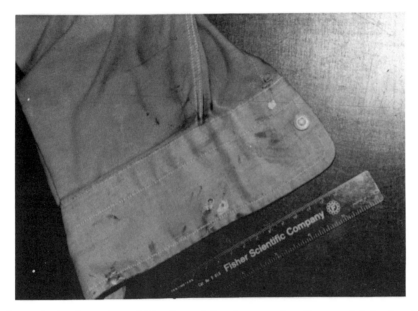

Figure 7-68   Smearing of blood on right sleeve and cuff area of defendant's shirt.

pattern with a uniform distribution of blood produced by a flat object and was felt to possibly represent a partial shoeprint produced by the assailant (Figure 7-67). Bloodstained shoes of the suspect were not recovered in this case.

The defendant's clothing in this case showed evidence of blood transfer on his exterior jacket produced by contact with a bloody source. Smearing of blood was present on the right sleeve and cuff area of his shirt (Figure 7-68). Medium-velocity blood spatter on the right collar area of the shirt of the defendant represented proximity to a source of blood that received impact (Figure 7-69). Bloodstains on the defendant's clothing were determined to be of the same group and genetic marker profile as that of the victim. The motive for this homicide was robbery. Prior to trial the defendant accepted a plea to first degree murder with a sentence of life in prison without parole.

This case demonstrates that activity of assailant and victim can be reconstructed through bloodstain interpretation at the scene and on clothing of victim and assailant. Blood transfer patterns including hair swipe patterns are frequently seen at crime scenes and provide useful information for the ultimate reconstruction of the case.

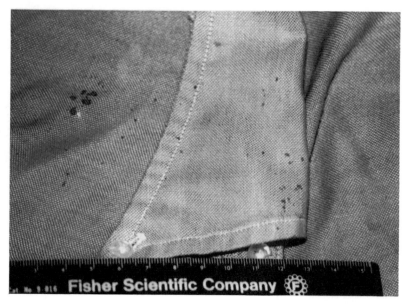

Figure 7-69   Medium-velocity blood spatter on right collar area of defendant's shirt.

Case 7

The importance of careful examination of the scene and clothing of the victim for evidence of bloodstains that may represent injury of an assailant has been previously demonstrated. This case represents one in which all the bloodstains at the scene and on the victim were deposited by the assailant. In a city in upstate New York, the police responded to a vehicular–pedestrian accident. The driver of the vehicle claimed that a male pedestrian ran into his path and the collision was unavoidable. The victim was taken to a local hospital and treated for minor injuries. The attending physician questioned the victim concerning a slashed wrist which required suturing but did not appear to be related to the vehicular accident. The individual was reluctant to offer an explanation to the physician, but later gave a statement to the police officer investigating the accident that his live-in girlfriend had slashed his wrist during an argument. He then grabbed her by the throat and pushed her away, and she fell to the floor unconscious. The boyfriend then panicked, became depressed, and attempted suicide in several ways. He first attempted to electrocute himself with the cord from a coffee maker and then drank a glass of cleaning solution. He then drove away from the house in his truck and a few miles down the

Figure 7-70 Medium-velocity blood spatter on left front of vehicle resulting from impact with previously injured boyfriend attempting to commit suicide.

road purposely crashed his vehicle into a tree. Still alive, and relatively uninjured, the boyfriend then ran in front of an oncoming vehicle which he also survived (Figure 7-70).

The 16-year-old girlfriend was found on the floor in the kitchen of the house shared by the couple (Figure 7-71). Postmortem examination revealed the cause of death to be asphyxiation. The pathologist determined that marks on the neck of the victim had been produced by sustained pressure on the neck with the neckline of the sweater utilized as a ligature. The front of the sweater and blue jeans of the victim were considerably bloodstained with transfer patterns of blood (Figure 7-72). A bloodstained towel was near her right shoulder. Several knives were scattered on the kitchen floor as well as numerous bloodstained paper towels. At the kitchen counter near the sink was found a coffee maker with the cord cut, but still in the electrical outlet. A metal fork was nearby (Figure 7-73). Circular spots of blood on the countertop represented bleeding from a source above the counter. A nearly empty glass containing a cleaning solution was found on the opposite side of the sink (Figure 7-74). All the bloodstains at the scene including those on the victim were found to be the type of the boyfriend. The girl sustained no blood-producing injuries. The scene examination did indicate that the boyfriend may have attempted suicide in the manners

218

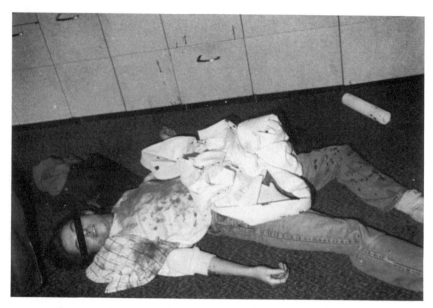

Figure 7-71 Victim on kitchen floor with bloodstained shirt and partially covered with paper towels.

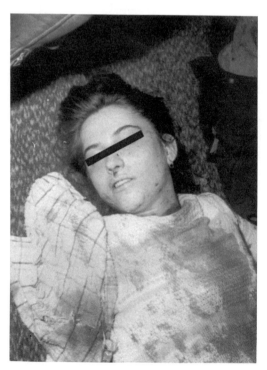

Figure 7-72 Closer view of blood transfer patterns on front shirt of victim that were determined to be the blood type of the boyfriend and not that of the victim.

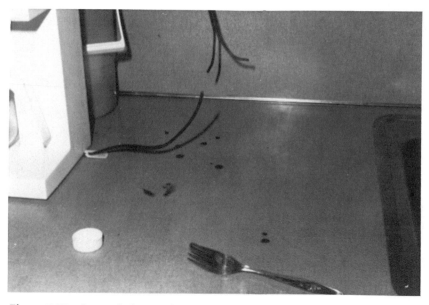

Figure 7-73 Severed electrical cord and fork utilized by boyfriend to unsuccessfully electrocute himself. Note blood drips on countertop from previously slashed wrist.

Figure 7-74 Glass on countertop containing cleaning fluid that boyfriend attempted to drink with additional blood drips nearby.

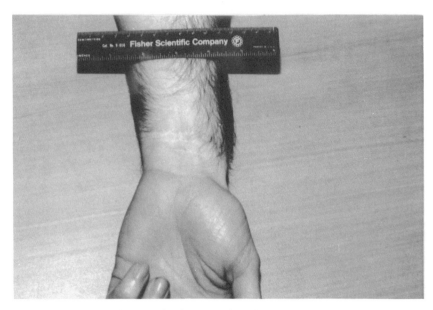

Figure 7-75   Healed scars of left wrist of boyfriend showing major wrist slash and parallel, healed hesitation wounds.

in which he claimed. However, he was convicted of homicide after a jury trial. The verdict in the first trial was appealed and eventually overturned. A new trial was ordered approximately two years later. The defense at this time requested a reevaluation of the physical evidence and bloodstain pattern interpretation. As part of this reinvestigation a request was made to examine the wrist of the defendant who was still in custody. The healed scar representing the wrist slash incurred two years previously was well defined. However, parallel to this major healed scar on the wrist were several superficial healed scars representing additional incised wounds (Figure 7-75). The presence of these classical hesitation wounds provided strong evidence that the wrist slash sustained by the defendant was self-inflicted. The location of the wrist slash was not in a typical location to be classified as a defensive wound. The defendant was convicted a second time by a jury without the benefit of testimony concerning the wrist or bloodstain interpretation since the defense attorney chose not to offer the testimony of his expert.

Case 8

Defensive injuries inflicted upon victims are common in cases associated with fatal wounds resulting from blunt force blows and cutting and stabbing trauma. In these types of death, defensive injuries are

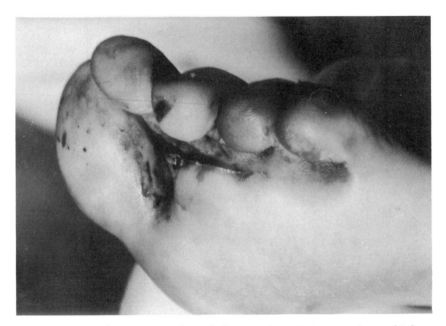

Figure 7-76 Defensive wounds on left toes of victim attempting to kick at knife-wielding assailant.

often represented by bruising or slashes on the upper extremities especially in the area of the hands and forearms. In those cases where the victims are prone and defending themselves with their feet, similar injuries may occur on the toes, ankles, or lower legs (Figure 7-76). Activities of the victim occurring after receiving blood-producing defensive injuries can often be documented by blood transfer patterns in the form of hand-, foot-, or shoeprints on surfaces including the clothing of the assailant.

Blood-producing injuries to assailants occur with some frequency and resultant bloodstains at a scene may be discernible from those produced by the victim through careful bloodstain interpretation and blood-grouping procedures. In addition to bloodstains an injured assailant may leave behind unique evidence.

During the postmortem examination of a female stabbing victim, the pathologist located an unattached, foreign fragment of skin on her leg. This skin fragment possessed ridge detail consistent with a fingertip (Figure 7-77). Investigators checked local hospital emergency rooms in the area and located a man who claimed to have been assaulted with a knife the night of the homicide. His injuries were limited to cuts on the right palm with a section of skin missing from a finger of the right hand. The skin fragment located on the victim was brought to the treating physician who matched it perfectly with the defect in the

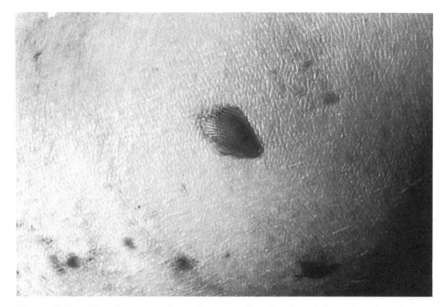

Figure 7-77 Skin fragment from finger with ridge detail found on leg of stabbing victim.

Figure 7-78 Mechanical match of fingertip skin found on victim with area of missing skin on finger of suspect.

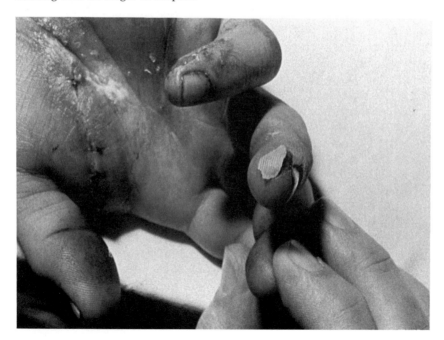

man's fingertip (Figure 7-78). Blood, matching the type of the victim, was also identified on his clothing. The suspect, a brother-in-law of the victim, was subsequently convicted of her murder.

Case 9

A middle-aged man from the Middle East was found dead in his jewelry-designing and manufacturing shop in the downtown area of a large city. He was lying on his back in a large pool of blood near gas cylinders (Figure 7-79). The body was found by family members after the deceased did not arrive home for dinner and did not respond to telephone calls to the place of business. The door to the premises was locked with no sign of forced entry. The family members admitted themselves with their own set of keys.

Death was considered to be due to massive external bleeding related to slash wounds of the wrists and backs of the knees (Figures 7-80 and 7-81). The wounds extended deeply to the bone in each area and severed tendons, arteries, veins, and nerves in the wrists and behind the

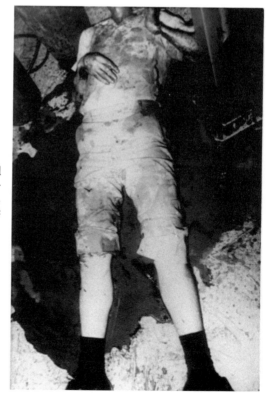

Figure 7-79 Victim as found lying in pool of blood in jewelry manufacturing shop. Note that trouser legs are rolled up.

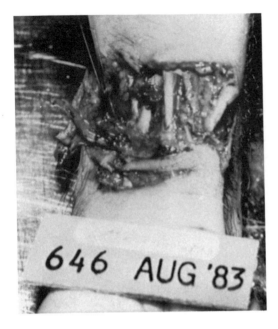

Figure 7-80 Deep, incised wound in right wrist of victim.

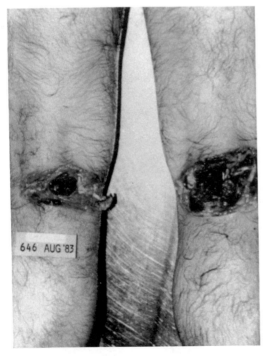

Figure 7-81 Deep, incised wounds behind both knees of victim.

Figure 7-82   Shoeprints in blood on floor leading away from the victim.

knees. In each location there was a single deep slash with no evidence of superficial hesitation cuts. The postmortem examination did not reveal any additional injuries to the victim nor evidence of restraint. Toxicology studies gave negative results.

Review of the scene photographs did not reveal evidence of the occurrence of a fight or struggle. The large pool of blood beneath and around the victim was relatively undisturbed (Figure 7-79). There were numerous bloody shoeprints on the floor leading away from the body (Figure 7-82). However, prior to the photographs having been taken the scene was accessible to the family, EMT personnel, and police investigators who likely tracked blood on the floor after approaching the body. There was an absence of blood on the shoes of the victim. The trouser legs of the victim were pulled up above the knees which would have exposed the site of injuries to the back of the knees. The slashes to these areas did not involve damage to the trousers. A scalpel with a plastic handle and number 11 blade was located between the legs of the victim at the level of the knees (Figures 7-83 and 7-84). The front of the victim's shirt was smeared with blood with evidence of blood spatter and cast-off bloodstains in the area of the front shoulders and extending onto the face of the victim (Figure 7-85). Blood flow and drip patterns on the floor to the left of the victim's left leg and waist were

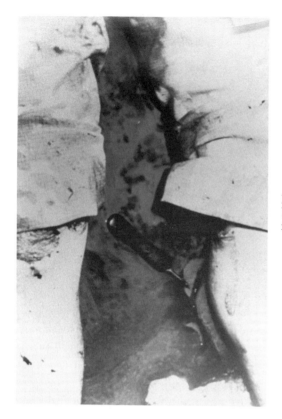

Figure 7-83 Scalpel located between legs of victim on floor.

Figure 7-84 View of scalpel with thick handle and No. 11 blade.

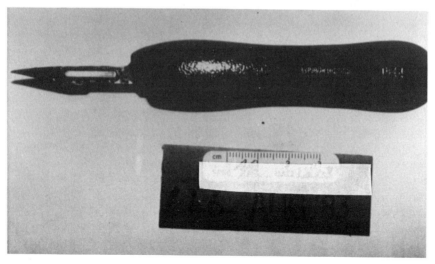

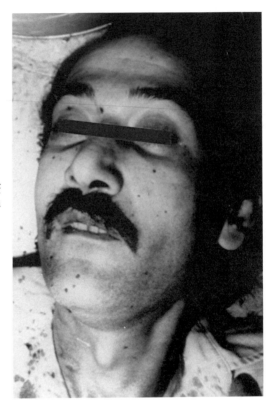

Figure 7-85   View of face of
victim showing distribution
of blood spatter.

observed in conjunction with some apparent arterial spurt patterns on
an adjacent table leg. These bloodstains would be consistent with the
victim sitting on the floor in that area prior to falling backward to his
final position.

The history of the victim indicated some evidence of despondency
and previous visits to a psychiatrist. An overdose of aspirin had been
ingested approximately three weeks prior to his death. Although there
was no evidence of a suicide note at the scene, this case was eventually
classified as a suicide. Many aspects of the investigation support this
conclusion. It is recognized that only 15–20 percent of suicide victims
leave notes. Prior attempts at self-destruction are not uncommon. The
areas of injury to the victim were accessible for him to inflict injury.
Exposure of the rear of the knees by raising the trouser legs prior to
slashing is consistent with self-infliction. The absence of hesitation
cuts is an unusual aspect of this case but on the other hand there was
no evidence of any of the injuries that were defensive in nature. The
fact that both wrists and rear of both knees were deeply slashed sever-
ing tendons and nerves as well as arteries and veins would tend to cast

doubt that the victim could have inflicted these injuries to the four locations himself. It was the opinion of some physicians that the victim could have self-inflicted the knee injuries and one wrist injury but not cut both wrists and knees in that fashion. How would he have been able to hold the scalpel in a hand that sustained severe tendon and nerve damage? There exist two possibilities that would be consistent with the bloodstains on the face of the victim. The scalpel could have been supported between the knees of the victim or held in the mouth and the blade then drawn across the wrist. Either scenario would account for the location of the scalpel between the legs of the victim. Neither the clothing nor the weapon was available for examination to further support these possibilities. An unusual blood transfer pattern on the left calf of the victim may be associated with the scalpel handle but unfortunately was not clearly resolved in the photographs made available for review.

A search of the forensic literature did not reveal a similar case of deep, bilateral slashing of the wrists and knees in the absence of hesitation cuts and thus this case is considered highly unusual. A theory that the victim declined to resist or was incapacitated by drug or chemical means prior to being slashed methodically by an unknown assailant was not substantiated by the postmortem examination nor other physical evidence.

Litigation in this case involved denial by an insurance company of a claim by the family for death benefits because of a suicide clause in the policy. The case was ultimately settled just prior to trial in civil court.

Blunt Force Trauma

Case 1

The victim in this case was a 22-year-old white woman found deceased on her bed at her residence in southern Pennsylvania. Since she had not reported for work at a local restaurant the previous day and did not answer the telephone, a co-worker came to her residence. The apartment was locked and there was no sign of forced entry. The victim's car was missing from the apartment parking lot. The co-worker and the apartment manager entered and discovered the body on a bed covered with a quilt (Figure 7-86).

At autopsy, the cause of death was determined to be due to blunt force craniocerebral injuries associated with three to seven lacerations of the occipital scalp (Figure 7-87). There were extensive open comminuted skull fractures with cerebral lacerations and contusions. Toxicological studies revealed a blood alcohol concentration of 0.069 percent ethanol. The time of death was estimated to be approximately 36 hours prior to the time she was discovered.

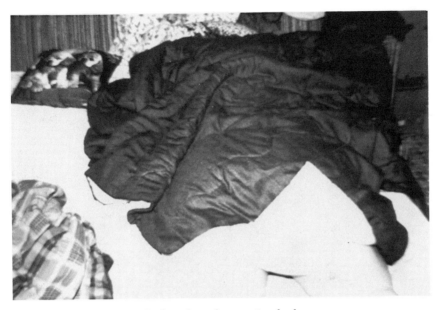

Figure 7-86   Victim on bed with quilt covering body.

Figure 7-87 View of victim's head at postmortem examination showing lacerations of the occipital scalp with underlying comminuted skull fractures.

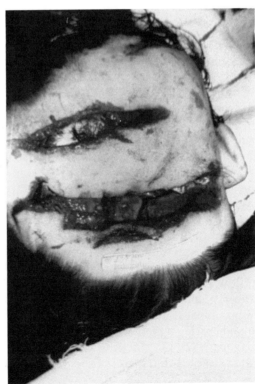

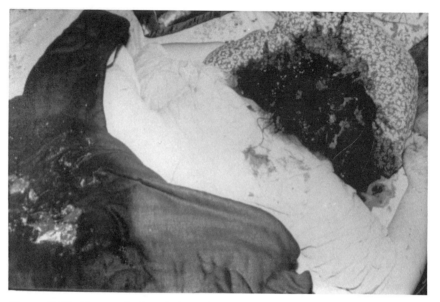

Figure 7-88 Removal of quilt from head of victim on bed with brain tissue adhering to underside of quilt.

The scene of this homicide was a small, two-room, one-bathroom apartment which was relatively undisturbed. There were no signs of a struggle's having taken place nor signs of a burglary. The victim was lying on a sofa-type foldout bed, face down, with a quilt over her body. Removal of the quilt revealed the extensive head injuries sustained by the victim and brain tissue embedded into the material on the underside of the area of the quilt that covered her head (Figure 7-88). This would indicate that some blows were struck to the head of the victim with the quilt over her head. Blood transfer patterns consistent with having been produced by bloody fingers were observed on the quilt that were felt to be associated with the assailant (Figure 7-89). The victim bled to a considerable extent on the bed. Blood had soaked through the mattress and onto the floor at the head of the bed. There was considerable medium-velocity blood spatter present on the arms of the victim as well as on the pillow upon which her head rested and on a second pillow forward on her head (Figures 7-90 and 7-91). Various stuffed animals and dolls positioned on the sofa above the head of the victim were undisturbed and received considerable circular medium-velocity blood spatter which originated from the area of the head of the victim (Figure 7-92). On the pillows and on the stuffed animals and dolls it was observed that some of the blood spatters contained small clots of

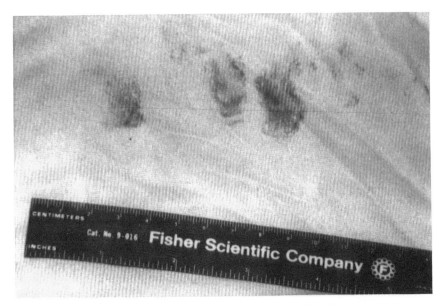

Figure 7-89 Blood transfer pattern on quilt produced by bloody fingers.

Figure 7-90 Medium-velocity blood spatter on pillow forward of head of victim on bed.

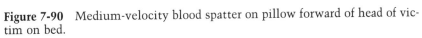

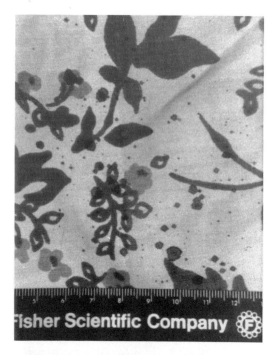

Figure 7-91 Closer view of medium-velocity blood spatter on pillow showing an impact of approximately 90 degrees.

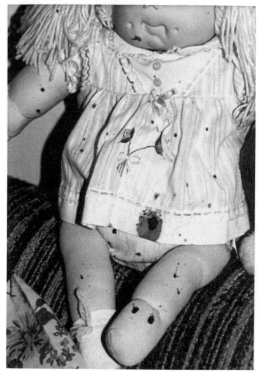

Figure 7-92 Medium-velocity blood spatter on doll located on top of sofabed forward of the head of the victim.

Figure 7-93 View of clotted blood spatter on doll.

blood in their central areas indicating that the source of blood receiving impact was at least partially clotted during administration of the blows (Figure 7-93). There were numerous cast-off bloodstain patterns present on the west wall to the left of the victim, on the south wall above the head of the victim, and on the east wall to the right of the victim (Figures 7-94, 7-95, and 7-96). The directionalities, convergences, and points of origin of these cast-off patterns were determined. The directionality of the bloodstains on the west wall was downward, those on the south wall upward, and those on the east wall downward. Study of the points of convergences and origins of these stains indicated that the source of blood was over the bed in the area of the victim receiving injury (Figure 7-97). It was consistent that the assailant administering the blows was positioned at the side of the bed to the left of the victim. The cast-off bloodstains present on the east wall of the bedroom were large and irregular and presented very unusual patterns produced by relatively large quantities of projected blood (Figure 7-98). This would indicate that the weapon utilized in this beating was a heavy blunt object and not swung in a rapid fashion. There were no cast-off bloodstains on the ceiling which would indicate that the

Figure 7-94 Cast-off bloodstain pattern on west wall of bedroom.

Figure 7-95 Convergences of bloodstains on south wall of bedroom.

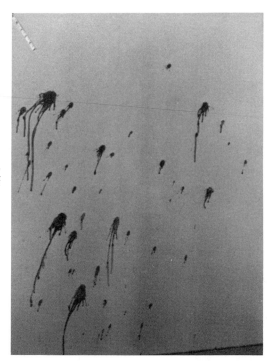

Figure 7-96 Cast-off blood-stain pattern on east wall of bedroom.

weapon was not swung over the head of the assailant as he was delivering blows to the victim.

The location of the medium-velocity blood spatter on the arms of the victim and on the nearby pillows and stuffed animals and dolls in conjunction with the locations of the cast-off bloodstains on the wall led to the conclusion that the victim was on the bed and in the same position as found when she was struck the fatal blows. There was no bloodstain evidence to indicate that she in any way fought or struggled with her assailant rather was likely taken by surprise or even have been asleep. The large amount of bleeding by the victim and the presence of the clotted blood spatter indicates a period of survival by the victim after receiving the initial blows. Additional blows were struck with the quilt placed over the head of the victim.

The boyfriend of the victim was developed as a suspect in this homicide. The victim's automobile was discovered at a motel about 20 miles from the scene where the suspect had secured a room using a credit card belonging to the victim. He fled the motel and avoided arrest for a few weeks until apprehended in a western state a few weeks later. However, a search of his motel room revealed a heavy 16.5-inch long crowbar which was found to contain human blood but in too small a quantity for grouping purposes (Figure 7-99). Also found in the

236

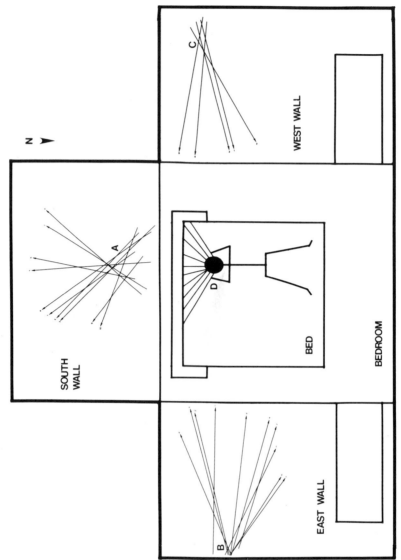

Figure 7-97 Diagram showing convergences of bloodstains on three walls of bedroom with point of origin's being the position of the victim on bed.

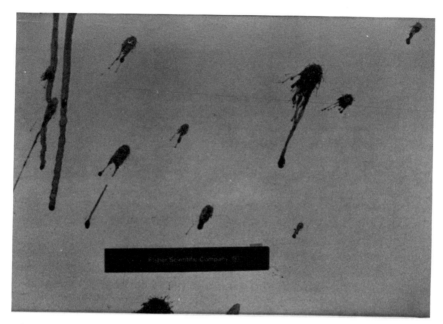

Figure 7-98 Close view of unusual cast-off bloodstain pattern on east wall produced by large quantities of blood projected from a heavy, blunt object.

Figure 7-99 Crowbar used to inflict injuries to victim.

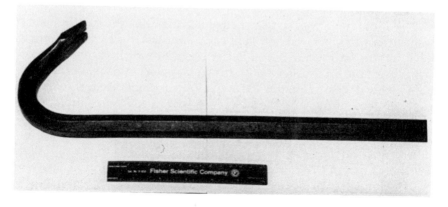

Figure 7-100   Canvas bag with bloodstains and brain tissue found at motel.

motel room were a set of clean clothes which were freshly washed and a green canvas bag. Analysis of the clothes did not reveal the presence of blood. However, analysis of stains and crusted material on the green canvas bag revealed brain tissue and human blood (Figure 7-100). The human blood was characterized as similar to that of the victim with respect to ABO grouping and genetic marker profile. The defendant subsequently pled guilty to first degree murder and is serving a life sentence in prison.

Case 2

A 42-year-old male was last seen alive leaving a topless bar at closing time with three young men in their early twenties. A short time later a police officer on routine patrol noticed the interior light of a vehicle parked with the driver's door open in an area adjacent to a lake near the main highway approximately three-quarters of a mile from the topless bar. The officer drove into the area to investigate and encountered two of the young men standing near the vehicle with the door open. A second but empty vehicle was parked nearby. During the course of questioning the men the officer looked down onto the frozen lake and saw the victim in this case lying on the ice in a pool of blood (Figure 7-101). He had been beaten and stabbed. The two men were subse-

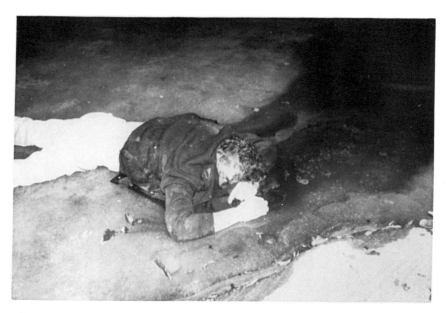

Figure 7-101 Victim of beating and stabbing on frozen pond. Note dilution of blood pool on ice.

quently arrested and investigation led to the arrest of the third individual several days later.

Postmortem examination revealed that the victim had suffered two stab wounds to the back to the upper and lower right side and one in the front epigastric region (Figure 7-102). The right pleural cavity contained approximately 1500 ml of fluid and clotted blood; the peritoneal cavity contained approximately 800 ml of blood. There was evidence of bruising in the rear shoulder area. The victim also sustained massive head injuries including multiple skull fractures and underlying brain injuries. Death was attributed to severe brain injury due to blunt force and internal hemorrhage resulting in injury to right lung and liver due to stab wounds.

Examination of the scene of this homicide revealed irregular blood transfer patterns on the ground near the victim's vehicle produced by contact with a source of blood with a relatively flat surface and associated with some movement (Figures 7-103 and 7-104). The rear of the victim's jacket contained heavy bloodstaining with dirt and debris in the area of the stab wounds in the back and most likely represented the source of the blood that produced these transfer bloodstains on the ground. The severe head injuries sustained by the victim did not occur in this location. There was no appreciable trail of blood from this point to the edge of the bank of the lake. It is possible that the victim was

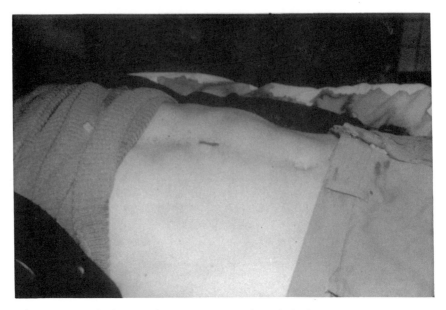

Figure 7-102 Stab wound in epigastric region of victim.

Figure 7-103 Blood transfer patterns on ground near victim's vehicle.

Figure 7-104   Closer view of blood transfer patterns on ground.

carried over to this point and thrown over the bank onto the ice. Half-way down the bank there was an additional area of blood transfer where the victim likely made contact on the way down the bank (Figure 7-105). The blunt force injuries that produced the massive skull fractures, brain injuries, and heavy bleeding occurred while the victim was in a prone position on the ice. There was evidence of medium-velocity blood spatter on the shoulder of the victim, on the ice adjacent to the body, and on the edge of the nearby bank. There were additionally present on the jacket of the victim and on the ice, fragments of brain tissue and skull. The blunt weapon in this case was an ax handle which was recovered from the defendant's vehicle. Evidence that this was the weapon involved is shown by the blood and tissue transfer pattern of the weapon on the jacket of the victim (Figure 7-106). Blood-stains consistent with the group and genetic marker profile of the victim were also demonstrated on the ax handle.

The three defendants offered differing versions of the homicide. They admitted drinking with the defendant in the topless bar and leaving with him at closing time with the promise of smoking mari-juana with the victim. This apparently was a ploy to rob him and possibly steal his Mercedes-Benz. The defendants agreed that the vic-tim became involved in a fight with the defendants at the parking area near the lake. One defendant claimed to have seen the others hit the

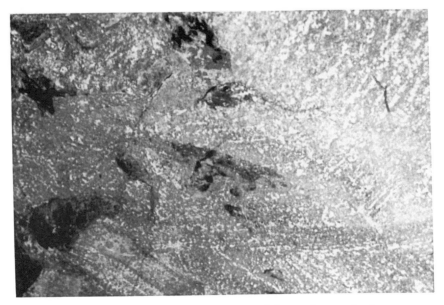

Figure 7-105 Blood transfer patterns on a rock located on embankment near edge of pond.

Figure 7-106 Blood and tissue transfer pattern of ax handle on jacket of victim.

victim with a stick and fists a few times and carry him over to the edge of the bank and throw him over. At this point this defendant did not want to get involved and ran off leaving the other two defendants. The remaining two defendants differed in their accounts of the beating and stabbing of the victim with each implicating the others.

The examination of the clothing and footwear of each of the defendants was helpful to the reconstruction of this case but did not provide answers to all questions. The defendant that ran off and was apprehended days later had washed his clothes so that their examination did not provide additional information. His boots did not show evidence of bloodstains but he had walked through mud during a rainstorm which could have removed bloodstains. Had this defendant stabbed the victim initially as claimed by another defendant he may not have received bloodstains on his clothing. A second defendant showed minimal smearing of blood on his clothing which was consistent with carrying the victim. The third defendant admitted that he stabbed the victim once and observed the other two beating the victim on the ice while he stood at the top of the bank. The top of the bank was approximately 50 feet away and 6 feet elevated from the location of the victim on the ice. This defendant's clothing and boots showed numerous small, circular spots of medium-velocity blood spatter on the lower right leg and boot, knee area of the right leg, and inside front area of the upper left thigh, and on the left arm of his jacket (Figures 7-107, 7-108, and 7-109). This

Figure 7-107 Medium-velocity blood spatter on lower right leg of jeans and right boot of defendant.

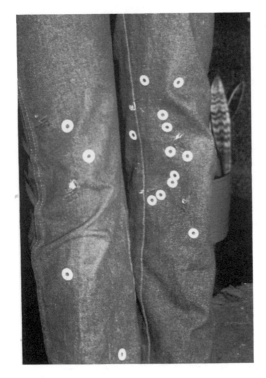

Figure 7-108 Medium-velocity blood spatter on right knee and left upper thigh of jeans of defendant.

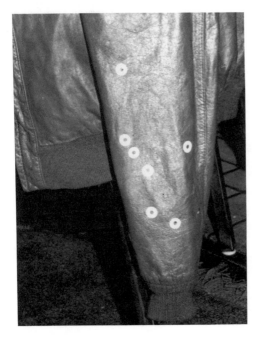

Figure 7-109 Medium-velocity blood spatter on left jacket sleeve of defendant.

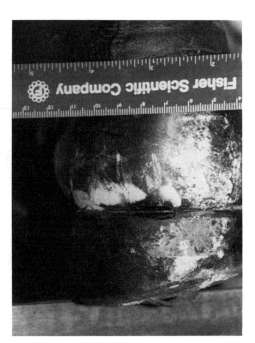

Figure 7-110 Bloodstains on rear heel of right boot of defendant.

array of blood spatter indicated proximity to and likely participation in the beating of the victim. The right boot in the area of the heel showed some medium-velocity blood spatter, blood crusts, and hair consistent with scalp hair of the victim and was likely produced by kicking the victim in the head (Figure 7-110). The version of events offered by this defendant was certainly refuted by the bloodstain evidence. This defendant was permitted to plead to a lesser charge of homicide and reduced sentence. He then testified for the prosecution against the other two defendants who were convicted and received life sentences in prison.

Case 3

Another instance in which the alertness and perception of a police officer on routine patrol resulted in the immediate apprehension of suspects in a homicide case occurred in Louisiana. Traveling on a two-lane highway parallel to a bayou canal, a police officer noticed two vehicles off the roadway near the bank of the canal. He stopped and noted that one vehicle was partially submerged in the water and the other was behind attempting to push the first vehicle farther into the water (Figure 7-111). The victim in this case was in the front passenger area of the first vehicle and had sustained fatal head injuries. The wife

Figure 7-111   Scene at edge of bayou canal with defendant's vehicle on muddy bank.

of the victim and a male acquaintance of hers were arrested and charged with homicide. A second female was arrested in conjunction with this case but eventually not charged with homicide.

The postmortem examination of the victim revealed multiple lacerations of the forehead and left side of the head with a circular, depressed fracture in the left temporal region of the skull with underlying injury to the brain due to beating with a blunt instrument (Figure 7-112). The semicircular laceration and circular depressed fracture of the skull were consistent with the blunt instrument's being a hammer (Figures 7-113 and 7-114). There were no defensive injuries or other trauma to the victim.

The reconstruction of this case was based upon evaluation of the scene where the victim was located and then the scene of the beating which was a bedroom of a trailer occupied by the victim and his wife. At the canal scene it was apparent that there was an attempt to dispose of the victim in his vehicle by pushing it into the bayou canal with a second vehicle. The canal was estimated to be approximately 20 feet deep; thus had the vehicle been successfully submerged, the case may never have been solved. The bank of the canal was a soft, wet, grassy area which caused difficulty with traction and thus with pushing the vehicle into the water. This problem was compounded by the fact that the first vehicle, with the victim in the front seat, was in parked gear

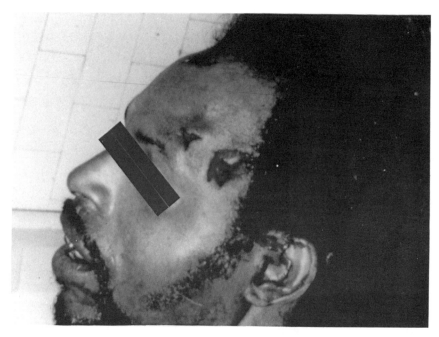

Figure 7-112 Lacerations on left side of head of victim.

Figure 7-113 Semicircular laceration in left temporal region of victim's head consistent with having been produced by a hammer.

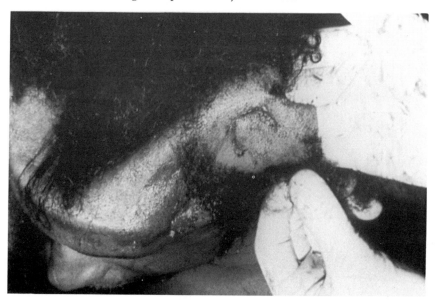

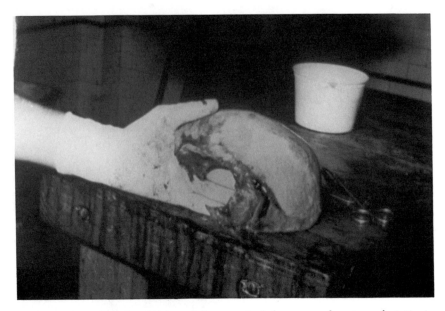

Figure 7-114 Circular depressed fracture in left temporal region of victim's skull below semicircular laceration.

during the attempts to push it. The victim had sustained injury prior to being placed into the vehicle as evidenced by the blood transfers and smears on the rear left fender of the vehicle (Figure 7-115). He most likely made contact with this area as he was being transported into the front seat.

The primary scene of this homicide was the trailer bedroom shared by the deceased and his wife. The trailer was orderly and there was no sign of a struggle's having taken place in any of the rooms. However, considerable effort had been taken to clean up the blood at the crime scene prior to the initial arrival of the investigators. The bed in the master bedroom was clean with fresh sheets and bedspread (Figure 7-116). No blood was visible in the room except on the ceiling. (An individual cleaning up a bloody crime scene often does not notice blood on ceilings.) Present in this case were two distinct cast-off bloodstain patterns on the ceiling. One pattern was located over the bed parallel to the wall at the head of the bed. Circular cast-off bloodstains were observed on the ceiling above the right upper area of the bed which became more oval or elongated as the pattern extended in a northerly direction (Figure 7-117). An assailant would have produced this pattern with overhead swings of a weapon while positioned on the left side of the bed. The second cast-off bloodstain pattern on the ceiling was observed as circular bloodstains above the right upper area of

Figure 7-115 Bloodstain pattern on left rear fender of victim's vehicle.

Figure 7-116 View of master bedroom and bed after scene was cleaned up.

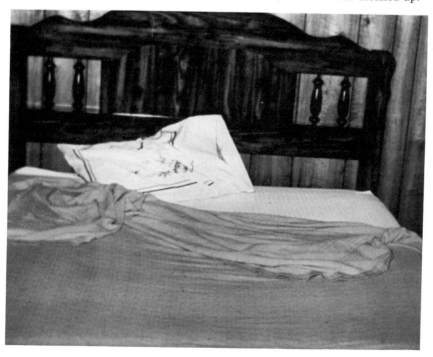

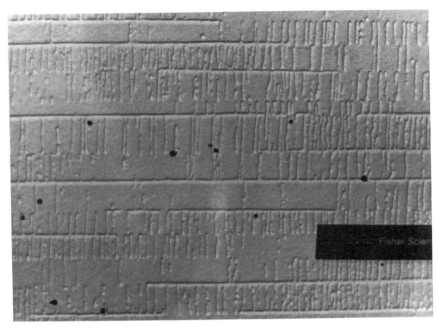

Figure 7-117 Cast-off bloodstains on ceiling above bed to the left of victim's position on bed.

the bed which became more oval or elongated as the pattern extended in an easterly direction towards the foot of the bed in the area of the overhead light and fan (Figures 7-118 and 7-119). An assailant would have produced this pattern with overhead swings of a weapon while positioned on the bed near the foot.

When the bed was stripped of the clean sheets and bedspread, and the mattress turned over, a large bloodstain was observed on the right upper area which coincided with the calculated position of the victim based upon the location of the cast-off bloodstains on the ceiling (Figure 7-120). Further search of the crime scene produced a plastic bag which was found to contain numerous bloodstained items including a mattress cover, bottom sheet, pillows, and pillow cases in addition to bloodstained towels, bloodstained shower cap, and a bloodstained claw-type hammer (Figure 7-121).

The bed was reconstructed with the sheet and pillows with their cases. The major bloodstain on the sheet coincided with the bloodstain on the mattress (Figure 7-122). This bloodstain was associated with some medium-velocity blood spatter and arterial spurt patterns which extended onto a heavily bloodstained pillow. This reconstruction further verified the position of the victim to be in a prone position on the bed when he was struck by multiple blows with a blunt instrument.

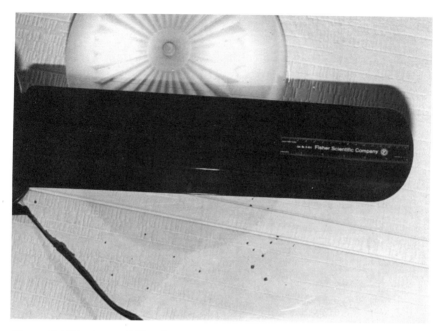

Figure 7-118 Cast-off bloodstains on ceiling above bed near light fixture and fan.

Figure 7-119 Closer view of cast-off bloodstains on ceiling above bed near light fixture.

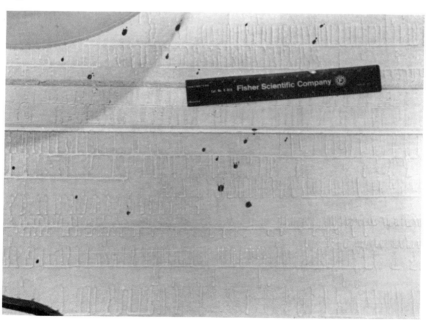

252

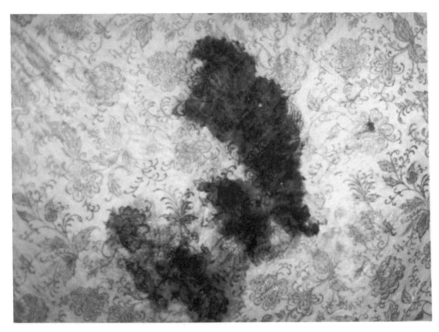

Figure 7-120 Large bloodstain on underside of mattress.

Figure 7-121 Plastic bag containing bloodstained sheets, towels, shower cap, and hammer.

Figure 7-122 Reconstruction of victim's bed with blood-stained sheets and pillows.

The second pillow was heavily bloodstained in conjunction with some brain tissue and was possibly placed over the head of the victim at some point after blood was shed.

The claw hammer and shower cap were interesting items of evidence in this case. The hammer was consistent in size and shape with having produced the injuries sustained by the victim. A trace of blood was detected on the hammer but was too limited in quantity for further testing. A hand towel from the garbage bag was considerably bloodstained and showed a transfer pattern in blood produced by a hammer (Figure 7-123). The plastic shower cap was considerably bloodstained on the inside surface and contained fragments of brain tissue. There was a semicircular defect in the shower cap which was consistent with having been produced by the hammer (Figure 7-124). This would indicate that the victim was beaten while wearing the shower cap. This is an important feature of the case in that the shielding effect of the plastic shower cap would be expected to greatly reduce the quantity of medium-velocity spatter produced during the beating. Relatively little of this type of spatter was seen on the sheet and pil-

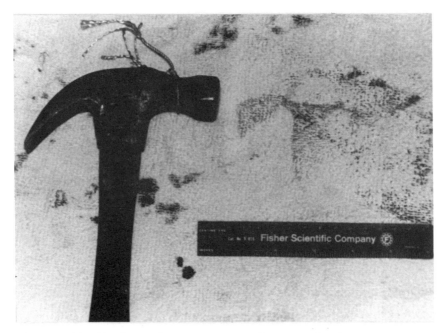

Figure 7-123 Blood transfer pattern on towel compared to hammer.

Figure 7-124 Shower cap worn by victim during beating on bed.

Figure 7-125 Front of shirt worn by male defendant showing blood pattern on right shoulder area produced by carrying victim from scene.

lows on the bed. Yet sufficient blood could accumulate on the hammer and be cast off the weapon during the back swing.

The male defendant in this case denied any role in the beating of the victim. He admitted to carrying the victim from the bed to the car at the request of the wife. Examination of the clothing of the male defendant did not show the presence of blood spatters nor cast-off patterns. There were transfer bloodstain patterns in the area of the right shoulder of the shirt which were consistent with this individual carrying the victim over his shoulder as he described (Figures 7-125 and 7-126).

The clothing of the wife worn at the time of arrest did not show a trace of blood. It is possible that she changed her clothes. At the scene in a smaller bedroom female slacks and a blouse were located which contained several types of bloodstain patterns. The slacks showed scattered areas of spatter and drips of blood on the mid- to lower leg area (Figure 7-127). On the blouse there was evidence of a small quantity of medium-velocity blood spatter on the left sleeve with smearing of blood on the right sleeve (Figures 7-128 and 7-129). Scattered small smears of blood were present on the front of the blouse (Figure 7-130). The rear of the blouse showed several cast-off bloodstains in the mid-

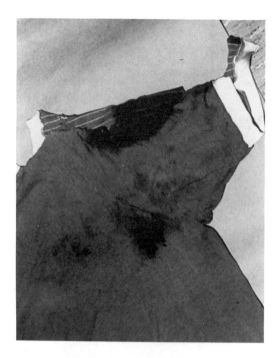

Figure 7-126 Rear of shirt worn by male defendant showing blood pattern on right shoulder area produced by carrying victim from scene.

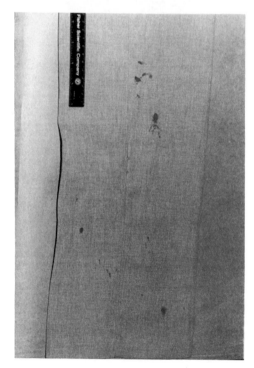

Figure 7-127 Blood spatter and drip pattern on right lower leg area of woman's slacks found at scene.

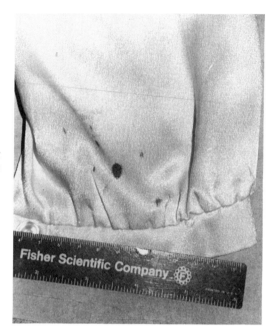

Figure 7-128 Blood spatter on left sleeve of woman's blouse found at scene.

Figure 7-129 Blood smears on right sleeve of woman's blouse found at scene.

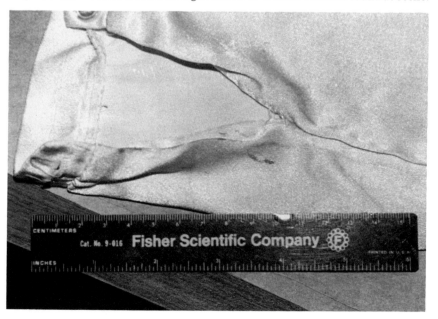

Figure 7-130 Bloodstains on front of woman's blouse found at scene.

back region which exhibited a downward directionality (Figures 7-131 and 7-132). This type of bloodstain pattern is frequently seen in this area of an assailant's shirt resulting from blood cast off a weapon as it is raised over the head similar to the manner in which cast-off blood-stains are produced on ceilings. Some of the blood droplets do not possess the energy to reach the height of the ceiling and fall downward in an arclike fashion. It was concluded that the wearer of the blouse either participated in the administration of the beating to the victim or was standing nearby with her back to the events taking place in order to receive the cast-off bloodstains on the rear of the shirt. The lack of medium-velocity blood spatter on the front of the blouse can be ex-plained by the shielding effect of the shower cap worn by the victim. There was not an abundance of blood spatter on the sheets nor pillow cases on the bed.

The wife of the victim in this case pleaded guilty to homicide prior to trial and is serving a life sentence in prison. Her male acquaintance later pled guilty to a lesser charge of manslaughter.

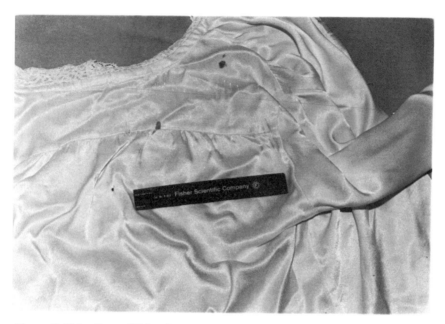

Figure 7-131 Cast-off bloodstains on upper rear of woman's blouse found at scene.

Figure 7-132 Cast-off bloodstains on lower rear of woman's blouse found at scene.

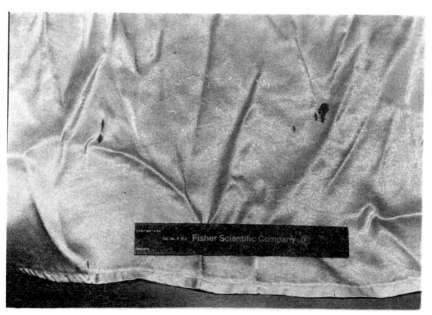

Case 4

A funeral home employee was charged with the homicide of his ex-wife. It was alleged that he had met with her on the pretext of shopping for Christmas presents, murdered her, then cremated her body at the funeral home where he worked as a greeter, and hid her remains in a friend's garage.

The remains, properly referred to as cremains, presented for postmortem examination consisted of numerous charred bone and debris (Figures 7-133 and 7-134). The bones were identified as human. Numerous fragments of skull, ribs, and vertebrae were recognizable. The pelvic bones were readily identifiable. The left iliac crest and upper femur appeared to have been exposed to a shearing trauma by a heavy, sharp surface. Portions of the femurs, tibias, and their articulation surfaces were present. Uneven burning of the bone suggested that flesh was on the bones during the burning process. The bones of the feet were identified and the phalanges noted to be delicate and small. Portions of the humerus, elbow, forearm, and hands were identified with some of the surfaces charred and others with unburned surfaces.

It was concluded that the cremains represented the body of a white

Figure 7-133 Cremains of victim at postmortem examination.

Figure 7-134   Closer view of cremains of victim.

woman with an approximate age of 32 years with previous pregnancies, the most recent occurring within the past two to three years. The irregular burning of the body suggested that the position of the body was not typical when placed in the crematorium or that the body was burned in large, separate portions. Positive identification of the victim in this case was accomplished by the examination of several charred teeth including several crowns and caps which were unburned and intact with black pegs in their bases. These were compared favorably with the premortem dental records of the victim. A gold necklace with a single white stone in a pendant was recovered intact. This jewelry item was identified by a friend of the deceased who had designed and made the necklace for her.

The crematorium consisted of a propane-fed furnace with dual apertures located on the interior side wall providing outlets for the flames. The temperature within the furnace may reach 1500 degrees Fahrenheit and normally reduce a body to ashes within a few hours (Figure 7-135). The deceased is normally placed in the crematorium over the center trough from which the cremains are eventually collected by raking into a tray below the furnace. The final weight of the cremains may be 3–4 pounds consisting of desiccated bone fragments which are usually pulverized prior to final disposition or burial (Figure 7-136).

Figure 7-135 Normal operation of crematorium with flame jets working properly.

Figure 7-136 View of cremains after normal cremation.

Figure 7-137 Crematorium with flame jet not operating properly.

The cremains of the victim in this case did not represent a complete cremation which greatly assisted the ultimate identification of the victim.

Investigation revealed that the flame port nearer the furnace opening was not operating properly and had a delayed ignition of approximately 2 hours (Figure 7-137). The pattern of residue on the floor of the furnace indicated that the victim had been placed just inside the door to the right of the trough and close to the right wall near the flame port that was malfunctioning (Figure 7-138). A blackish stained area was present on the wall just below and to the right of this flame port. This stained area represented an impact pattern with a downward directionality from approximately eleven o'clock to five o'clock (Figure 7-139). This was produced by a previously exposed source of liquid. Sufficient liquid originated from this source to permit the formation of a flow pattern toward the floor surface. It is possible that these stain patterns were produced from an exposed source of blood from the victim such as a head wound as she was being placed into the furnace. The source of blood would have to have been available from prior exposure rather than produced at the time of impact with the wall.

At the funeral home there was evidence that blood had been cleaned from the floor but no patterns were recognizable near the crematorium. This was however, an indication that the victim received blood-producing injury prior to being placed into the furnace. The husband

Figure 7-138 Dark residue representing body outline of victim on floor of crematorium.

Figure 7-139 Impact pattern on wall of crematorium above body outline.

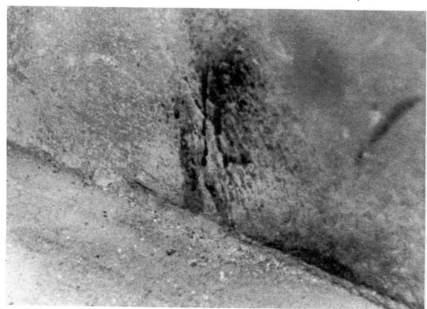

was convicted of first degree murder at trial despite his continued claim of innocence.

Case 5

A husband was charged with the murder of his wife who was found dead in the laundry room of their apartment building in the early evening hours. The husband stated that he had accompanied his wife to the laundry room and stayed with her until the wash cycle had started on the washing machine. He then returned to their apartment to watch television. When his wife did not return to the apartment he grew concerned and returned to the laundry room and discovered his wife lying on her back on the floor in a pool of blood, her head crushed. The husband went on to state that he lifted the head of his wife, felt for a pulse, and realized that she was dead. In frustration he slammed his hands to the bloody floor, wiped them on his coat, and ran to a neighbor's apartment to summon the police. He returned to the laundry room with the neighbor and again attempted to pull his wife up by placing is hands behind her head. He was restrained by the neighbor who also placed a towel over the face of the victim prior to the arrival of the police (Figure 7-140).

At autopsy it was determined that the victim sustained severe lacerations in the right frontal, parietal, and occipital areas of the scalp with

Figure 7-140 Victim on floor of laundry room as found by police upon arrival at scene.

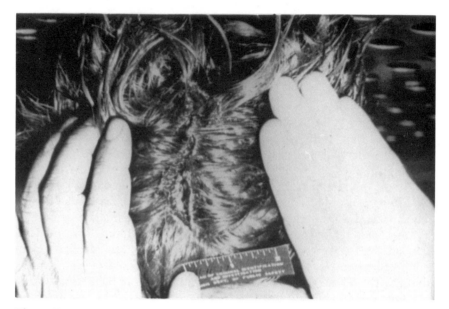

Figure 7-141 Severe scalp laceration sustained by victim.

underlying cerebral contusions (Figure 7-141). There was no evidence of skull fracture. A small laceration and bruising was noted on the right forehead area. Bruising was also noted bilaterally in the subman-dibular region of the face and the central portion of the neck. Superfi-cial lacerations were noted in the midline of the neck (Figure 7-142). Extensive areas of hemorrhage were noted in the soft tissues of the neck and upper sternal area with no evidence of fractures. Fractures were noted in the left second and fifth ribs. The immediate cause of death was attributed to respiratory failure due to manual strangula-tion. There was no evidence of sexual assault associated with this homicide.

The scene of this homicide was a laundry room with three washing machines along one wall and two dryers along the other with the victim positioned in the center area of the room. The radiating me-dium-velocity bloodstain pattern showed a point of convergence at the victim's head (Figure 7-143). This bloodstain pattern impacted on the floor, wall, washing machine, and dryer nearest the head of the victim. The bloodstains within this radiating pattern were confined to a short distance above the level of the floor and resulted from repeated impact of the victim's head with the floor while in that position.

Bloodstains which resulted from free-falling drops of blood impacted on top of the washing machine (Figure 7-144). It is likely that the victim received initial injury to the head while standing at the washing

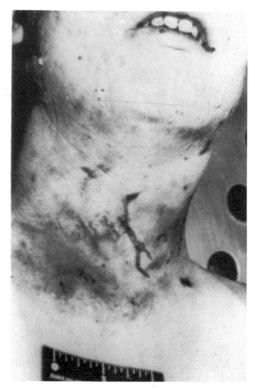

Figure 7-142 Bruises and superficial lacerations on neck of victim.

Figure 7-143 Medium-velocity bloodstain pattern impacting on wall a short distance above floor in a radial or spokelike pattern. The origin of these bloodstains is the area of the victim's head on the floor.

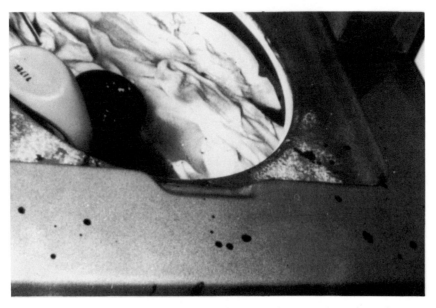

Figure 7-144   Bloodstains on top of washing machine resulting from dripping from above.

machine. This resulted in blood drops falling to the washing machine surface. Additional drops of blood fell to the top surface of the dryers and garbage can top on the opposite side of the room which are consistent with bleeding from the head of the victim while standing. A blood swipe pattern was present on a dryer which likely represented contact by the bloody hand of the victim prior to falling to her final position (Figure 7-145). There was no evidence of bloodstain patterns on the floor near the victim that could be associated with the statement of the husband that he had slapped is hands in blood on the floor after raising the head of his wife.

There were numerous bloody shoeprints on the floor of the laundry room which were found to be consistent with having been produced by a sole pattern similar to shoes worn by the husband. He had previously stated that he had entered the premises on two occasions after blood had been shed. The directionality of the shoeprints shows them to be erratic in movement rather than simply in and out of the room (Figure 7-146). More important to the reconstruction of this case was the examination of close-up photographs of the bloody shoeprints near the body. There was medium-velocity blood spatter superimposed over several of the shoeprints (Figure 7-147). The formation of the bloody shoeprint must have preceded the production of the medium-velocity spatter. It was concluded that the person wearing the shoes that produced that shoeprint in blood was present in the laundry room near or

Figure 7-145 Blood swipe patterns on clothes dryer.

Figure 7-146 Shoeprints in blood on floor of laundry room.

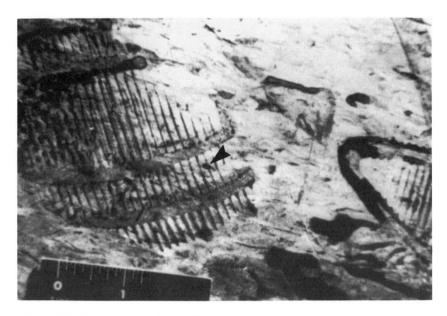

Figure 7-147   Medium-velocity blood spatter impacted on top of shoeprint in blood.

at the time of the struggle that produced bloodshed. This observation was not consistent with the version of events given by the husband.

The jacket worn by the husband contained considerable bloodstaining which was determined to be the type of his wife. Bloodstains consistent with medium-velocity impact spatter were located on the right sleeve and chest. Extending over the right shoulder area and down the back of the jacket were cast-off bloodstains which are typically produced during the administration of a beating and not by slapping one's hands in blood on the floor (Figure 7-148). On the right sleeve of the husband's jacket was a palmar transfer pattern in blood which was produced by a relatively small hand (Figure 7-149). This was likely produced by the victim as she attempted to defend herself during the course of the struggle in the laundry room.

The husband was convicted of the homicide of his wife. This case provides an excellent demonstration of the value of bloodstain evidence that clearly refuted the version of events described by the accused and provided strong physical evidence for the prosecution at trial.

Case 6

A platoon of soldiers stationed at an army base in the Republic of South Korea went on leave to a Korean ski resort for the weekend. On

Figure 7-148 Jacket of husband with blood spatter on front surface.

Figure 7-149 Palmar transfer pattern in blood on sleeve of husband's jacket.

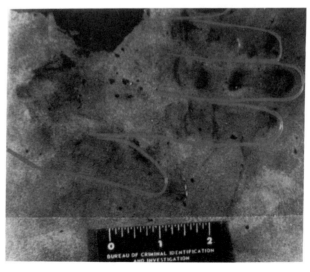

Sunday night several of the group were at a disco, drinking and dancing until late in the evening. Early the next morning one of the soldiers was found dead outside, adjacent to a hotel and parking lot not far from the disco where the group had been the previous evening (Figures 7-150 and 7-151). Initial investigation indicated that the victim had suffered blunt force injuries to the head area. The victim's wallet was found some distance from the body and initially robbery was suspected as a motive for the slaying. A companion of the victim was questioned and admitted that he and the victim had gotten into an argument in the street after leaving the disco and a fight had ensued after the victim had kicked him in the groin. The companion stated that at some point during the fight he picked up a wooden board and struck the victim while he was standing near the curb. The victim then staggered over to the area near the wall of the hotel where he was later found. The companion admitted that he may have stepped on the victim's face and may have jabbed him in the face with the board while he was on the ground. He denied striking the prone victim in the head repeatedly with the board and maintained that he did not inflict lethal injury to the victim nor take his wallet. He was arrested for this homicide. The postmortem examination of the victim revealed death to be due to blunt force injuries of the head which included: (1) multiple lacerations, contusions, and abrasions of the face (Figures 7-152 and 7-153); (2) fractures of the maxilla, nasal bone, and ethmoid bone; and (3) contusions of the brain with subarachnoid and intracerebral hemorrhages of the brain. Also noted were abrasions of the right wrist and knuckles of the right hand.

The scene of this homicide was a dirt area with sapling trees growing adjacent to the outside wall of a hotel. The trees were supported in a tripod fashion with wooden boards. The body was located close to and parallel to the hotel wall (Figure 7-154). To the right of the head and feet of the body were two large rocks. The curb of the street and entrance to an underground parking ramp was several feet in front of the feet of the victim. Scattered bloodstains and flow patterns were present on the curb of the street which were consistent with the victim having bled in that area for a short time (Figure 7-155). There was no bloodstain evidence of repeated blows with a blunt object's having been inflicted on the victim in this area. A few scattered bloodstains in the snow were noted farther inward of the curb but a continuing pattern of blood or other physical evidence representing the victim's path to his final position could not be identified in photographs provided. The victim was lying on his back with his left arm resting against the adjacent wall. There was considerable blood spatter present on the open jacket of the victim and on the ground near his right shoulder. On the wall to his left was an area of medium-velocity blood spatter and

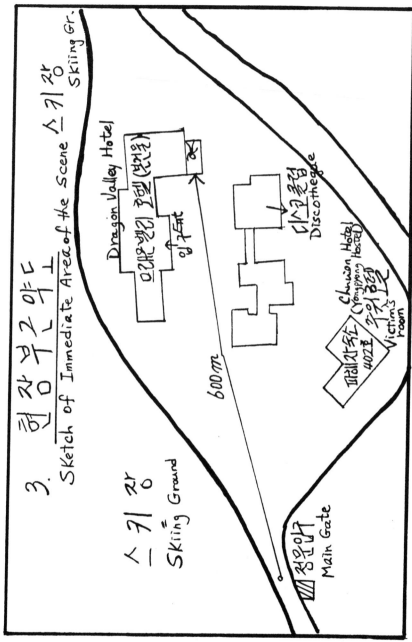

Figure 7-150 Korean police sketch of immediate area at scene.

274

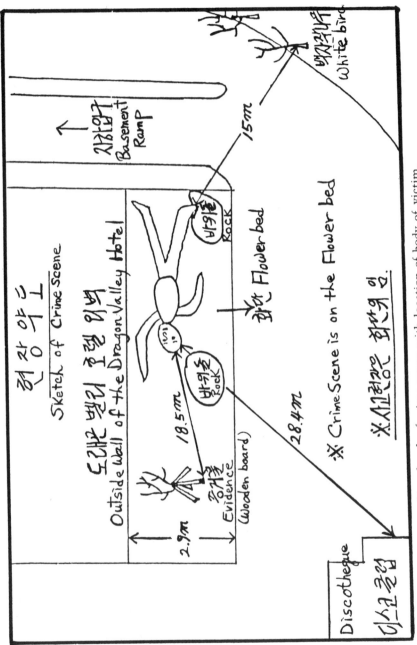

Figure 7-151 Korean police sketch of crime scene with location of body of victim.

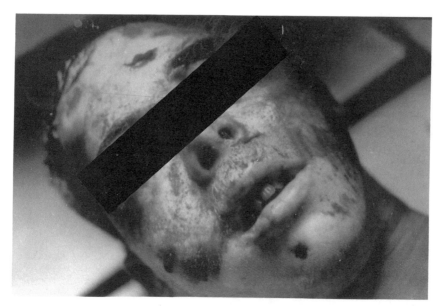

Figure 7-152 Face of victim showing lacerations and contusions.

Figure 7-153 Left side of face of victim showing abrasions on left cheek. Photograph was taken during second autopsy performed after embalming of body.

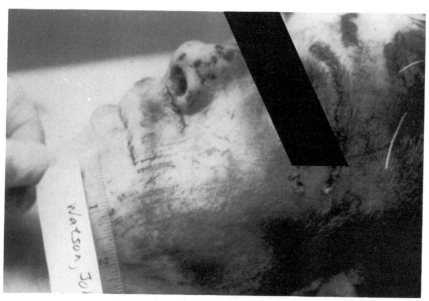

Figure 7-154 Location of victim at scene. Note gloves of victim are neatly placed between legs.

Figure 7-155 Blood drip patterns on curb where altercation began that have flowed onto the street.

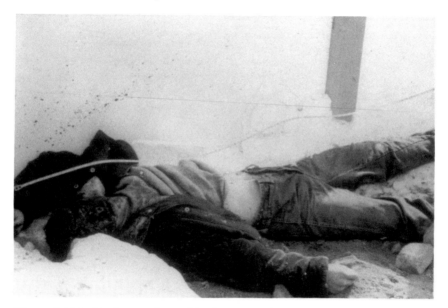

Figure 7-156 Medium-velocity bloodstains and cast-off pattern on wall to left of victim's head.

cast-off bloodstaining (Figure 7-156). Additionally, the large rock to the right of the victim's head contained considerable medium-velocity blood spatter (Figure 7-157). These areas of blood spatter were relatively close to the ground and were consistent with having been produced by repeated blows to the head of the victim while he was in a prone position in that location. These bloodstains could not have been produced by stepping on the face of the victim nor poking him in the face with a board as described by the defendant.

The weapon utilized to inflict blunt force injuries to the victim in this case was determined to be a wooden board approximately 70 inches long and 1¾ inches wide. The source of this board was determined to be a support beam for one of the young trees nearby (Figure 7-158). The board surface at one end contained areas of medium-velocity blood spatter. Additionally, a large splinter of wood found on the face of the victim matched a defect in the board.

Examination of the trousers of the defendant revealed that the front areas of both legs between the knee and the cuff contained numerous, circular medium-velocity blood spatters which were determined to be the same blood group and genetic marker profile as the victim (Figure 7-159). The location of these medium-velocity blood spatters was consistent with their having been received while either administering a beating to the prone victim or being in proximity to this event at the time it was taking place. This blood spatter could not have been pro-

Figure 7-157 Medium-velocity bloodstains on rock to right of victim on ground. Note areas of impact of blood on lower edge of rock.

Figure 7-158 Wooden board utilized as weapon found at scene.

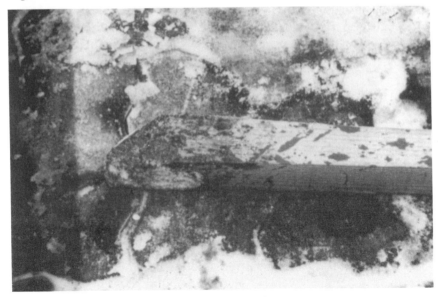

Figure 7-159 Location of medium-velocity blood spatters on lower left leg of defendant's trousers. Because of lack of contrast between the bloodstains and fabric, the blood spatters have been enhanced for photographic purposes. The section of trouser was removed by the crime laboratory for blood identification purposes.

duced by the act of stepping on the face of the victim or poking him in the face with the board as stated by the defendant. The defendant was convicted of homicide by court martial and sentenced to life in prison.

This case again illustrates the importance of the examination and correlation of bloodstains at the crime scene, on the weapon, and on victim's and defendant's clothing, with the autopsy findings. In this instance the evidence clearly refuted the version of events offered by the defendant.

Case 7

The body of a 75-year-old man was discovered by two young boys near a garage approximately one and a half blocks from his home in a quiet residential neighborhood of a northern city. The victim, who lived alone, was a self-employed junk dealer and had been reported missing

Figure 7-160   Pool of blood located on ground of victim's property.

six days previously by a concerned friend. Police investigators had searched the victim's residence on the day he was reported missing. In his backyard area they discovered a pool of blood on the ground with spots of blood leading away from his property in the general direction of where he was found (Figure 7-160). The body was in a frozen condition and partially covered with snow (Figure 7-161). There were no shoeprints visible in the snow except for those produced by the two boys who had initially discovered the body (Figure 7-162). The ground beneath the body was dry and devoid of snow (Figure 7-163). The victim was fully clothed with a buttoned overcoat. A bloodstained handkerchief was located beneath the head of the victim (Figure 7-164).

The time of death of the victim was estimated to have been approximately six days previously coincident with the time of his disappearance. Postmortem examination revealed multiple contused lacerations of the scalp with underlying contusions of the brain and cerebral edema (Figures 7-165 and 7-166). The wounds were described as follows: (1) a 1¼-inch laceration was present in the left frontal area extending upward from the left edge of the eyebrow; (2) a 1½-inch gaping laceration was present on the left frontal and parietal area along the coronal suture line; (3) a 2¼-inch closed laceration was present just to

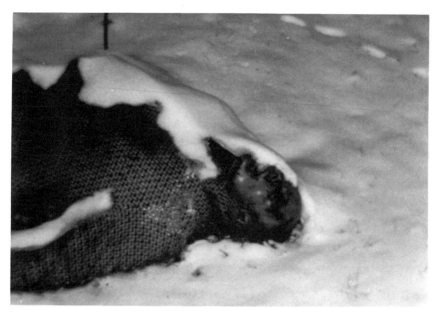

Figure 7-161   Victim at scene partially covered with snow approximately two blocks from his property.

Figure 7-162   Tracks in snow produced by two boys who discovered victim.

Figure 7-163 Body outline of victim indicating likely presence of victim prior to snowfall.

Figure 7-164 Location of bloodstained handkerchief beneath head of victim.

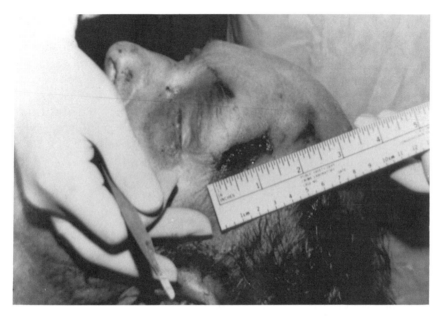

Figure 7-165 Laceration in left frontoparietal region of victim's head.

Figure 7-166 Lacerations on top of head of victim.

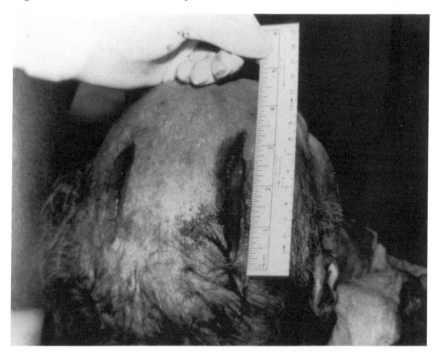

the left of midline in the parietal area; and (4) a 3¾-inch gaping laceration was noted to the right of midline from the right frontal area running into the right parietal area. The cause of death was established to be cerebral contusions and edema due to blunt force injury of the head. The pathologist concluded that there could have been a period of consciousness between the infliction of the wounds and the last loss of consciousness with the victim capable of walking during that time. It was then theorized that the victim received injury outside his residence and in an effort to seek assistance was physically able to walk the one and one half blocks before eventual fatal collapse. This would account for the bloodstained handkerchief beneath the head of the victim apparently used to stem the flow of blood from his head injuries.

Bloodstain patterns on the clothing of the victim were consistent with moderate-to-severe bleeding from the head as evidenced by the soaking of blood in the neck and collar areas of the overcoat, vest, shirt, and T shirt (Figure 7-167). Blood had dripped onto the chest area of the vest, shirt, and blue jeans at a time when the victim was in a sitting or standing position as shown by their downward directionalities (Figures 7-168, 7-169, and 7-170). The front of the vest and shirt also exhibited

Figure 7-167 Blood-soaked collar area of victim's exterior.

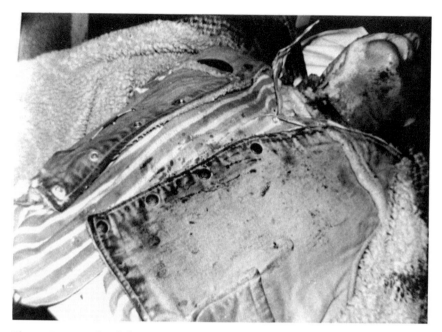

Figure 7-168 Blood drip pattern on front of vest of victim.

Figure 7-169 Blood drip pattern on front of victim's shirt.

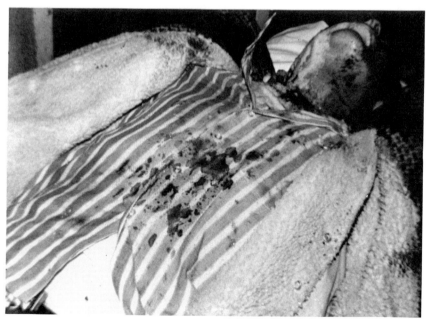

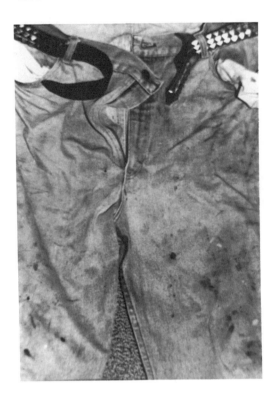

Figure 7-170 Bloodstains on front of victim's blue jeans.

some areas of medium-velocity blood spatter deposited as a result of receiving blunt force injury or other physical activity. The presence of medium-velocity blood spatter on the cuff area of the right sleeve of the shirt would place the right wrist close to the site of impact (Figure 7-171). With blunt force injury to the victim having occurred, the presence of this blood spatter may have been deposited during a defensive gesture by the victim. Further indication that the victim was alive and conscious for a period of time after sustaining injury is demonstrated by the presence of transfer bloodstains on objects including eye glasses in the pockets of his vest and shirt as well as the transfer bloodstain on the inside of the left front pocket of the blue jeans (Figures 7-172 and 7-173). These bloodstains would be produced by a hand, wet with blood from contact with an injured area, reaching into the pockets.

The absence of dripped blood patterns on the front of the victim's overcoat and the fact that this coat was buttoned up over the blood-stained front areas of the vest and shirt when the victim was found, indicate that the coat was not buttoned on the victim at the time he received injury to the head. The coat was buttoned after blood had been deposited on the vest and shirt from the bleeding source.

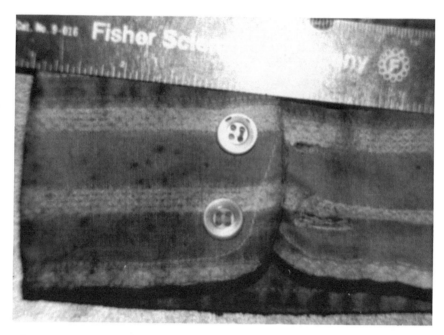

Figure 7-171 Medium-velocity blood spatter on cuff area of right sleeve of victim.

Figure 7-172 Blood transfer and smearing on eye glasses found in shirt pocket.

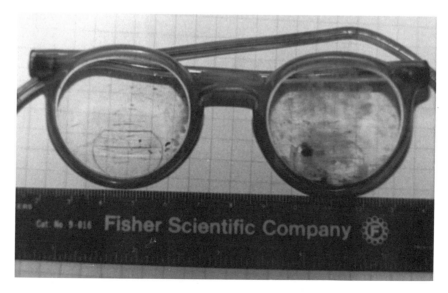

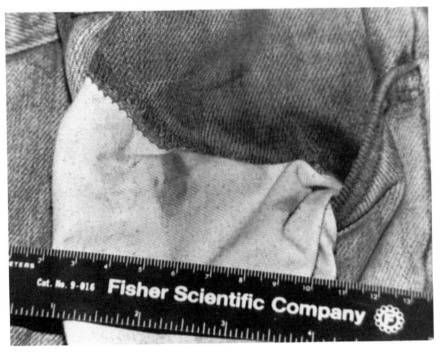

Figure 7-173 Blood transfer staining in left front pocket of victim's blue jeans.

An acquaintance of the deceased was developed as a suspect in this case and ultimately gave a statement that he struck the victim once with a large aluminum pipe after an argument outside the victim's residence. He denied striking the victim more than once. The suspect led investigators to a nearby location where the pipe was recovered from dense underbrush.

The aluminum pipe measured 5 feet in length and was 2 inches in width with a weight of approximately 8 pounds. The bloodstain patterns on the aluminum pipe represented multiple impacts to an exposed source of blood (Figure 7-174). There were distinct areas of blood transfer, smearing, and medium-velocity blood spatter present on the shaft of the pipe. A single blow to a victim administered with an object of this type would not be expected to produce medium-velocity blood spatter or significant blood transfer unless the source of blood was previously exposed. The first blow may produce injury that will bleed such as a laceration but successive blows and impact with exposed blood would be required to transfer and spatter blood onto the object and immediate area. The wide area of blood transfer stains was also consistent with multiple impacts to a blood source.

Figure 7-174 Bloodstained pipe utilized to inflict injuries to victim.

This case demonstrates survival time and mobility of a victim for a period of time after receiving lethal head injuries with the conclusion of the pathologist supported by the bloodstain evidence. Additionally, careful examination of a blunt force weapon may help establish that a particular weapon was used to administer more than a single blow to a victim.

Case 8

On a Halloween night a 20-year-old man had been drinking at a local tavern which was hosting a costume party for its patrons. At the conclusion of the festivities the man proceeded to walk his girlfriend to her home which was located a few blocks away. The girlfriend stated that he did not appear to be intoxicated and that after seeing her to her door walked back towards the tavern where his car was located in an adjacent parking lot. There was no argument and the boyfriend appeared to be in good spirits when he departed.

The boyfriend was found dead in the road approximately halfway between his girlfriend's house and the tavern parking lot apparently

Figure 7-175 Pedestrian victim of hit-and-run accident on pavement with eviscerated brain in foreground.

having been struck by a hit and run driver. The brain of the victim was completely eviscerated and lying near the body on the pavement located in the northbound lane of a two-lane road (Figure 7-175). It was determined at the scene of the accident that the initial impact occurred in the southbound lane from a vehicle traveling in the same direction. Plastic grill fragments and a hubcap were recovered at the scene. The victim was clad in a white lab coat and white slacks and apparently was wearing a felt hat which was also located near the body (Figure 7-176).

Postmortem examination at a local hospital revealed that the victim had sustained severe trauma to the head which had resulted in evisceration of the brain and massive bleeding. An extensive area of the left side of the skull was missing with the remaining areas extensively fractured including the zygomatic arch and mandible (Figure 7-177). There was a diagonal tract of abrasion extending from the left shoulder downward and to the right across the chest. No other external injuries were identified. Several ribs were fractured on the left and right side which contributed to bilateral hemothorax. The spleen was also noted to be ruptured. The blood alcohol content of the victim was determined to be 0.18 percent ethanol.

Figure 7-176 Another view of victim at scene of accident with hat in foreground.

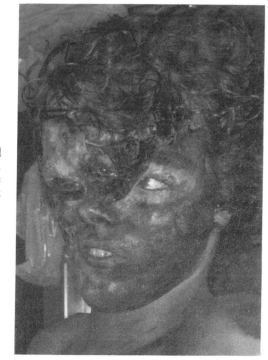

Figure 7-177 Massive head injury sustained by victim. The dark residue on the face of the victim is black makeup for Halloween.

Several months later a suspect vehicle was identified and a young man arrested and charged with vehicular homicide and leaving the scene of an accident. The defendant gave a statement indicating that he and a friend had consumed alcoholic beverages on the night of the accident but denied intoxication. The defendant was driving in the southbound lane of the road and observed what he perceived to be a pile of rags in the road ahead. He claimed to have taken some evasive action but heard a thump and realized that he had made contact with something in the road with the left front of his vehicle. He thought then that it may have been a body but panicked and drove home and did not report the incident. The basis for the arrest included matching of the plastic grill pieces to the grillwork in the front of the defendant's vehicle and the matching of red paint fragments and smears from the hat and left shoulder of the victim's jacket with red paint from the vehicle. Additionally, the hubcap found at the scene was determined to have originated from the defendant's vehicle.

The original autopsy report from the hospital pathologist did not address the critical issue concerning the position of the pedestrian-victim at the time of impact. Review of this case by a forensic pathologist consultant did not reveal indications of classical injuries that are frequently sustained by an erect, adult pedestrian when struck by an automobile. There being no apparent injuries or fractures of the lower extremities, the head was considered the primary impact site. Furthermore, the massive skull fractures and brain evisceration were not consistent with the victim's head merely striking the pavement. The forensic pathologist concluded that the head injury was produced by forceful impact of the front bumper of the vehicle thus bursting the skull with the brain projected from the cranial vault at that point. The remainder of the injuries sustained by the victim were attributed to rotation of the body and subsequent impact with the roadway prior to its final resting place in the northbound lane of traffic. It was concluded that the head of the victim would have to have been positioned above the pavement while the victim was prone, parallel to the center line and facing oncoming traffic in the southbound lane. This would be consistent with the victim attempting to raise himself just prior to impact with the bumper of the oncoming vehicle. The victim was not run over and the injuries were attributed to impact with a single vehicle. The bloodstain evidence on the roadway provided correlation with the conclusions of the pathologist. An initial impact site of the head of the victim on the road was identified just inside the southbound lane that resulted from forceful contact with an exposed source of blood (Figure 7-178). The resultant pattern is represented as a conically shaped splash pattern consisting of blood, brain, and skull fragments radiating towards the victim's final position. At the approximate mid-

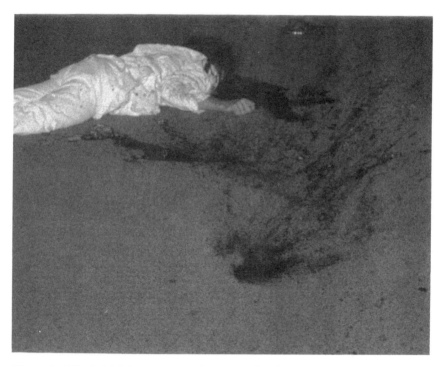

Figure 7-178   Initial impact site of victim's head on roadway.

point of this pattern is a secondary smeared pattern traveling tangentially towards right thigh of the victim where the brain rests which represents the skidding of the brain on the pavement after projection from the cranial vault (Figure 7-179). A large flow pattern and pool of blood has formed near the right shoulder of the victim in his final position as a result of the massive head injuries. Considerable blood spatter is present on the arms and shoulder areas of the victim's jacket with the trousers relatively free of bloodstains (Figure 7-180). The hat of the victim located near the body was torn in the front left area, and the inside surface contained considerable blood and brain tissue.

An experiment was developed to further explore the probable position of the victim at the time of impact. A styrofoam wig head was halved and then hollowed with a propane torch. After refitting with severed portions, the wig head was then covered with plaster of Paris approximately ⅓–½ inch thick (Figure 7-181). Through an entry hole in the top was added gelatin which would represent brain tissue. After setting of the gelatin was accomplished, approximately 50 ml of anti-coagulated human blood was added to the formed skull cavity and sealed. The head was then attached to a simulated body which was

Figure 7-179 Bloodstain representing skidding of brain to its final location near body.

Figure 7-180 Blood spatter on right sleeve of victim's white jacket.

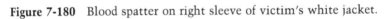

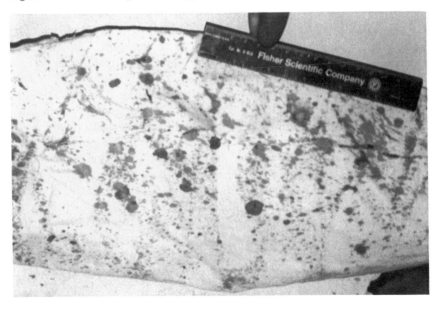

Figure 7-181 Styrofoam head encased in plaster of Paris.

composed of a canvas work suit filled with sand and newspaper to an approximate weigh of 135 pounds. The head was fastened to a wooden dowel through the hole in the base of the wig head. The dowel extended down into the body cavity to the extent that the head was held firmly in place.

The body was prepared for impact by placing it in the approximate position as concluded by the pathologist with the head elevated approximately 12 inches from the pavement (Figure 7-182). At this height the bumper of the vehicle being utilized in the experiment would be expected to impact the head. The vehicle was driven at approximately 30 MPH and impact of the head with the left bumper was accomplished. This was repeated several times on different areas of a roadway with fresh heads and with exchange of fresh white T shirts on the upper torso of the body.

The results of the experiments with the simulated head and torso were consistent with the conclusions of the pathologist and the blood-

Figure 7-182 Position of simulated victim prior to impact.

stain interpretation of the scene. A similar impact site with resultant splash pattern was observed consisting of blood, gelatin, and plaster of Paris fragments (Figure 7-183). In fact, the wound sustained by the plaster of Paris head was quite similar to that sustained by the victim (Figure 7-184). The body was propelled forward and similar blood spatters were produced on the arms and shoulders of the white T shirts (Figure 7-185). A difficulty encountered in this type of experiment was the inability to reproduce the rotation of a body with the use of a sand-filled canvas suit. Additionally, it was felt that a more flexible neck would be appropriate. Although a very basic concept and experiment, the results were considered to be useful and provided at least some experimental data to support the conclusions of the forensic pathologist and the bloodstain interpretation that the victim was in a near-prone position on the road when struck by the defendant's vehicle. The defense provided this information to the prosecutor's office with a result that the defendant was permitted to plead guilty to leaving the scene of an accident in fulfillment of all charges pending against him.

Figure 7-183 Bloodstain patterns on roadway produced by impact of vehicle bumper with simulated victim. Note final position of victim.

Figure 7-184 Damage to simulated head produced by impact with vehicle bumper.

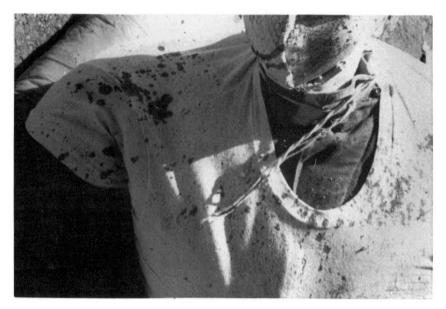

Figure 7-185 Blood spatter on right arm and front of shirt of simulated victim.

The reason the victim was prone on the roadway is not clear. His blood alcohol content of 0.18 percent may have been a contributing factor. A drug screen was never performed. Therefore the combination effect of drugs and alcohol could not be assessed. No inherent medical problem could be substantiated either through autopsy or past medical history. An intentional act on the part of the victim could not be proven.

APPENDIX A
PRECAUTIONS FOR INFECTIOUS DISEASES: AIDS AND HEPATITIS B
HENRY C. LEE, PhD

Introduction

The widespread apprehension and controversy over exposure to various infectious diseases, such as AIDS and hepatitis B, have resulted in the development of guidelines and precautions for law enforcement personnel. Today, with AIDS and hepatitis B infections virtually epidemic, police officers, crime scene investigators, and forensic laboratory examiners are more likely than ever before to encounter these infectious blood or other body fluids during routine activities.

Acquired immunodeficiency syndrome (AIDS) has a variety of manifestations that range from asymptomatic, and signs of AIDS-related complex (ARC), to severe immunodeficiency and life-threatening secondary infections. The virus that causes the disease is known by several names. In nontechnical literature, it is frequently referred to as the human immunodeficiency virus (HIV). In scientific literature, it is usually identified as HTLV-III/LAV, which stands for "human T-lymphotropic virus type III/lymphadenopathy-associated virus." The virus is a "retrovirus" which invades the victim's immunity system, destroys it, and causes the patient to become highly susceptible to secondary infections. The AIDS virus has been isolated from blood, bone marrow, saliva, lymph nodes, brain tissue, semen, plasma, vaginal fluids, cervical secretions, tears, and human milk. The mode of transmission generally involves direct contact of contaminated blood and body fluids with open cuts, wounds, lesions, or mucous membranes. There is currently no cure for AIDS.

Hepatitis B is an infectious disease of the liver. Hepatitis B is a type of serum hepatitis that will result in jaundice, cirrhosis, and sometimes cancer of the liver. The virus may be found in human blood, urine, semen, cerebrospinal fluid, saliva, and vaginal fluid. Injection into the bloodstream, droplet exposure of mucous membranes, and contact with broken skin are the primary hazards. There is a vaccine currently against hepatitis B.

The following guidelines are established based on the current scientific and medical knowledge. By practicing these precautions laboratory examiners and police officers may perform their duties as required by law, while minimizing the risk of accidental infection, whether administering cardiopulmonary resuscitation (CPR) at the scene of an accident, collecting evidence at crime scenes, examining physical evidence at the laboratory, or dealing with individuals who are high-risk carriers.

Precautionary Measures

The precautions specified below should be enforced routinely, regardless of whether the persons involved are known to be AIDS or hepatitis B infected.

1. All blood and body fluids are to be considered infectious whether wet or dry.
2. All needles, syringes, blades, razor blades, knives, and sharp instruments should be handled with caution and placed in puncture-resistant containers.
3. Good personal hygiene is the best protection against infectious diseases. Wash hands with soap and water after each assignment.
4. Know your skin integrity. Keep all wounds carefully bandaged while on duty. Use a bandage that provides a complete impermeable 360 degree coverage. Change the bandage if it becomes soiled or dirty.
5. Latex gloves should be worn when handling blood specimens, body fluids, materials, and objects exposed to contamination. Dispose of gloves after one use.
6. Gowns, masks, and eye protectors should be worn when clothing may be soiled by blood or body fluids or when procedures are being performed that may involve extensive exposure to blood or potentially infectious body fluids (such as the transport of the victim's body, laboratory examination specimens, postmortem examinations).
7. Avoid all hand-to-face contact including eating, smoking, and drinking where the possibility of transmission exists.
8. Hands and skin area must be washed immediately and thoroughly if they accidentally become contaminated with blood or body fluids.
9. Contaminated surfaces and objects should be cleaned up with a one (1) part household bleach to nine (9) parts water (1:10 dilution). An alcohol pad or soap and water can be used as a subsequent cleaning solution and to remove the odor of bleach.
10. Constantly be alert for sharp objects. When handling hypodermic needles, knives, razors, broken glass, nails, broken metal, or any

other sharp object bearing blood, use the utmost care to prevent a cut or puncture of the skin.

Specific Guidelines for the Laboratory Examiner

1. When handling and examining contaminated blood or body fluids, the examiner shall wear double latex gloves, lab coat, mask, and eye coverings.
2. Cover the lab bench with a protective sheet and remove instruments from the lab bench before examining any blood or body fluids.
3. Sharp instruments, such as needles, knives, scalpels, blades, broken glass, broken metal, auto lens, nails and other objects shall be handled by the examiner with deliberate care to prevent infection from accidental cuts or punctures.
4. After completing the examination:
   a. Any sharp objects should be packaged carefully and properly.
   b. Any liquid blood and body fluids should be diluted with equal amounts of sodium hypochlorite solution and disposed of properly.
   c. The lab bench should be cleaned with 1:10 sodium hypochlorite solution and rinsed with soap and water.
5. Hands must be washed after removing gloves, gowns and masks before leaving the examination area.
6. Any spills should be cleaned promptly with soap and water, or household detergent.

Specific Guidelines for the Crime Scene Investigator

1. Crime scene investigators should wear latex gloves and coverall gowns when conducting crime scene searches.
2. Surgical masks should be worn when aerosol or airborne particles may be encountered, for example, blood droplets, dried blood particles, and so forth.
3. Double latex gloves, surgical masks, and protective eyewear should be used when collecting or handling liquid blood, body fluids, dried blood particles, blood-contaminated evidence, or bodies of the deceased.
4. Latex gloves, eye-coverings, surgical masks, and a gown should be worn when attending an autopsy.
5. When processing the crime scene, constantly be alert for sharp objects and broken objects or surfaces.

6. Do not place your hands in areas where you are unable to see when conducting a search.
7. Under no circumstances should anyone at the crime scene be allowed to smoke, eat, or drink.
8. When liquid blood and body fluids are collected in bottles or glass vials, these containers must be labeled prominently "Blood Precautions."
9. Blood and body fluid-stained clothing and objects must be dried and packaged in double bags and labeled properly. If evidence collected from a possibly infected person, the package should be labeled "Caution Potential AIDS (Hepatitis) Case."
10. If practical, use only disposable items at a crime scene where infectious blood is present. All nondisposable items must be decontaminated after each use.
11. Any reports, labels, or evidence tag splashed with blood should be destroyed with the information copied on clean forms.
12. After completing the search of a scene, investigators should clean their hands with diluted household bleach solution and with soap and water solution. Any contaminated clothing and footwear should be disposed of properly.

Specific Guidelines for the Police Officer

1. Whenever the slightest possibility of exposure exists, the officer should wear latex gloves, protective gown, and face mask.
2. In addition to latex gloves, disposable footwear protection should be worn at motor vehicle accidents where the possibility of contamination exists.
3. Special masks are to be used when administering cardiopulmonary resuscitation (CPR). It is the officer's responsibility to see that the mask is disinfected after each use.
4. Precautionary measures should always be applied to avoid being bitten or assaulted during arrests or questioning witnesses or suspects.
5. When searching areas that are not clearly visible, a flashlight or baton should be used to illuminate the area. Do not place your hands between car seats or under car seats.
6. When searching a suspect, a cautionary pat search should be conducted. If possible, the suspect should be directed to empty his pockets and socks.
7. Physical evidence containing blood or body fluids should be marked and handled using the same guidelines as previously described.
8. Any contamination of exposed skin should be immediately

washed with 1:10 bleach solution and rinsed well with soap and water.

9. Any contaminated clothing and gloves should be discarded properly. Other nondisposable material should be decontaminated with bleach solution and washed thoroughly.

10. If an accidental exposure occurs, the incident is to be reported immediately to the supervisor or proper authority, and physician.

APPENDIX B
SUPREME COURT DECISIONS RELATING TO
BLOODSTAIN INTERPRETATION

1. STATE OF CALIFORNIA VS. THOMAS CARTER, 48C, 2nd 737, 312 P. 2nd 665, June 1957.
2. REGINA VS. SPARROW, 51 CCC, 2nd 449, Ontario Court of Appeal, December 1979.
3. STATE OF ILLINOIS VS. ERICKSON, No. 79-186, App., 411 N.E. 2nd 44, September 1980.
4. STATE OF IOWA VS. HALL, Iowa N.W., 2nd 80, No. 62176, September 1980.
5. STATE OF TENNESSEE VS. MELSON, Tenn. 638 S.W., 2nd 342, August 1982.
6. STATE OF MAINE VS. HILTON, Me., 431 A, 2nd 1296, January 1981.

APPENDIX C
COMPUTER PROGRAM FOR BLOODSTAIN
PATTERN INTERPRETATION

```
1       PAGE
5       INIT
6       GO TO 6000
10      PRINT 'BLOODSTAIN PATTERN ANALYSIS'
20      PRINT
30      PRINT
40      PRINT 'CHOOSE A ONE-LETTER COMMAND FOR THE ACTION
        YOU WISH TO TAKE.'
50      PRINT 'FOR INFORMATION ON HOW TO USE THIS PROGRAM,
        ENTER H (RETURN).'
60      PRINT
70      PRINT
80      PRINT 'COMMAND   ACTION'
90      PRINT
100     PRINT 'H   HELP'
110     PRINT 'E   ENTER BLOODSTAIN WIDTH, LENGTH, AND
                  DISTANCE'
120     PRINT 'FROM POINT OF CONVERGENCE.'
130     PRINT 'D   DISPLAY ALL BLOODSTAINS ON A GIVEN WALL OR'
140     PRINT 'FLOOR WITH LINES EXTRAPOLATED BACK TO THEIR'
150     PRINT 'POINT OF ORIGIN.'
160     PRINT 'S   DISPLAY A THREE-DIMENSIONAL SCATTER DIAGRAM
                  OF ALL'
165     PRINT 'CALCULATED POINTS OF ORIGIN.'
170     PRINT 'Q   QUIT PROGRAM.'
175     PRINT
180     PRINT
185     PRINT 'ENTER COMMAND HERE:'
190     INPUT A$
195     IF A$='H' THEN 1000
200     IF A$='E' THEN 2000
205     IF A$='D' THEN 3000
```

```
210    IF A$='S' THEN 4000
215    IF A$='Q' THEN 5000
220    PAGE
230    GO TO 10
1000   PAGE
1020   PRINT 'THIS PROGRAM WILL CALCULATE AND DISPLAY THE
       POINT OF ORIGIN'
1030   PRINT 'OF A GROUP OF BLOODSTAINS.'
1040   PRINT
1050   PRINT 'YOU WILL NEED TO PROVIDE THE PROGRAM WITH...'
1060   PRINT '1) THE WIDTH AND LENGTH OF THE BLOODSTAIN, IN
           MM'
1070   PRINT '2) THE DISTANCE FROM THE STAIN TO THE POINT OF'
1080   PRINT 'CONVERGENCE IN MM'
1090   PRINT
1100   PRINT 'THE DISTANCE FROM THE STAIN TO THE POINT OF
       CONVERGENCE IS'
1110   PRINT 'DETERMINED AS FOLLOWS. ASSUME THERE ARE
       SEVERAL BLOODSTAINS'
1120   PRINT 'ON THE FLOOR OR A WALL. THESE BLOODSTAINS WILL
       BE OVAL,'
1130   PRINT 'UNLESS THEY STRUCK THE WALL OR FLOOR
       PERPENDICULARLY. DRAW'
1140   PRINT 'A LINE THROUGH EACH BLOODSTAIN, BISECTING IT
       LENGTHWISE.'
1150   PRINT 'THESE LINES SHOULD INTERSECT EACH OTHER
       APPROXIMATELY AT THE'
1160   PRINT ' "POINT OF CONVERGENCE." MEASURE THE DISTANCE
       FROM EACH STAIN'
1170   PRINT 'TO THE "POINT OF CONVERGENCE." '
1180   PRINT
1190   PRINT 'THE DISPLAY COMMAND (D) DISPLAYS ALL THE STAINS
       FROM ONE'
1200   PRINT 'SURFACE, ALONG WITH AN AVERAGED DISTANCE FROM
       THE POINT OF'
1210   PRINT 'ORIGIN TO THE SURFACE, MEASURED ALONG THE AXIS
       CONNECTING'
1211   PRINT 'THE POINT OF CONVERGENCE WITH THE POINT OF
       ORIGIN.'
1220   PRINT
1230   PRINT 'THE SCATTERGRAM COMMAND (S) PROVIDES A
       COMPARISON OF THE'
```

```
1240      PRINT 'POINT OF ORIGIN AMONG DIFFERENT SURFACES
          WHICH YOU HAVE'
1250      PRINT 'ENTERED INTO THE PROGRAM. IN ORDER TO USE THIS
          COMMAND,'
1260      PRINT 'YOU WILL NEED TO PROVIDE THE PROGRAM WITH THE
          DIMENSIONS'
1270      PRINT 'OF THE ROOM IN QUESTION.'
1280      PRINT
1290      PRINT 'THIS PROGRAM CAN BE USED WITH SURFACES WHICH
          ARE NOT'
1300      PRINT 'HORIZONTAL OR VERTICAL. HOWEVER, THESE SLANTED
          SURFACES'
1310      PRINT 'CANNOT BE DISPLAYED WITH THE (S) COMMAND.'
1320      PRINT
1360      PRINT 'HIT (RETURN) TO GO BACK TO THE MAIN SCREEN.'
1370      INPUT A$
1375      PAGE
1380      GO TO 10
2000      PAGE
2001      PRINT 'DO YOU ALREADY HAVE DATA STORED ON DISK WHICH
          YOU WANT TO'
2002      PRINT 'RETRIEVE AND ADD TO? (Y/N)'
2003      INPUT A$
2004      IF A$='Y' THEN 7000
2005      PRINT
2010      PRINT 'FOR THE PURPOSES OF THIS PROGRAM, YOU CAN
          ENTER BLOODSTAINS'
2015      PRINT 'ON ANY OF 6 VERTICAL SURFACES ("WALLS") AND 6
          HORIZONTAL'
2020      PRINT 'SURFACES ("FLOORS" OR "CEILINGS"). THE PROGRAM
          WILL'
2025      PRINT 'CALCULATE THE POINT OF ORIGIN FROM ANY OF
          THESE SURFACES'
2030      PRINT 'INDIVIDUALLY.'
2031      PRINT
2032      PRINT 'BLOODSTAIN WIDTH IS THE WIDTH OF THE
          BLOODSTAIN AT ITS'
2033      PRINT 'WIDEST POINT. LENGTH IS THE LENGTH OF THE
          BLOODSTAIN ALONG THE'
2034      PRINT 'AXIS CONNECTING IT TO THE POINT OF CONVERGENCE
          DISTANCE'
2035      PRINT 'IS THE DISTANCE FROM THE STAIN TO THE POINT OF
          CONVERGENCE.'
```

```
2036      PRINT
2040      PRINT 'YOU CAN ENTER UP TO 20 BLOODSTAINS ON EACH OF
          THE 12'
2045      PRINT 'AVAILABLE SURFACES.'
2050      PRINT
2055      PRINT 'TO CHOOSE A SURFACE, ENTER W1, W2, W3, W4, W5,
          OR W6 FOR A'
2060      PRINT 'VERTICAL WALL, OR F1, F2, F3, F4, F5, OR F6 FOR A
          HORIZONTAL'
2065      PRINT 'FLOOR.'
2070      PRINT
2200      PRINT 'CHOOSE A SURFACE;'
2210      INPUT S
2211      IF S$<>'W1' THEN 2214
2212      I=W1(1,21)
2213      GO TO 2265
2214      IF S$<>'W2' THEN 2217
2215      I=W1(2,21)
2216      GO TO 2265
2217      IF S$<>'W3' THEN 2220
2218      I=W1(3,21)
2219      GO TO 2265
2220      IF S$<>'W4' THEN 2223
2221      I=W1(4,21)
2222      GO TO 2265
2223      IF S$<>'W5' THEN 2226
2224      I=W1(5,21)
2225      GO TO 2265
2226      IF S$<>'W6' THEN 2229
2227      I=W1(6,21)
2228      GO TO 2265
2229      IF S$<>'F1' THEN 2232
2230      I=W1(7,21)
2231      GO TO 2265
2232      IF S$<>'F2' THEN 2235
2233      I=W1(8,21)
2234      GO TO 2265
2235      IF S$<>'F3' THEN 2238
2236      I=W1(9,21)
2237      GO TO 2265
2238      IF S$<>'F4' THEN 2241
```

```
2239        I=W1(10,21)
2240        GO TO 2265
2241        IF S$()'F5' THEN 2244
2242        I=W1(11,21)
2243        GO TO 2265
2244        IF S$()'F6' THEN 2247
2245        I=W1(12,21)
2246        GO TO 2265
2247        PRINT 'ERROR IN CHOOSING SURFACE. CHOOSE AGAIN.'
2248        GO TO 2210
2265        PAGE
2267        PRINT 'WHEN DONE ENTERING BLOODSTAINS TO SURFACE
            ';S$;', ENTER 0'
2268        PRINT 'UNDER BLOODSTAIN WIDTH. YOU CAN RETURN TO
            ';S$;' TO ENTER'
2269        PRINT 'MORE STAINS ANY TIME.'
2270        PRINT
2271        I=I+1
2272        IF I(21 THEN 2280
2273        PRINT 'I CANNOT STORE ANY MORE BLOODSTAINS TO THIS
            SURFACE. SORRY!'
2274        GO TO 2200
2280        PRINT 'BLOODSTAIN WIDTH, MM'
2285        INPUT W
2290        IF W=0 THEN 2292
2291        GO TO 2295
2292        PAGE
2293        GO TO 10
2295        PRINT 'BLOODSTAIN LENGTH, MM'
2300        INPUT L
2301        IF W,=L THEN 2305
2302        PRINT 'WIDTH CANNOT BE GREATER THAN LENGTH.''
2303        GO TO 2280
2305        PRINT 'DISTANCE TO AXIS OF ORIGIN, MM'
2310        INPUT D
2315        P=ASN(W/L)*180/PI
2320        T=TAN(P*PI/180)
2325        H=D*T
2330        PRINT 'WIDTH, MM   LENGTH, MM   DISTANCE, MM'
2335        PRINT W,L,D
2340        PRINT 'ANGLE  TANGENT  HEIGHT, MM'
```

```
2345    PRINT P,T,H
2346    PRINT
2347    PRINT 'HIT (RETURN) TO CONTINUE.'
2348    INPUT A$
2350    PRINT
2430    IF S$()'W1' THEN 2436
2431    W1(1,I)=H
2432    X1(1,I)=P
2433    Y1(1,I)=D
2434    W1(1,21)=I
2435    GO TO 2265
2436    IF S$()'W2' THEN 2442
2437    W1(2,I)=H
2438    X1(2,I)=P
2439    Y1(2,I)=D
2440    W1(2,21)=I
2441    GO TO 2265
2442    IF S$()'W3' THEN 2448
2443    W1(3,I)=H
2444    X1(3,I)=P
2445    Y1(3,I)=D
2446    W1(3,21)=I
2447    GO TO 2265
2448    IF S$()'W4' THEN 2454
2449    W1(4,I)=H
2450    X1(4,I)=P
2451    Y1(4,I)=D
2452    W1(4,21)=I
2453    GO TO 2265
2454    IF S$()'W5' THEN 2460
2455    W1(5,I)=H
2456    X1(5,I)=P
2457    Y1(5,I)=D
2458    W1(5,21)=I
2459    GO TO 2265
2460    IF S$()'W6' THEN 2466
2461    W1(6,I)=H
2462    X1(6,I)=P
2463    Y1(6,I)=D
2464    W1(6,21)=I
2465    GO TO 2265
```

```
2466    IF S$()'F1' THEN 2472
2467    W1(7,I)=H
2468    X1(7,I)=P
2469    Y1(7,I)=D
2470    W1(7,21)=I
2471    GO TO 2265
2472    IF S$()'F2' THEN 2478
2473    W1(8,I)=H
2474    X1(8,I)=P
2475    Y1(8,I)=D
2476    W1(8,21)=I
2477    GO TO 2265
2478    IF S$()'F3' THEN 2484
2479    W1(9,I)=H
2480    X1(9,I)=P
2481    Y1(9,I)=D
2482    W1(9,21)=I
2483    GO TO 2265
2484    If S$()'F4' THEN 2490
2485    W1(10,I)=H
2486    X1(10,I)=P
2487    Y1(10,I)=D
2488    W1(10,21)=I
2489    GO TO 2265
2490    IF S$()'F5' THEN 2496
2491    W1(11,I)=H
2492    X1(11,I)=P
2493    Y1(11,I)=D
2494    W1(11,21)=I
2495    GO TO 2265
2496    IF S$()'F6' THEN 2247
2497    W1(12,I)=H
2498    X1(12,I)=P
2499    Y1(12,I)=D
2500    W1(12,21)=I
2501    GO TO 2265
3000    PAGE
3005    PRINT 'WHICH WALL OR FLOOR WOULD YOU LIKE DISPLAYED?
        YOU CAN'
3010    PRINT 'CHOOSE FROM.'
3015    PRINT
```

```
3020      PRINT 'W1,  W2,  W3,  W4,  W5,  W6'
3025      PRINT 'OR'
3030      PRINT 'F1,  F2,  F3,  F4,  F5,  F6'
3035      PRINT
3040      PRINT 'TYPE IN YOUR CHOICE HERE:'
3041      INPUT A$
3042      PRINT 'YOU CAN CHOOSE THE SCALING FOR YOUR GRAPH. A
          SMALLER NUMBER'
3043      PRINT 'WILL MAGNIFY THE RESULTS ON THE GRAPH. A
          LARGER NUMBER WILL'
3044      PRINT 'SHRINK THE RESULTS INTO THE LOWER LEFT CORNER.
          A GOOD FIRST'
3045      PRINT 'GUESS ON THE SCALING FACTOR IS 20...'
3046      PRINT
3047      PRINT 'WHAT SCALING FACTOR WOULD YOU LIKE?'
3048      INPUT Z
3050      PAGE
3051      MOVE 0,0
3055      WINDOW 0,4000,0,4000
3060      VIEWPORT 10,100,20,80
3062      SCALE Z,Z
3065      AXIS 100,100
3066      IF A$()'F1' THEN 3120
3070      FOR I=1 TO W1 (7,21)
3075      MOVE Y1(7,I),0
3080      DRAW 0,W1(7,I)
3085      NEXT I
3090      C$='F1'
3095      Q=0
3097      FOR I=1 TO W1(7,21)
3100      Q=Q+W1(7,I)
3105      NEXT I
3110      Q=Q/10/W1(7,21)
3115      GO TO 3500
3120      IF A$()'F2' THEN 3144
3122      FOR I=1 TO W1(8,21)
3124      MOVE Y1(8,I),0
3126      DRAW 0,W1(8,I)
3128      NEXT I
3130      C$='F2'
3132      Q=0
```

```
3134      FOR I = 1 TO W1(8,21)
3136      Q=Q+W1(8,I)
3138      NEXT I
3140      Q=Q/10/W1(8,21)
3142      GO TO 3500
3144      IF A$()'F3' THEN 3168
3146      FOR I=1 TO W1(9,21)
3148      MOVE Y1(9,I),0
3150      DRAW 0,W1(9,I)
3152      NEXT I
3154      C$='F3'
3156      Q=0
3158      FOR I=1 TO W1(9,21)
3160      Q=Q+W1(9,I)
3162      NEXT I
3164      Q=Q/10/W1(9,21)
3166      GO TO 3500
3168      IF A$()'F4' THEN 3192
3170      FOR I=1 TO W1(10,21)
3172      MOVE Y1(10,I),0
3174      DRAW 0,W1(10,I)
3176      NEXT I
3178      C$='F4'
3180      Q=0
3182      FOR I=1 TO W1(10,21)
3184      Q=Q+W1(10,I)
3186      NEXT I
3188      Q=Q/10/W1(10,21)
3190      GO TO 3500
3192      IF A$()'F5' THEN 3216
3194      FOR I=1 TO W1(11,21)
3196      MOVE Y1(11,I),0
3198      DRAW 0,W1(11,I)
3200      NEXT I
3202      C$='F5'
3204      Q=0
3206      FOR I=1 TO W1(11,21)
3208      Q=Q+W1(11,I)
3210      NEXT I
3212      Q=Q/10/W1(11,21)
3214      GO TO 3500
```

```
3216    IF A$()'F6' THEN 3700
3218    FOR I=1 TO W1(12,21)
3220    MOVE Y1(12,I),0
3222    DRAW 0,W1(12,I)
3224    NEXT I
3226    C$='F6'
3228    Q=0
3230    FOR I=1 TO W1(12,21)
3232    Q=Q+W1(12,I)
3234    NEXT I
3236    Q=Q/10/W1(12,21)
3500    VIEWPORT 0,130,0,100
3505    WINDOW 0,130,0,100
3510    MOVE 40,15
3515    PRINT 'DISTANCE FROM AXIS, 100 MM'
3520    MOVE 125,80
3525    PRINT 'H'
3530    MOVE 125,77
3535    PRINT 'E'
3540    MOVE 125,74
3545    PRINT 'I'
3550    MOVE 125,71
3555    PRINT 'G'
3560    MOVE 125,68
3565    PRINT 'H'
3570    MOVE 125,65
3575    PRINT 'T'
3580    MOVE 125,59
3585    PRINT '1'
3590    MOVE 125,56
3595    PRINT '0'
3610    MOVE 125,50
3615    PRINT 'C'
3620    MOVE 125,47
3635    PRINT 'M'
3630    MOVE 40,90
3635    PRINT 'DISPLAY OF FLOOR ';C$
3645    MOVE 40,87
3650    PRINT 'AVERAGE HEIGHT: ';Q;' CM'
3653    MOVE 40,84
3655    PRINT 'HIT (RETURN) TO CONTINUE.'
```

```
3660      INPUT A$
3665      PAGE
3670      GO TO 10
3700      IF A$()'W1' THEN 3712
3701      FOR I=1 TO W1(1,21)
3702      MOVE 0,Y1(1,I)
3703      DRAW W1(1,I),0
3704      NEXT I
3705      C$='W1'
3706      Q=0
3707      FOR I=1 TO W1(1,21)
3708      Q=Q+W1(1,I)
3709      NEXT I
3710      Q=Q/10/W1(1,21)
3711      GO TO 3850
3712      IF A$()'W2' THEN 3724
3713      FOR I=1 TO W1(2,21)
3714      MOVE 0,Y1(2,I)
3715      DRAW W1(2,I),0
3716      NEXT I
3717      C$='W2'
3718      Q=0
3719      FOR I=1 TO W1(2,21)
3720      Q=Q+W1(2,I)
3721      NEXT I
3722      Q=Q/10/W1(2,21)
3723      GO TO 3850
3724      IF A$()'W3' THEN 3736
3725      FOR I=1 TO W1(3,21)
3726      MOVE 0,Y1(3,I)
3727      DRAW W1(3,I),0
3728      NEXT I
3729      C$='W3'
3730      Q=0
3731      FOR I=1 TO W1(3,21)
3732      Q=Q+W1(3,I)
3733      NEXT I
3734      Q=Q/10/W1(3,21)
3735      GO TO 3850
3736      IF A$()'W4' THEN 3748
3737      FOR I=1 TO W1(4,21)
```

```
3738        MOVE 0,Y1(4,I)
3739        DRAW W1(4,I),0
3740        NEXT I
3741        C$='W4'
3742        Q=0
3743        FOR I=1 TO W1(4,21)
3744        Q=Q+W1(4,I)
3745        NEXT I
3746        Q=Q/10/W1(4,21)
3747        GO TO 3850
3748        IF A$()'W5' THEN 3760
3749        FOR I=1 TO W1(5,21)
3750        MOVE 0,Y1(5,I)
3751        DRAW W1(5,I),0
3752        NEXT I
3753        C$='W5'
3754        Q=0
3755        FOR I=1 TO W1(5,21)
3756        Q=Q+W1(5,I)
3757        NEXT I
3758        Q=Q/10/W1(5,21)
3759        GO TO 3850
3760        IF A$()'W6' THEN 3950
3761        FOR I=1 TO W1(6,21)
3762        MOVE 0,Y1(6,I)
3763        DRAW W1(6,I),0
3764        NEXT I
3765        C$='W6'
3766        Q=0
3767        FOR I=1 TO W1(6,21)
3768        Q=Q+W1(6,I)
3769        NEXT I
3770        Q=Q/10/W1(6,21)
3850        VIEWPORT 0,130,0,100
3851        WINDOW 0,130,0,100
3852        MOVE 40,15
3853        PRINT 'HEIGHT, 10 CM'
3854        MOVE 125,80
3855        PRINT 'D'
3856        MOVE 125,77
```

0	V(2,4)=D3
1	V(2,5)=D4
2	IF A$⟨⟩'W3' THEN 4268
63	V(3,1)=1
64	V(3,2)=D1
65	V(3,3)=D2
66	V(3,4)=D3
67	V(3,5)=D4
68	IF A$⟨⟩'W4' THEN 4274
69	V(4,1)=1
70	V(4,2)=D1
71	V(4,3)=D2
72	V(4,4)=D3
73	V(4,5)=D4
74	IF A$⟨⟩'W5' THEN 4280
75	V(5,1)=1
76	V(5,2)=D1
77	V(5,3)=D2
78	V(5,4)=D3
79	V(5,5)=D4
80	IF A$⟨⟩'W6' THEN 4286
81	V(6,1)=1
82	V(6,2)=D1
83	V(6,3)=D2
84	V(6,4)=D3
85	V(6,5)=D4
86	IF A$⟨⟩'F1' THEN 4292
87	V(7,1)=1
88	V(7,2)=D1
89	V(7,3)=D2
290	V(7,4)=D3
291	V(7,5)=D4
292	IF A$⟨⟩'F2' THEN 4298
293	V(8,1)=1
294	V(8,2)=D1
295	V(8,3)=D2
296	V(8,4)=D3
297	V(8,5)=D4
298	IF A$⟨⟩'F3' THEN 4304
299	V(9,1)=1
300	V(9,2)=D1

3857	PRINT 'I'
3858	MOVE 125,74
3859	PRINT 'S'
3860	MOVE 125,71
3861	PRINT 'T'
3862	MOVE 125,68
3863	PRINT '.'
3864	MOVE 125,62
3865	PRINT 'F'
3866	MOVE 125,59
3867	PRINT 'M'
3868	MOVE 125,53
3869	PRINT 'A'
3870	MOVE 125,50
3871	PRINT 'X'
3872	MOVE 125,47
3873	PRINT 'I'
3874	MOVE 125,44
3875	PRINT 'S'
3876	MOVE 125,38
3877	PRINT '1'
3878	MOVE 125,35
3879	PRINT '0'
3880	MOVE 125,32
3881	PRINT '0'
3882	MOVE 125,26
3883	PRINT 'M'
3884	MOVE 125,23
3885	PRINT 'M'
3886	MOVE 40,90
3887	PRINT 'DISPLAY OF WALL ';C$
3888	GO TO 3645
3950	MOVE 300,300
3951	PRINT 'ERROR IN CHOOSING SURFACE. HIT ⟨RETURN⟩ TO CONTINUE.'
3952	INPUT A$
3953	GO TO 3000
4000	PAGE
4001	PRINT 'TO PRODUCE THE FOLLOWING DIAGRAM, YOU WILL NEED TO INPUT THE'

```
4005    PRINT 'LOCATION OF EACH POINT OF CONVERGENCE YOU
        WISH DISPLAYED.'
4010    PRINT 'TO MEASURE THESE LOCATIONS, BEGIN AT 0,0,0 IN THE
        SW CORNER'
4015    PRINT 'OF THE ROOM. MEASURE THE DISTANCE IN CM FROM
        THIS CORNER'
4020    PRINT 'NORTH TO THE POINT OF CONVERGENCE, EAST FROM
        THE CORNER TO'
4025    PRINT 'THIS SAME POINT, AND VERTICALLY FROM THE
        CORNER TO THE'
4030    PRINT 'POINT OF CONVERGENCE. YOU WILL NEED TO INPUT
        THESE THREE'
4035    PRINT 'MEASUREMENTS FOR EACH SURFACE YOU WANT
        DISPLAYED. ALSO, THE'
4040    PRINT 'PROGRAM WILL NEED TO KNOW IN WHICH DIRECTION
        THE AXIS EXTENDS'
4045    PRINT 'OUT FROM THE WALL OR FLOOR FROM THE POINT OF
        CONVERGENCE'
4046    PRINT 'TOWARD THE POINT OF ORIGIN, THAT IS: NORTH,
        SOUTH, EAST,'
4049    PRINT 'WEST, UP OR DOWN.'
4050    PRINT
4051    PRINT 'YOU CAN CHOOSE A SCALE FACTOR FOR THIS DISPLAY
        AS WELL.'
4052    PRINT 'A SCALE FACTOR OF 16 MAY WORK WELL HERE...'
4053    PRINT 'WHAT SCALE FACTOR WOULD YOU LIKE?'
4054    INPUT Z
4055    MOVE 0,0
4056    WINDOW 0,4000,0,4000
4057    VIEWPORT 10,100,20,80
4058    SCALE Z,Z
4088    PAGE
4089    DIM V(12,5)
4090    FOR I=1 TO 12
4091    FOR J=1 TO 5
4092    V(I,J)=0
4093    NEXT J
4094    NEXT I
4095    PRINT 'CHOOSE A WALL OR FLOOR YOU WOULD LIKE
        DISPLAYED. YOU CAN'
4096    PRINT 'CHOOSE FROM'
4097    PRINT
4098    PRINT 'W1,W2,W3,W4,W5,W6'
4099    PRINT 'OR'
4100    PRINT 'F1,F2,F3,F4,F5,F6'
4101    PRINT 'OR'
4102    PRINT 'X TO TERMINATE THE DISPLAY.'
4135    PRINT
4140    PRINT 'TYPE IN ONE CHOICE HERE:'
4145    INPUT A$
4146    MOVE 0,0
4147    WINDOW 0,4000,0,4000
4148    VIEWPORT 10,100,20,80
4149    SCALE Z,Z
4150    PAGE
4155    IF A$()'X' THEN 4225
4165    GO TO 10
4225    PRINT 'HOW FAR NORTH, IN CM, IS THE POINT OF
        CONVERGENCE'
4226    PRINT 'OF ';A$;' FROM THE SW CORNER OF THE RO
4227    INPUT D2
4228    PRINT 'HOW FAR EAST, IN CM, IS THE POINT OF
        CONVERGENCE'
4229    PRINT 'OF ' ;A$;' FROM THE SW CORNER OF THE R
4230    INPUT D1
4231    PRINT 'HOW FAR ABOVE THE FLOOR AT THE SW CC
        THE ROOM IS THE'
4232    PRINT 'POINT OF CONVERGENCE OF ';A$;'?'
4233    INPUT D3
4234    PRINT 'ENTER A ONE-LETTER CODE FOR THE DIREC
        POINT OF'
4235    PRINT 'CONVERGENCE EXTENDS OUT FROM ';A$;',
        2=SOUTH  3=EAST'
4236    PRINT' 4=WEST  5=UP  6=DOWN'
4237    INPUT D4
4250    IF A$()'W1' THEN 4256
4251    V(1,1)=1
4252    V(1,2)=D1
4253    V(1,3)=D2
4254    V(1,4)=D3
4255    V(1,5)=D4
4256    IF A$()'W2' THEN 4262
4257    V(2,1)=1
4258    V(2,2)=D1
4259    V(2,3)=D2
```

```
4301    V(9,3)=D2
4302    V(9,4)=D3
4303    V(9,5)=D4
4304    IF A$()'F4' THEN 4310
4305    V(10,1)=1
4306    V(10,2)=D1
4307    V(10,3)=D2
4308    V(10,4)=D3
4309    V(10,5)=D4
4310    IF A$()'F5' THEN 4316
4311    V(11,1)=1
4312    V(11,2)=D1
4313    V(11,3)=D2
4314    V(11,4)=D3
4315    V(11,5)=D4
4316    GO TO 4375
4317    V(12,1)=1
4318    V(12,2)=D1
4319    V(12,3)=D2
4320    V(12,4)=D3
4321    V(12,5)=D4
4375    PAGE
4376    MOVE 0,0
4377    AXIS 100,100
4378    SET DEGREES
4379    ROTATE 45
4380    RDRAW 4000,0
4381    MOVE 0,0
4382    I=100
4383    RMOVE 100,0
4384    RDRAW 0,10
4385    RMOVE 0, -10
4386    I=I+100
4387    IF A<4100 THEN 4383
4410    FOR I=1 TO 12
4411    IF V(I,1)=0 THEN 4455
4412    Q=0
4413    FOR K=1 TO W1(I,21)
4414    Q=Q+W1(I,K)
4415    NEXT K
4416    Q=Q/10/W1(I,21)
```

```
4417      MOVE V(I,2)V(I,4)
4418      SET DEGREES
4419      ROTATE 45
4420      RMOVE V(I,3),0
4421      ROTATE 0
4422      IF V(I,5)⟨⟩1 THEN 4428
4423      ROTATE 45
4424      RDRAW Q,0
4425      RDRAW −Q/10,+Q/10
4426      ROTATE Q
4427      GO TO 4455
4428      IF V(I,5)⟨⟩2 THEN 4434
4429      ROTATE 45
4430      RDRAW −Q,0
4431      RDRAW +Q/10,−Q/10
4432      ROTATE Q
4433      GO TO 4455
4434      IF V(I,5)⟨⟩3 THEN 4438
4435      RDRAW Q,0
4436      RDRAW −Q/10,+Q/10
4437      GO TO 4455
4438      IF V(I,5)⟨⟩4 THEN 4442
4439      RDRAW −Q,0
4440      RDRAW +Q/10,−Q/10
4441      GO TO 4455
4442      IF V(I,5)⟨⟩5 THEN 4446
4443      RDRAW 0,Q
4444      RDRAW +Q/10,−Q/10
4445      GO TO 4455
4446      IF V(I,5)⟨⟩6 THEN 4450
4447      RDRAW 0,−Q
4448      RDRAW −Q/10,+Q/10
4449      GO TO 4455
4450      PAGE
4451      PRINT 'ERROR IN INPUTTING THE DIRECTION IN WHICH THE
          POINT OF'
4452      PRINT 'CONVERGENCE EXTENDS.'
4453      PRINT
4454      GO TO 4376
4455      NEXT I
4456      VIEWPORT 0,130,0,100
```

```
4457      WINDOW 0,130,0,100
4458      MOVE 0,90
4459      PRINT 'TIC MARKS ARE IN 100 CM INTERVALS'
4460      PRINT 'HIT (RETURN) TO CONTINUE.'
4464      INPUT A$
4465      PAGE
4466      GO TO 4095
5000      PAGE
5001      PRINT 'YOU CAN SAVE ALL THE NUMBERS YOU HAVE ENTERED
          TO DISK.'
5010      PRINT 'DO YOU WANT TO DO THIS? (Y/N)'
5020      INPUT A$
5030      IF A$='N' THEN 5100
5040      IF A$='Y' THEN 5500
5050      PRINT 'WHAT? (Y/N)'
5060      GO TO 5020
5100      PRINT 'OK. THE TERMINAL IS NOW YOURS.'
5110      END
5500      PRINT 'PUT A DISK IN DISK DRIVE #0. HIT (RETURN) WHEN
          READY.'
5505      INPUT A$
5506      PRINT 'HERE IS A DIRECTORY OF THE DISK. PLEASE CHOOSE A
          FILENAME'
5507      PRINT '(THE PART AFTER THE SCRATCHLIB/) WHICH IS NOT
          LISTED BELOW'
5508      PRINT 'OTHERWISE, THIS PROGRAM WILL ABORT.'
5509      PRINT
5510      DIRECTORY
5511      PRINT
5512      PRINT 'WHAT WOULD YOU LIKE TO NAME YOUR DATA FILE
          (8 CHARACTERS)?'
5513      INPUT A$
5520      UNIT 0
5530      CREATE A$;6000,0
5540      OPEN A$;1,'F' ,M$
5545      PRINT M$
5550      WRITE #1:W1
5560      WRITE #1:X1
5570      WRITE #1:Y1
5579      CLOSE 1
5580      PAGE
```

```
5585      PRINT 'INFORMATION STORED IN FILE ';A$;'.'
5590      PRINT 'THE TERMINAL IS ALL YOURS.'
5595      END
6000      DIM W1(12,21),X1(12,20),Y1(12,20)
6060      FOR I=1 TO 20
6070      FOR J=1 TO 12
6110      X1(J,I)=0
6120      Y1(J,I)=0
6130      W1(J,I)=0
6420      NEXT J
6430      NEXT I
6440      FOR I=1 TO 12
6450      W1(I,21)=0
6460      NEXT I
6560      GO TO 10
7000      PRINT 'TURN ON DISK DRIVE 0 AND PUT YOUR DISK IN.'
7010      PRINT 'HIT (RETURN) WHEN READY.'
7020      INPUT A$
7030      PRINT 'HERE IS A DIRECTORY OF YOUR DISK. WHICH FILE DO
          YOU WISH'
7040      PRINT 'TO RETRIEVE? ENTER THE NAME STARTING WITH THE
          PORTION AFTER'
7050      PRINT 'THE WORK "SCRATCHLIB/".'
7055      PRINT
7060      PRINT 0
7070      DIRECTORY
7080      PRINT
7090      PRINT 'FILE TO RETRIEVE:'
7100      INPUT A$
7120      OPEN A$:1,'F' ,M$
7130      PRINT M$
7140      READ #1:W1
7160      READ #1:X1
7180      READ #1:Y1
7200      CLOSE 1
7210      PRINT 'DATA HAS BEEN RETRIEVED FROM FILE ';A$;','
7220      PRINT 'HIT (RETURN) TO CONTINUE.'
7230      INPUT A$
7240      PAGE
7250      GO TO 2010
```

APPENDIX D
TRIGONOMETRIC TABLES—SINE FUNCTION

Angle in degrees	Sine of angle	Angle in degrees	Sine of angle	Angle in degrees	Sine of angle
0.0	.0000	18.5	.3173	37.0	.6018
0.5	.0087	19.0	.3256	37.5	.6088
1.0	.0175	19.5	.3338	38.0	.6157
1.5	.0262	20.0	.3420	38.5	.6225
2.0	.0349	20.5	.3502	39.0	.6293
2.5	.0436	21.0	.3584	39.5	.6361
3.0	.0523	21.5	.3665	40.0	.6428
3.5	.0610	22.0	.3746	40.5	.6494
4.0	.0698	22.5	.3827	41.0	.6561
4.5	.0785	23.0	.3907	41.5	.6626
5.0	.0872	23.5	.3987	42.0	.6691
5.5	.0958	24.0	.4067	42.5	.6756
6.0	.1045	24.5	.4147	43.0	.6820
6.5	.1132	25.0	.4226	43.5	.6884
7.0	.1219	25.5	.4305	44.0	.6947
7.5	.1305	26.0	.4384	44.5	.7009
8.0	.1392	26.5	.4462	45.0	.7071
8.5	.1478	27.0	.4540	45.5	.7173
9.0	.1564	27.5	.4617	46.0	.7193
9.5	.1650	28.0	.4695	46.5	.7254
10.0	.1736	28.5	.4772	47.0	.7314
10.5	.1822	29.0	.4848	47.5	.7373
11.0	.1908	29.5	.4924	48.0	.7431
11.5	.1994	30.0	.5000	48.5	.7490
12.0	.2079	30.5	.5075	49.0	.7547
12.5	.2164	31.0	.5150	49.5	.7604
13.0	.2250	31.5	.5225	50.0	.7660
13.5	.2234	32.0	.5299	50.5	.7716
14.0	.2419	32.5	.5373	51.0	.7771
14.5	.2504	33.0	.5446	51.5	.7826
15.0	.2588	33.5	.5519	52.0	.7880
15.5	.2672	34.0	.5592	52.5	.7934
16.0	.2756	34.5	.5664	53.0	.7986
16.5	.2840	35.0	.5736	53.5	.8039
17.0	.2924	35.5	.5807	54.0	.8090
17.5	.3007	36.0	.5878	54.5	.8141
18.0	.3090	36.5	.5948	55.0	.8192

(continued)

Angle in degrees	Sine of angle	Angle in degrees	Sine of angle	Angle in degrees	Sine of angle
55.5	.8241	67.5	.9239	79.5	.9833
56.0	.8290	68.0	.9272	80.0	.9848
56.5	.8339	68.5	.9304	80.5	.9863
57.0	.8387	69.0	.9336	81.0	.9877
57.5	.8434	69.5	.9367	81.5	.9890
58.0	.8480	70.0	.9397	82.0	.9903
58.5	.8526	70.5	.9426	82.5	.9914
59.0	.8572	71.0	.9455	83.0	.9925
59.5	.8616	71.5	.9483	83.5	.9936
60.0	.8660	72.0	.9511	84.0	.9945
60.5	.8704	72.5	.9537	84.5	.9954
61.0	.8746	73.0	.9563	85.0	.9962
61.5	.8788	73.5	.9588	85.5	.9969
62.0	.8829	74.0	.9613	86.0	.9976
62.5	.8870	74.5	.9636	86.5	.9981
63.0	.8910	75.0	.9659	87.0	.9986
63.5	.8949	75.5	.9681	87.5	.9990
64.0	.8988	76.0	.9703	88.0	.9994
64.5	.9026	76.5	.9724	88.5	.9997
65.0	.9063	77.0	.9744	89.0	.9998
65.5	.9100	77.5	.9763	89.5	1.0000
66.0	.9135	78.0	.9781	90.0	1.0000
66.5	.9171	78.5	.9799		
67.0	.9205	79.0	.9816		

Glossary

Angle of impact The internal angle at which blood strikes a target surface relative to the horizontal plane of that target surface.

Arterial spurting Characteristic bloodstain patterns on a target surface resulting from blood exiting under pressure from a breached artery. These patterns are characterized by their specific appearance and shape.

Backspatter Blood that is directed back towards its source of energy. Backspatter is often associated with gunshot wounds of entrance.

Bloodstain Blood that has come in contact with a surface.

Cast-off pattern Blood that has been projected onto a surface from other than an impact site. This pattern is produced when blood is thrown from a bloody object in motion.

Clot A blood clot is formed by a complex mechanism involving the plasma protein fibrinogen, platelets, and other clotting factors. It is observed visually as a network of fibrous material (fibrin and red blood cells). Subsequently, the blood clot begins to retract causing a separation of the remaining liquid portion which is now referred to as serum.

Directionality Relating to or indicating the direction a drop of blood traveled in space from its point of origin.

Drawback effect The presence of blood in the barrel of a firearm that has been drawn backward owing to the effect created by discharged gasses. This is seen frequently in close-range-contact gunshot injuries.

Drip pattern Blood that drips into blood resulting in round, satellite blood spatters, 0.1–1.0 mm in diameter, around the periphery of the central bloodstain.

Forward spatter Blood that travels in the same direction as the source of energy or force causing the spatter. Forward spatter is often associated with gunshot wounds of exit.

High-velocity impact spatter A bloodstain pattern caused by a high-velocity force characterized by a mistlike dispersion which, owing to the low density of the blood particles, has traveled only a short distance in flight. A high-velocity impact is considered to be approximately 100 feet per second or greater such as produced by gunshot and high-speed machinery. Individual stains within the mistlike dispersion are usually 0.1 mm or smaller in diameter but may be seen in association with larger bloodstains.

Impact site The point on a bloody object or body which receives a blow. Often, impact site is used interchangeably with point of origin. Impact site may also refer to an area on the surface of a target which is struck by blood in motion.

Low-velocity impact spatter Bloodstains produced on a surface when the blood source has been subjected to a low-velocity force approximately 5 feet per second or less.

Medium-velocity impact spatter Bloodstains produced on a surface when the blood source has been subjected to a medium-velocity force between approximately 5 and 25 feet per second.

Origin, point of The location from which the blood that produced a bloodstain originated. This is determined by projecting angles of impact of well-defined bloodstains back to an axis constructed through the point of convergence.

Parent drop A drop of blood from which a wave castoff or satellite spatter originates.

Point of convergence A point to which a bloodstain pattern can be projected. This point is determined by tracing the long axis of well-defined bloodstains within the pattern back to a common point or source.

Projected blood pattern A pattern created when a force other than a low-velocity impact acts upon a quantity of blood approximately 0.10 ml or greater.

Satellite spatter Small droplets of blood that are projected around or beside a drop of blood upon impact with a surface. A wave castoff is also considered a form of satellite spatter.

Secondary splash or ricochet The deflection of large volumes of blood after impact with a target surface to another target surface.

Serum stain A clear, yellowish stain with a shiny surface often appearing around a bloodstain after the blood has retracted due to clotting.

Smudge A bloodstain that has been distorted to a degree so that further classification is not possible.

Spine The pointed edge characteristics that radiate away from the center of a bloodstain. Their formation depends upon impact velocity and surface texture.

Splash A stain pattern created by a low-velocity impact upon a quantity of blood approximately 0.10 ml or greater striking a surface.

Swipe or smear The transfer of blood onto a surface not already contaminated with blood. One edge is usually feathered which may indicate the direction of travel.

Target A surface upon which blood has been deposited.

Terminal velocity The maximum speed to which a free-falling drop of blood can accelerate in air which is approximately 25.1 feet per second.

Transfer pattern A contact bloodstain created when a wet, bloody surface contacts a second surface. A recognizable mirror image or at least a recognizable portion of the original surface may be transferred to the second surface.

Wave castoff A small blood droplet that originates from a parent drop of blood due to the wavelike action of the liquid in conjunction with striking a surface at an angle less than 90 degrees.

Wipe A bloodstain pattern created when an object moves through an existing bloodstain removing blood from the original stain and altering its appearance.

This glossary has been adapted from suggested terminology compiled by the Terminology Committee of the International Association of Bloodstain Pattern Analysts. Input was received from many individuals throughout the forensic community both in the United States and Canada. An official list of bloodstain terminology has not yet been officially adopted by this organization. It should be recognized that the terminology utilized in this manual is not all-inclusive and variations may exist in different texts and other sources. It is felt that the terminology presented here does represent a significant agreement and consensus of opinion of many individuals. There is a need for consistent and uniform terminology in reports and testimony in order to avoid confusion and misleading interpretation in the evaluation of written conclusions and oral testimony in court.

The definition of angle of impact or angle of incidence of a blood drop as the internal angle at which it strikes a surface relative to the horizontal plane of that impacting surface is widely but not universally used. DeForest, Gaensslen and Lee, in their text *Forensic Science—An Introduction to Criminalistics,* prefer to define angle of impact as the angle of incidence conforming to the optical reflection and refraction of light rays. The authors measure the angle of incidence relative to the "normal" of the impacting surface rather than the horizontal plane of the surface itself. The "normal" of a surface is an imaginary line perpendicular (90 degrees) to the horizontal plane of the surface. A straight-on impact of a blood drop along the normal to a surface would be said to have an angle of incidence of 0 degrees rather than a 90-degree angle of impact. A 10-degree angle of incidence relative to the normal in this system would correspond to an 80-degree angle of impact relative to the plane of the horizontal surface. To determine angle of incidence relative to the normal from the width to length ratio, the cosine function must be utilized rather than the sine function. To convert the angle of incidence relative to the normal to the more universal angle of impact relative to the horizontal plane of the surface, it must be subtracted from 90 degrees. It is very important to realize which system is being utilized in a bloodstain interpretation to avoid confusion. Perhaps it is better in this instance to maintain the classical definition of angle of impact relative to the horizontal plane of the impacting surface, which is more familiar to investigators as a means of maintaining consistency and uniformity.

Bibliography

Acherkan, N., et al. 1979. Determination of the erythrocyte acid phosphatase groups in dried blood. *Sudebno-Meditsinskaia Ekspertiza* 22(2), 25–27, April–June (Russia).

———. 1984. Transaminase groups in fresh and dried blood. *Sudebno-Meditsinskaia Ekspertiza* 27(4), 36–38, October–December (Russia).

Akashi, S. 1965. Studies on the group-specific double combination method. *Japan Journal of Legal Medicine* (19), 177–187, May.

Alfultis, H.M. 1965. A microtitration method for grouping dried bloodstains. *Journal of Forensic Sciences* 10, 319–334, July.

Alsawaf, K., et al. 1985. Isotachophoretic analysis of bloodstains: Differentiation of human, menstrual, bovine, and ovine blood. *Journal of Forensic Sciences* 30(3), 922–930, July.

Ameno, S., et al. 1983. Personal identification of human bloodstains by crossed electroimmunodiffusion. *Nippon Hoigaku Zasshi* 37(1), 6–15, February (Japan).

American Association of Blood Banks, 1970. *Technical Methods and Procedures,* 5th Edition, Chicago, Illinois.

Anastasov, B. 1969. Identification of Gm blood groups in bloodstains. *God Zborn Med. Fak Skopje* 15, 399–404.

Andre, A., et al. 1984. Importance of the choice of the means in the study of bloodstains. *Haematologia* (Budapest) 17(2), 311–315.

Andrus, R.H. 1981. Phenotyping of carbonic anhydrase II in fresh blood and bloodstains on cellulose acetate membrane. *Journal of Forensic Sciences* 26(1), 181–183, January.

Arai, N., et al. 1982. Hyperphenylanalinemia due to dihydropteridine reductase deficiency: Diagnosis by enzyme assays on dried blood spots. *Pediatrics* 70(3), 426–430, September.

Arefev, I.M., et al. 1979. Establishment of the species classification of blood and the expertise of discharges by using a laser indicator of immunological reactions. *Sudebno-Meditsinskaia Ekspertiza* 22(4), 43–45, October–December (Russia).

——. 1982. Laser mass-spectrometric analysis of element composition of bloodstains on the metal. *Sudebno-Meditsinskaia Ekspertiza* 25(3), 35–36, July–September. (Russia).

——. 1978. Determination of the species specificity of blood by a light-mixing spectroscopic method. *Sudebno-Meditsinskaia Ekspertiza* (21)1, 26–28, January–March (Russia).

Asano, M., et al. 1972. Identification of menstrual bloodstains by the electrophoretic pattern of lactate dehydrogenase isozymes. *Journal of Forensic Sciences* 1, 327–332, September.

Aye, U.T. 1977. Detection of residual ABO substances in serologically used glass test tubes by absorption-elution method. *Journal of Forensic Science* 9(2), 155, March–April.

——. 1978. The reliability of ABO grouping of bloodstains contaminated with sweat. *Journal of the Forensic Science Society* 18(3–4), 193–195, July–October.

Balthazard, V., et al. 1939. Etude des gouttes de sang projecte. *Annales Med. Leg. Criminol.* 19, 265 (France).

Bar, W., et al. 1983. Evaluation of blood traces under field conditions and their preparation for analysis: Introduction to the formation of an inexpensive single use instrument. *Archiv Fur Kriminologie* 172(5–6), 166–170, November–December (Germany).

Bargagna, M., et al. 1968. The determination of the haptoglobin type in bloodstains by means of electrophoresis. *Minerva Medica* 88, 183–186, May–August (Italy).

——. 1967. A study of absorption-elution as a method of identification of rhesus antigens in dried bloodstains. *Journal of the Forensic Science Society* 7, 123–130, July.

——. 1982. The detection of Rh antigens (D,C, c,E,e,) on bloodstains by a micro-elution technique using low ionic strength solution (LISS) and papain-treated red cells. *Forensic Sci. Inter.* 19(2), 197–203, March–April.

Barinova, L.I. 1975. Serological diagnosis of pregnancy by bloodstains with the use of the domestic preparation, Gravidadiagnosticum. *Sudebno-Meditsinskaia Ekspertiza* 18(3), 24–25, July–September (Russia).

Barnard, P.A., et al. 1979. Alteration of electrophoretic mobility of hemoglobin in bloodstains. *Journal of Forensic Sciences* 24(2), 384–388, April.

Barsegiants, L.O. 1967. Differentiation of excretions of the human organism by emission spectral analysis. *Sudebno-Meditsinskaia Ekspertiza* 10, 30–34, October–December (Russia).

Batstone, G.F., et al. 1984. Measuring theophylline on dried blood spots. *Lancet* 2(8394), 99, July 14.

Baxter, M., et al. 1982. A method of phenotyping group specific component protein from dried bloodstains by immunofixation thin layer polyacrylamide gel isoelectric focusing. *Journal of the Forensic Science Society* 22(4), 367–371, October.

——. 1984. A method for the identification and typing of the subtypes of the Gc 1 allele from dried bloodstains. *Journal of the Forensic Science Society* 24(5), 453–458, September–October.

Baxter, S.J. 1982. The subtyping of haptoglobin in blood samples in dried and liquid state. *Journal of the Forensic Science Society* 22(3), 263–265, July.

———. 1985. Electrophoresis in forensic sciences. *Journal of Forensic Sciences* 30(4), 994–995, October.

Baxter, S.J., et al. 1974. The immunological identification in infanticide and associated crimes. *Med. Sci., Law* 14(3), 163–167, July.

———. 1974. Simultaneous haptoglobin and haemoglobin typing of blood and bloodstains using gradient polyacrylamide gel electrophoresis. *Med. Sci., Law* 14(4), 231–236, October.

———. 1974. The use of anti-human hemoglobin in forensic serology. *Med. Sci., Law* 14(3), 159–162, July.

Benciolini, P., et al. 1977. Problems in determining A2B group specific properties in bloodstains. *Journal of Legal Medicine* 79(4), 285–288, May (Germany).

Berg, S., et al. 1979. Detectability of Tf C- and PGM-1 subtypes in old blood samples. *Archiv Fur Kriminologie* 164(3–4), 101–106, September–October (Germany).

Berghaus, G., et al. 1983. Possibilities of the use of miniaturized ultra thin isoelectric focusing for bloodstain examination. *Beitr. Gerichtl. Med.* 41, 185–189 (Germany).

———. 1983. Electrofocusing of PGM1 subtypes in bloodstains on a 100 micrometer polyacrylamide gel over a 4 cm distance. *Journal of Legal Medicine* 90(4), 293–296 (Germany).

———. 1984. Possibilities for identifying blood traces using multidimensional electrophoresis procedures. *Beitr. Gerichtl. Med.* 42, 245–249 (Germany).

———. 1986. Recent electrophoretic methods in the analysis of bloodstains. *Beitr. Gerichtl. Med.* 44, 63–66 (Germany).

Bernardelli, B., et al. 1976. Ascending one dimensional thin layer chromatography in specific blood diagnosis. *Acta Bio-Medica De L Ateneo Parmense* 47(5), 597–604, September–October (Italy).

———. 1976. High performance thin layer chromatography in specific blood diagnosis. *Acta Bio-Medica De L Ateneo Parmense* 47(6), 685–692, November–December (Italy).

Berns, B., and Lotterie, J. 1988. Micromethod for MN antigen grouping of dried bloodstains. *Journal of Forensic Sciences* Vol. 33, No. 1, January.

Bevel, T. 1983. Geometric bloodstain interpretation. *FBI Law Enforcement Bulletin*, Office of Congressional and Public Affairs, Vol. 52, No. 5, 7–10, May.

Bhatnagar, R.K., et al. 1974. Preservation effects in forensic ABO determinations using analysis of results as evidence in criminal cases. *Archiv Fur Kriminologie* 154(3–4), 91–99, September–October (Germany).

———. 1980. Phosphoglucomutase (PGM) typing of bloodstains. *Indian Journal of Medical Research* 71, 627–631, April.

Bialowas, M. 1980. Curiosa haematologica IV. *Wiadomosci Lekareskie* 33(14), 1179–1180, July (Poland).

Blake, E.T., et al. 1978. Haptoglobin typing of bloodstains—electrophoresis of immunoprecipitated haptoglobin. *Journal of the Forensic Science Society* 18(3–4), 237–244, July–October.

Blazek, V., et al. 1982. Spectroscopic age determination of bloodstains—new technical aspects. *Acta Med. Leg. Soc.* (Liege) 32, 613–616 (Germany).

Blumenfeld, O.O., and Adamany, A.M. 1978. Structural polymorphism within the amino-terminal region of MM, NN, and MN glycoproteins (glycophorins) of the human erythrocyte membrane. Proceedings of the National Academy of Sciences. Vol. 75, No. 6, pp. 2727–2731, June.

Boissezon, J.F., et al. 1966. Identification of human bloodstains by the immunoelectrosyneresis method. *Ann. Med. Leg.* (Paris) 46, 453–456, November–December (France).

Boudreau, A.J., et al. 1982. Cause of an aberrant phenotype—an interesting dilemma. *Journal of Forensic Sciences* 27(4), 938–941, October.

Bourguignon, J.P., et al. 1986. Variations in dried blood spot immunoreactive trypsin in relation to gestational age and during the first week of life. *Europ. J. Pediatr.* 144(6), 547–549, April.

Boyd, W.C. 1966. *Fundamentals of Immunology*. 4th Edition. New York, NY: Interscience Publishers.

Brettel, H.F., et al. 1982. Determination of the volume of blood puddles. *Archiv Fur Kriminologie* 169(1–2), 12–16, January–February (Germany).

Brewer, C.A., et al. 1976. A low ionic strength hemagglutinating autoanalyzer for rhesus typing of dried bloodstains. *Journal of Forensic Sciences* 21(4), 811–815, October.

Briggs, T.J. 1978. The probative value of bloodstains on clothing. *Med. Sci., Law* 18(2), 79–83, April.

Brinkmann, B., et al. 1985. Characterization of microtraces of blood. *Journal of Legal Medicine* 94(3), 237–244 (Germany).

———. 1979. Typing ACP isoenzymes in bloodstains—test limits and temperature dependency. *Journal of Legal Medicine* 84(1), 1–6 (Germany).

———. 1981. Determination of Gc phenotype from bloodstains. *Archiv Fur Kriminologie* 168(1–2), 53–57, July–August (Germany).

———. 1986. Factors affecting the morphology of bloodstains. *Beitr. Gerichtl. Med.* 44, 67–73 (Germany).

———. 1976. White bloodstains. *Archiv Fur Kriminologie* 157(3–4), 114–118, March–April (Germany).

———. 1969. Determination of phosphoglucomutase types in blood traces. *Deutsche Z Ges Gerichtl. Med.* 66, 31–34 (Germany).

Bronnikova, M.A. 1966. A new method of determination of the group of bloodstains—preliminary report. *Sudebno-Meditsinskaia Ekspertiza* 9, 38–40, October–December (Russia).

Brown, B.L. 1981. The determination of the sex of an individual from a dried bloodstain using radioimmunoassay of testosterone, progesterone, and estradiol-17-beta. *Journal of Forensic Sciences* 26(4), 766–781, October.

Brownlie, A.R. 1965. Blood and the blood groups—A developing field for expert evidence. *Journal of the Forensic Science Society* 5, 124–174, July.

Brzecka, K., et al. 1966. Attempted determination of Gc factor in human bloodstains. *Ann. Med. Leg.* (Paris) 46, 250–254, July–August (France).

———. 1967. Attempted detection of haptoglobins in bloodstains. *Atti. Acad. Fisiocr. Siena* (Medicofis) 16, 624–628 (France).

Bucklin, R. 1982. The shroud of turin—a pathologist's viewpoint. *Journal of*

Legal Medicine 33–39; *Journal of the Mississippi Medical Association* 24(4), 95–98, April.

Budiakov, O.S. 1967. On the possibility of using serum gamma globulin Gm factors in forensic medical expertise. *Sudebno-Meditsinskaia Ekspertiza* 10, 41–45, January–March (Russia).

Budowle, B. 1984. A method to increase the volume of sample applied to isoelectric focusing gels. *Forensic Sci. Int.* 24(4), 273–277, April.

Budowle, B., et al. 1985. Transferrin subtyping of human bloodstains. *Forensic Sci. Int.* 28(3–4), 269–275, August.

———. 1985. Discontinuous polyacrylamide gel electrophoresis for typing haptoglobin in bloodstains. *Journal of Forensic Sciences* 30(3), 893–897, July.

Burago, I., et al. 1986. Isoantigenic differentiation by the ABO system of mixed human and livestock bloodstains. *Sudebno-Meditsinskaia Ekspertiza* 29(3), 36–37, July–September (Russia).

Butt, R.W. 1983. Identification of human bloodstains by radioimmunoassay. *Journal of the Forensic Science Society* 23(4), 291–296, October.

Caffiaux 1965. Blood groups M and N. *Laval Med.* 36, 425–430, May (France).

Camps, F.E., Ed. 1968. *Gradwohl's Legal Medicine.* Baltimore, MD: Williams and Wilkins Co.

Carracedo, A., et al. 1983. A silver staining method for the detection of polymorphic proteins in minute bloodstains after isoelectric focusing. *Forensic Sci. Int.* 23(2–3), 241–248, November–December.

———. 1982. Phosphoglucomutase subtypes in human bloodstains. *Acta Med. Leg. Soc.* (Liege) 32, 589–592.

———. 1982. The typing of alpha 1-antitrypsin in human bloodstains by isoelectric focusing. *Forensic Sci. Int.* 19(2), 181–184, March–April.

Castilla, J., et al. 1972. Analysis of haptoglobin types by means of acrylamide gel disk vertical electrophoresis—application to the diagnosis of bloodstains. *Med. Leg. Domm Corpor* (Paris) 5, 52–55, January–March.

Charyni, V.I. 1969. Differentiation of bloodstains of phylogenetically closely related animals through immunoelectrophoresis. *Sudebno-Meditsinskaia Ekspertiza* 12, 27–31, January–March (Russia).

Chatterji, P.K. 1978. A simplified mixed agglutination technique for ABO grouping of dried bloodstains using cellulose acetate sheets. *Journal of the Forensic Science Society* 17(2–3), 143–144, April–July.

Cheetham, R.C., et al. 1983. The sexing of bloodstains by testosterone total protein ration determination. *Forensic Sci. Int.* 22(2–3), 195–201, August–September.

Chernov, V.P. 1966. Establishing the species origin of blood by the precipitation reaction and recording on chromatographic paper. *Sudebno-Meditsinskaia Ekspertiza* 9, 36–38, October–December (Russia).

Chisum, W.J. 1971. A rapid method for grouping dried bloodstains. *Journal of the Forensic Science Society* 205–206, Vol. 11.

Clausen, P.K., et al. 1980. Differentiation of fetal and adult bloodstains by pyrolysis-gas liquid chromatography. *Journal of Forensic Sciences* 25(4), 765–778, October.

Coe, J. 1974. Postmortem chemistry: Practical considerations and literature review. *Journal of Forensic Sciences* 19, 1.

Coombs, R., et al. 1945. Detection of weak or incomplete Rh agglutinins. *Lancet* 2, 15.

Crossley, J.R., et al. 1979. Dried blood spot screening for cystic fibrosis in the newborn. *Lancet* 1(8114), 472–474, March.

———. 1966. Haptoglobin types in dried bloodstains. *Nature* (London) 211, 872–873, August.

———. 1967. The determination of phosphoglucomutase (PGM) types in bloodstains. *Journal of the Forensic Science Society* 7, 131–133, July.

———. 1971. The examination of and typing of bloodstains in the crime laboratory. National Institute of Law Enforcement and Criminal Justice, December.

Culliford, B.J., and Nickolls, L.C. 1964. The benzidine test—a critical review. *Journal of Forensic Sciences* 9, 175.

Culliford, B.J., et al. 1968. Adenylate kinase (AK) types in bloodstains. *Journal of the Forensic Science Society* 8, 79–80, October.

Davie, M.J. 1979. ABO, Gm and Km grouping of bloodstains on microtitre plates. *Journal of the Forensic Science Society* 19(1), 59–64, January.

DeForest, P.R., Gaensslen, R.E., and Lee, H.C. 1983. *Forensic Science—An Introduction to Criminalistics*. New York, NY: McGraw-Hill, 1983.

Denault, G.C., Takimoto, H.H., Kwan, Q.Y., and Pallos, A. 1980. Detectability of selected genetic markers in dried blood on aging. *Journal of Forensic Sciences*, Vol. 25, No. 3, pp. 479–498, July.

DeRobertis, M., et al. 1982. Identification of hepatitis B virus surface antigen (HBsAg) in bloodstains—preliminary results. *Acta Med. Leg. Soc.* (Liege) 32, 465–468.

Divall, G.B. 1985. Esterase D typing of bloodstains by nonequilibrium focusing. *Forensic Sci. Int.* 28(3–4), 277–285, August.

Dixon, T.R., et al. 1976. A scanning electron microscope study of dried blood. *Journal of Forensic Science* 21(4), 797–803, October.

Dodd, B. 1968. "Immunological Aspects of Forensic Science." In *Clinical Aspects of Immunology*, 2nd Edition, by P. Gell and R. Coombs. Philadelphia, PA: F.A. Davis Company.

Dorrill, M., et al. 1979. The species identification of very old human bloodstains. *Forensic Sci. Int.* 13(2), 111–116, March–April.

Douglas, R., et al. 1969. Rh and kell typing of dried bloodstains. *Journal of Forensic Sciences* 14, 255–262, April.

Dowd, R., et al. 1983. Erythrocyte diphorases DIA1 and DIA2 in bloodstains. *Journal of Legal Medicine* 91(2), 123–127.

Driesen, H.H., et al. 1973. Isolation of M and N antigens from dried bloodstains. *Archiv Fur Kriminologie* 151, 180–183, May–June (Germany).

Ducos, J., et al. 1969. Demonstration of antigen VW in dry bloodstains. *Revue Francais De Transfusion Et Immuno-Hemotologie* 12(Suppl.) 189–193 (France).

———. 1969. Demonstration of factor Gm3 in dry bloodstains—importance for the identification of their racial origin. *Revue Francais De Transfusion Et Immuno-Hemotologie* 12(Suppl.) 183–188 (France).

———. 1969. Demonstration of factors I and i in dry bloodstains. *Revue Francais De Transfusion Et Immuno-Hemotologie* 12(Suppl.), 195ff (France).

Ishizu, H. 1984. Identification of Y chromosome in bloodstains. *Nippon Rinsho* 42(10), 2385–2394, October (Japan).

Ishizu, H., et al. 1983. Y chromosome fluorescence in 10-year-old bloodstains. *Nippon Hoigaku Zasshi* 37(4), 387–391.

———. 1983. Differentiation of sex origin of bloodstains by radioimmunoassay of sex hormones. *Nippon Hoigaku Zasshi* 37(2), 127–132, April.

Ito, S., et al. 1985. Identification of a human hemoglobin tryptic peptide (alpha-T4) from a bloodstain by fast protein liquid chromatography—determination of human origin. *Nippon Hoigaku Zasshi* 39(1), 23–26, February.

Itoh, Y. 1979. Absorption test using latex particles for the indicator system for the species identification of bloodstains and muscles. *Journal of Forensic Sciences* 24(3), 561–568, July.

Iudina, G.S. 1972. Absorption-elution reactions applicable to the detection of M and N antigens in bloodstains. *Sudebno-Meditsinskaia Ekspertiza* 15, 37–40, July–September (Russia).

———. 1975. Difficulties in differentiating groups M and N in bloodstains. *Sudebno-Meditsinskaia Ekspertiza* 18(1), 32–35, January–March (Russia).

———. 1979. Simultaneous detection of M, N, A, and B antigens in bloodstains by means of absorption-elution. *Sudebno-Meditsinskaia Ekspertiza* 22(2), 37–39, April–June (Russia).

Iwasa, M., et al. 1979. Preparation of anti-alpha 2-macroglobulin using canavalia lineata DC lectin for differentiating species specificity of bloodstains. *Tohoku Journal of Experimental Medicine* 127(3), 209–215, March.

Jarco, S. 1968. Malaria and murder (Joseph Jones, 1878). *Bulletin of the New York Academy of Medicine* 44, 759–760, June.

Jay, B.W., et al. 1979. A stability study of the esterase D isoenzymes. *Journal of Forensic Sciences* 24(1), 193–199, January.

Johnson, D.A., et al. 1985. Antibiotic therapy based on stained peripheral blood smear. *Archives of Internal Medicine* 145(2), 369, February.

Jones, D.A. 1972. Blood samples—probability of discrimination. *Journal of the Forensic Science Society* 12, 355–359, April.

Jones, L.V. 1959. *Scientific Investigation and Physical Evidence*. Ch. 11. Springfield, IL: Charles C. Thomas Co.

Joshi, H., et al. 1980. Studies on three biochemical polymorphic systems—phosphoglucomutase (locus one) PGM1, adenylate kinase AK and pseudocholinesterase (E2 locus) PCE2 in human bloodstains subjected to tropical and temperate climatic conditions. *Indian Journal of Biochemistry and Biophysics* 17(1), 67–71, February.

———. 1979. Persistence of typable activity of pseudocholinesterase (E2 locus)-C5 component polymorphism in human bloodstains under Indian climatic conditions. *Indian Journal of Experimental Biology* 17(3), 258–261, March.

Kanter, E., et al. 1986. Analysis of restriction fragment length polymorphisms in deoxyribonucleic acid (DNA) recovered from dried bloodstains. *Journal of Forensic Sciences* 31(2), 403–408, April.

Kanter, E., Baird, M., Shaler, R., and Balazs, I. 1986. Analysis of restriction fragment length polymorphisms in deoxyribonucleic acid (DNA) recovered from dried bloodstains. *Journal of Forensic Sciences*, Vol. 31, No. 2, 403–408, April.

Kashimura, S., et al. 1984. An experimental study of the identification of the person of origin of a bloodstain by crossed immunoelectrophoresis. *Forensic Sci. Int.* 25(2), 147–154, June.

———. 1979. Identification from crossed electroimmunodiffusion patterns of serum. *Tohoku Journal of Experimental Medicine* 129(2), 169–176, October.

Katsumata, Y., et al. 1985. Identification of fetal bloodstains by enzyme-linked immunoabsorbant assay for human alpha-feto protein. *Journal of Forensic Sciences* 30(4), 1210–1215, October.

———. 1984. Detection of thyroglobulin in bloodstains as an aid in the diagnosis of mechanical asphyxia. *Journal of Forensic Sciences* 29(1), 299–302, January.

———. 1979. Identification of fetal bloodstains by radioimmunoassay of alpha 1-fetoprotein. *Journal of Legal Medicine* 82(4), 323–326, March.

Keil, W., et al. 1986. Quantitative IgD measurement for discrimination of human bloodstains. *Forensic Sci. Int.* 31(2), 73–78, June.

———. 1984. First results with the treponema pallidum hemagglutination (TPHA) test in bloodstains. *Journal of Legal Medicine* 91(4), 247–253 (Germany).

Khalap, S., et al., 1976. Gm and Inv grouping of bloodstains. *Med. Sci., Law* 16(1), 40–43, January.

———. 1979. Gm(5) grouping of dried bloodstains. *Med. Sci., Law* 19(2), 86–88, April.

———. 1978. The sequential determination of Gm/Km and ABO blood groups from the same piece of bloodstained thread. *Journal of Forensic Sciences* 11(1), 41–45, January–February.

Kharamov, S., et al. 1986. Diagnosis of menstrual bloodstains by the characteristics of the lactate dehydrogenase isoenzyme spectrum. *Sudebno-Meditsinskaia Ekspertiza* 29(3), 30–32, July–September (Russia).

Kido, A., et al. 1984. A stability study on Gc subtyping in bloodstains—comparison by two different techniques. *Forensic Sci. Inter.* 26(1), 39–43, September.

———. 1984. Determination of Tf C subtypes by isoelectric focusing and its demonstration from bloodstains. *Nippon Hoigaku* 38(1), 5–8, February.

Kijewski, H., et al. 1985. A new method for the determination of carboxyhemoglobin in fluid and dried blood using fourier transformation infrared spectrometry. *Journal of Legal Medicine* 95(1), 67–74 (Germany).

Kijewski, S., et al. 1975. The influence of soil differences in determining the quantity and recognizability of serological properties of blood traces in the earth. *Journal of Legal Medicine* 75(4), 253–263 (Germany).

Kimura, H., et al. 1983. The typing of group-specific component (Gc Protein) in human bloodstains. *Forensic Sci. Int.* 22(1), 49–55, July.

Kimura, S. 1967. Studies on the species specificity of human blood IV—application of the serum hemoglobin precipitation reaction to the medicolegal practices. *Japan Journal of Legal Medicine* 21, 104–113, January (Japan).

Kind, S.S. 1962. The ABO grouping of bloodstains. *Journal of Criminal Law, Criminal and Police Science* 53, 367–374.

———. 1976. Absorption-elution groupings of dried blood smears. *Nature* CLXXXVIII, 397.

Kind, S.S., et al. 1976. An investigation into the possible sources of adventitious ABH substances in bloodstain grouping. *Journal of the Forensic Science Society* 16(2), 155–161, April.

———. 1969. The use of ammoniacal bloodstain extracts in ABO groupings. *Journal of the Forensic Science Society* 9, 131–134, December.

———. 1973. The estimation of bloodstain age from the spectrophotometric properties of ammoniacal bloodstain extracts. *Journal of Forensic Sciences* 2, 325–332, August.

———. 1976. Some observations on the ammoniacal extraction method in bloodstain grouping and its comparison with other extractive and non-extractive methods. *Journal of the Forensic Science Society* 16(1), 47–54, January.

King, L.A. 1974. The identification of anti-parasitic antibodies in bloodstains using an indirect fluorescent antibody technique. *Journal of the Forensic Science Society* 14, (2), 117–121, April.

———. 1974. The value of biochemical profiling for the discrimination of bloodstains. *Journal of the Forensic Science Society* 14(4), 323–327, October.

———. 1979. The fluorometric detection of salicylate in bloodstains. *Journal of Forensic Sciences* 24(2), 317–318, April.

King, L.A., et al. 1975. The differentiation of an adult's bloodstain from that of a child using an indirect fluorescent antibody technique. *Journal of Forensic Sciences* 6(3), 197–203, December.

———. 1976. Antibody profiling of bloodstains. *Journal of Forensic Sciences* 8(2), 151–154, September–October.

Kipps, A.E., et al. 1978. The detection of mixtures of blood and other body secretions in stains. *Journal of the Forensic Science Society* 18(3–4), 189–191, July–October.

Kirk, P.L. 1974. *Crime Investigation, 2nd Edition*, pp. 167–181. New York, NY: John Wiley and Sons.

Kirk, P.L., and Grunbaum, B. 1969. "Individuality of Blood and Its Forensic Significance." In *Legal Medicine Annual*, Cyril Wecht, Ed. New York, NY: Appleton-Century-Crofts Co.

Kirk, P.L. 1955. Affidavit Regarding State of Ohio vs. Samuel Sheppard, Court of Common Pleas, Criminal Branch, No. 64571, 26 April.

———. 1974. *Crime Investigation*. Ch. 15. New York, NY: John Wiley and Sons.

———. 1967. "Blood—A Neglected Criminalistics Research Area." In *Law Enforcement Science and Technology, Vol. 1* pp. 267–272. London: Academic Press.

Kissling, E., et al. 1972. Determination of H substances in dried bloodstains using the absorption method and demonstration of weak agglutinins in the agglutinin reaction test using lattes method. *Archiv Fur Kriminologie* 150(5–6), 141–145, November–December (Germany).

Klir, P. 1979. Changes of various proteins in older bloodstains. *Cesk Patol* 24(2), 17–19, May (Czechoslovakia).

Klir, P., et al. 1980. Determination of subgroups A1–A2 in bloodstains. *Soud Lek* 25, Supp. 3, 44–45 (Czechoslovakia).

———. 1984. Study of the Rh system in bloodstains. *Soud Lek* 29(1), 12–13, February (Czechoslovakia).

Knight, B. 1977. "Blood Identification." In *Forensic Medicine*, Vol. II, Tedeschi, C.G., Eckert, W.G., and Tedeschi, L.G., Eds. Philadelphia, PA: W.B. Saunders Co.

Kohler, U., et al. 1977. On the suitability of spectrophotometric analyses for the estimation of bloodstain age. *Journal of Legal Medicine* 79(3), 183–187, April (Germany).

Kolokolova, G.P. 1974. Possibility of determining with the aid of protectins, antigen B in blood spots and saliva using an absorption-elution reaction. *Sudebno-Meditsinskaia Ekspertiza* 17(3), 19–21, July–September (Russia).

———. 1980. Determination of antigen Gm(1) in bloodstains using goat immune sera. *Sudebno-Meditsinskaia Ekspertiza* 23(1), 36–37, January–March (Russia).

Komatsu, N., et al. 1985. Polymorphism of EsD by isoelectric focusing—description of the new allele EsD*KoFu and phenotyping in bloodstains. *Journal of Legal Medicine* 95(4), 227–233 (Germany).

Kotowski, T.M., et al. 1986. The use of microspectrophotometry to characterize microscopic amounts of blood. *Journal of the Forensic Science Society* 31(3), 1079–1085, July.

Kringsholm, B., et al. 1977. Fluorescent Y-chromosomes in hairs and bloodstains. *Journal of Forensic Sciences* 9(2), 117–126, March–April.

Kuo, M.C. 1982. Linking a bloodstain to a missing person by genetic inheritance. *Journal of Forensic Sciences* 27(2), 438–444, April.

Kuprina, T.A. 1980. Forensic medical importance of the serological determination of hemoglobin in blood traces (a review of the literature). *Sudebno-Meditsinskaia Ekspertiza* 23(1), 42–43, January–March (Russia).

Laber, T.L. 1985. Diameter of a bloodstain as a function of origin, distance fallen and volume of drop. *I.A.B.P.A. News*, Vol. 2, No. 1, 12–16.

Laber, T.L., and Epstein, B. 1983. *Experiments and Practical Exercises in Bloodstain Pattern Analysis*. Minneapolis, MN: Callen Publishing Company.

LaCavera, A. 1972. Medicolegal identification of bloodstains by means of precipitating serums. *Med. Leg. Domm. Corpor.* (Paris) 5, 41–42, January–March (France).

———. 1972. Medicolegal investigation of mixed bloodstains by means of animal anti-hemoglobin immune serums. *Med. Leg. Domm. Corpor.* (Paris) 5, 43–44, January–March (France).

LaCavera, A., et al. 1972. Identification of ABO blood groups by an absorption-elution micro method. *Med. Leg. Domm. Corpor.* (Paris) 5, 55–56, January–March (France).

Landsteiner, K. 1903. Individual blood differences in forensic practice. *Zeit fur Medizinalbeamte* 16, (3):85.

———. 1901. Agglutination differences of human blood. *Wein Klin Woch* XLVI.

Landsteiner, K., and Levine, P. 1927. Further observations on individual differences of human blood. *Proceedings of the Society of Experimental Biology and Medicine*, 24, 941.

———. 1927. New agglutinable factor differentiating individual human bloods. *Proceedings of the Society for Experimental Biology and Medicine* XXIV, 600.

Landsteiner, K., and Weiner, A.S. 1940. An agglutinable factor in human blood recognized by immune sera for rhesus blood. *Proceedings of the Society for Experimental Biology and Medicine* XLIII, 43.

Lang, B.G. 1976. The assay of ABO antisera intended for use in the grouping of bloodstains. *Journal of the Forensic Science Society* 16(1), 55–60, January.

———. 1976. The use of bovine serum albumin for H antigen typing in bloodstains. *Journal of the Forensic Science Society* 16(1), 61–66, January.

Lappas, N.T. 1981. The identification of human bloodstains by means of thin layer immunoassay—a preliminary report. *Journal of the Forensic Science Society* 21(4), 301–305, October.

Lappas, N.T., et al. 1981. The identification of human bloodstains by means of a micro-thin layer immunoassay procedure. *Journal of Forensic Sciences* 26(3), 564–569, July.

Lattes, L. 1923. Diagnosis of individual blood groups. *Ann. Med. Leg. et Crim.* V, 1923.

Laux, D.L., et al. 1983. The relative indices of efficiency for selected methods of bloodstain analysis. *Journal of Forensic Sciences* 28(4), 1000–1003, October.

Lee, H.C. 1982. "Identification and Grouping of Bloodstains." In *Forensic Science Handbook*, Richard Saferstein, Ed. Englewood Cliffs, NJ: Prentice-Hall, Inc.

———. 1986. Estimation of original volume of bloodstain. *IAI News*, July.

———. 1986. Estimation of original volume of bloodstains. *Identification News*, July.

Lee, H.C., et al. 1985. Simultaneous identification and determination of species origin, ABH antigens, and isoenzyme markers in the same bloodstain. *Forensic Sci. Int.* 29(3–4), 191–198, November–December.

———. 1976. A precipitin inhibition test on denatured bloodstains for the determination of human origin. *Journal of Forensic Sciences* 21(4), 804–810, October.

Lee, H.C., Gaensslen, R.E., and Pagliaro, E.M. 1983. Determination of the volume of a single bloodstain. AAFS, 38th Annual Meeting, Abstract B-12.

Lee, H.C., Gaensslen, R.E., and Pagliaro, E.M. 1986. Bloodstain volume estimation. *I.A.B.P.A. News*, Vol. 3, No. 2, 47–54.

Lenoir, L., et al. 1972. Identification of the chemical, serologic, and immunologic characteristics of human bloodstains on clothing dry cleaned by a standard method. *Med. Leg. Domm Corpor.* (Paris) 5, 71–73, January–March (France).

———. 1966. Determination of Gm groups on bloodstains. *Ann. Med. Leg.* (Paris) 46, 191–193, May–June (France).

LeRoy, H.A. 1983. Bloodstain pattern interpretation. *Identification Newsletter of the Canadian Identification Society*, January.

Levkov, J.S. 1987. A method for the determination of MN antigens in dried blood. *Journal of Forensic Sciences*, Vol. 32, No. 2, pp. 357–363, March.

Lincoln, P.J. 1980. Blood Group Evidence for the Defense. *Med. Sci., Law* 20(4), 239–245, October.

Lincoln, P.J., and Dodd, B. 1968. ABH groups in hair: Mixed agglutination. *Med., Sci., Law* 8:1, 41.

Lincoln, P.J., et al. 1984. "Experience in the detection of red cell antigens and HLA antigens in bloodstains. *Haematologia* 17(2), 299–305 (Budapest).

———. 1979. Psychic surgery—a serological investigation. *Lancet* 1(8127), 1187–1198, June.

———. 1968. The detection of the Rh antigens C, Cw, c,D,E,e, and the antigen S of the MnSs system in bloodstains. *Med., Sci., Law* 8, 288–295, October.

———. 1975. The application of a micro-elution technique using anti-human globulin for the detection of the S, s, K, Fya, Fyb, and Jka antigens in stains. *Med. Sci., Law* 15(2), 91–101, April.

Lins, G., et al. 1982. The use of remission analysis for direct colorometric determination of age of bloodstains. *Journal of Legal Medicine* 88(1–2), 13–22 (Germany).

Liu, J.H., et al. 1980. An exploratory study on the characterization of A1 and A2 bloodstains using a fluorescence immunoassay. *Journal of Forensic Sciences* 25(3), 686–690, July.

Liubinskaia, S.I., et al. 1975. Study of the Y chromatin in bloodstains. *Sudebno-Meditsinskaia Ekspertiza* 18(3), 17–20, July–September (Russia).

Logvinenko, A.G. 1975. Possibility of determining the age of bloodstains by a colorimetric method. *Sudebno-Meditsinskaia Ekspertiza* 18(4), 12–16, October–December (Russia).

———. 1985. Relation between the principle parameters of the color of bloodstains, storage conditions, and time of formation. *Sudebno-Meditsinskaia Ekspertiza* 28(3), 26–28, July–September (Russia).

———. 1978. Modification of a comparison colorimetry method for establishing the age of bloodstains. *Sudebno-Meditsinskaia Ekspertiza* 21(1), 31–33, January–March (Russia).

Longia, H.S. 1976. Dried blood typing—hinged antibody technique for antigen detection. *Indian Journal of Experimental Biology* 14(3), 336–338, May.

Lontai, I., et al. 1979. Who drove the automobile. *Morphologiai Es Igazsagugyi Orvisi Szemle* 19(2), 152, April (Hungary).

Lotterle, J. 1982. HLA typing of bloodstains—a comparison of methods (absorption method, absorption-elution methods). *Acta Med. Leg. Soc.* (Liege) 32, 581–584 (Germany).

———. 1981. HLA typing of bloodstains—investigations with an absorption test—preliminary report. *Journal of Legal Medicine* 87(3), 217–224 (Germany).

Lotterle, J., et al. 1986. Study of the antigens of the ABO system in bloodstains with monoclonal antisera. *Beitr. Gerichtl. Med.* 44, 87–92 (Germany).

———. 1985. Scanning electron microscopy and biochemical studies on the adhesion of dried blood to cotton. *Beitr. Gerichtl. Med.* 43, 265–270 (Germany).

———. 1986. Micromethod for the detection of erythrocyte antigens in bloodstains. *Journal of Legal Medicine* 96(3), 163–171 (Germany).

Lytle, L.T., et al. 1978. Chemiluminescence in the visualization of forensic bloodstains. *Journal of Forensic Sciences* 23(3), 550–562, July.

MacDonald, J.E. 1954. The shape of rain drops. *Scientific American,* February.

MacDonell, H.L. 1977. Preserving bloodstain evidence at crime scenes. *Law and Order,* Vol. 25, pp. 66–69, April.

———. 1982. Bloodstain pattern interpretation. Laboratory of Forensic Science, Corning, New York.

———. 1981. "Criminalistics—Bloodstain Examination." In *Forensic Sci-*

ences, Vol. 3, Cyril Wecht, Ed., pp. 37-1–37-26. New York, NY: Mathew Bender.

———. 1977. Reconstruction of a homicide. *Law and Order*, Vol. 25, No. 7, 26–31, July.

———. 1971. "Interpretation of Bloodstains: Physical Considerations." In *Legal Medicine Annual*, Cyril Wecht, Ed., pp. 91–136. New York, NY: Appleton-Century-Crofts.

MacDonell, H.L., and Bialousz, L. 1971. Flight characteristics and stain patterns of human blood. United States Department of Justice, Law Enforcement Administrative Assistance Administration, Washington, DC.

———. 1973. *Laboratory Manual on the Geometric Interpretation of Human Bloodstain Evidence*. Laboratory of Forensic Sciences, Corning, New York.

MacDonell, H.L., and Brooks, B. 1977. "Detection and Significance of Blood in Firearms." In *Legal Medicine Annual*, Cyril Wecht, Ed., pp. 185–199. New York, NY: Appleton-Century-Crofts.

MacDonell, H.L., and Panchou, C. 1979. Bloodstain patterns on human skin. *Journal of the Canadian Society of Forensic Science*, Vol. 12, No. 3, 134–141, September.

———. 1979. Bloodstain pattern interpretation. *Identification News*, Vol. 29, 3–5, February.

Madea, B., et al. 1986. Morphologic analysis of bloodstains in a histologic section. *Beitr. Gerichtl. Med.* 44, 81–85 (Germany).

Madivale, M.S., et al. 1971. An improved absorption-elution method for ABO group identification in bloodstains. Archiv Fur Kriminologie 147, 168–175, May–June (Germany).

———. 1972. Determination of blood group from bloodstains using the isoenzyme test. Archiv Fur Kriminologie 150(5–6), 160–166, November–December (Germany).

Magnushevskaia, E.L. 1976. Possibility of species determination of bloodstains treated with alcohol and acridine orange. *Sudebno-Meditsinskaia Ekspertiza* 19(3), 39, July–September (Russia).

Majsky, A. 1986. Detection of HLA antigens in bloodstains. *Cas Lek Cesk* 125(28), 865–868, July (Czechoslovakia).

Manunza, P., et al. 1966. Immunofluorescent technics in the diagnosis of species from bloodstains—preliminary note. *Minerva Medicolegal* 86, 184–5, July–August (Italy).

Marcinkowski, T. 1968. Attempts of using immunoelectrophoresis for identification of blood traces. *Wiadomosci Lekarskie* 21, 1027–1030, June (Poland).

Mardesic, D., et al. 1983. Estimation of 17-alpha-hydroxyprogesterone in dried blood spots for mass screening of newborn infants with congenital adrenal hyperplasia. *Acta Med. Iugosi* 37(2), 95–100.

Marsters, R., and Schlein, F. 1958. Factors affecting the deterioration of dried bloodstains. *Journal of Forensic Sciences* 3, 288–302.

Martin, E.W. 1971. "Hazards of Medication." In *Adverse Drug Reactions—Blood Dyscrasias*, p. 338. Philadelphia, PA: J.B. Lippincott Company.

Martin, P.D. 1978. A manual method for the detection of the Rh antigen in dried bloodstains. *Journal of the Forensic Science Society*, 17(2–3), 139–142, April–July.

Marziano, E. 1968. Research on the immunological diagnosis of pregnancy using urine and bloodstains of various ages. *Minerva Medicoleg.* 88, 55–58, January–April (Italy).

McDowall, M.J., et al. 1978. Increased sensitivity of tests for the detection of blood group antigens in stains using a low ionic strength medium. *Med. Sci., Law* 18(1), 16–23, January.

———. 1978. Observations of the use of an autoanalyzer and a manual technique for the detection of the red cell antigens C, D, E, c, K, and S in bloodstains. *Journal of Forensic Sciences* 11(2), 155–164, March–April.

Menczer, G., et al. 1982. Pregnancy specific beta-1-glycoprotein (SP1) in bloodstains. *Morphologiai Es Igazsagugyi Orvosi Szemle* 22(2), 151–153, April (Hungary).

Merli, S., et al. 1967. Determination in bloodstains of the factors of the Inv system—preliminary findings on Inv (1). *Zacchia* 3, 249–255, April–June (Italy).

Messler, H., et al. 1982. The effect of textile technical parameters of a bloodstained fabric on its absorption of blood. Arch. Kriminol, 169(3–4), 99–113, March–April (Germany).

Mihailovic, M., et al. 1972. "Who was Driving an Automobile." *Archiv Fur Kriminologie* 149, 155–157, May–June (Germany).

Mikama, Y., et al. 1966. Consecutive application of preliminary blood test, fibrin plate method, and group specific double combination method for the identification of human blood type with a minute quantity of bloodstained material. *Japan Journal of Legal Medicine* 20, 207–212, March.

Misawa, S. 1968. Selection of anti-sera for stain grouping and the significance of IgM, Ig, and IgG-Globulin antibody in the absorption test, elution test, and mixed agglutination method. *Japan Journal of Legal Medicine* 22, 431–453, September (Japan).

Miscicka, D., et al. 1977. Determination of phenotypes of phosphoglucomutase (PGM1) in bloodstains by cellulose acetate electrophoresis. *Journal of Legal Medicine* 79(4), 297–300, May (Germany).

Mittmeyer, H.J. 1983. Studies on determining transformations in the Gm and inv system. *Beitr. Gerichtl. Med.* 41, 191–197 (Germany).

Moenssens, A.A., Inbau, F.E. 1978. *Scientific Evidence in Criminal Cases, 2nd Edition.* Mineola, NY: The Foundation Press, Inc.

Mokashi, R.H., et al. 1974. Isoenzyme methods in the differentiation of human and monkey blood. *Archiv Fur Kriminologie* 153(1–2), 48–53, January–February (Germany).

Moller, M.R., et al. 1977. Radioimmunological detection of morphine in stains of blood and urine. *Journal of Legal Medicine* 79(2), 103–107, March.

Montaldo, S., et al. 1982. Chronological diagnosis of bloodstains by alpha s ratio method extracted in pH 7.9 and 9.8 buffered solutions. *Acta Med. Leg. Soc.* (Liege) 32, 599–604.

Moreau, P., and Dodinval, D. 1962. Classic Methods for Identification of Blood Groups. 29th International Congress of Med. Leg. and Med. Sociale, Marseilles, France.

Morgan, B.R., et al. 1967. Sub-typing of group A bloodstains. *Med., Sci., Law* 7, 82–83, April.

Morrison, R., et al. 1985. Immunofixation of complement component C3 phenotypes in bloodstains after cellulose acetate electrophoresis. *Journal of Forensic Sciences* 30(4), 1221–1225, October.

Moureau, P. 1963. "Determination of Blood Groups in Bloodstains." In *Methods of Forensic Science, Vol. 2.* New York, NY: Interscience Publishing Co.

Mudd, J.L. 1958. A microplate method for reverse ABO typing of bloodstains. *Journal of Forensic Science* 31(2), 418–425, April.

Muller, M., 1958. Antibody-antigen reactions in gel. *Larc Medicale,* XXX 4, 218 (France).

Muller, M., et al. 1966. Identification of the biological characteristics of bloodstains on garments submitted to dry cleaning technics. *Ann. Med. Leg.* (Paris) 46, 188–190, May–June (France).

Muller, P.H., et al. 1972. Value and limitations of present methods of medicolegal identification of bloodstains. *Med. Leg. Domm. Corpor.* (Paris) 5, 3–35, January–March (France).

Myhre, B.A. 1984. The change in criminalistic methods for bloodstain analysis in California. *Haematologia* 17(2), 307–310 (Budapest).

Nelson, M.S., et al. 1983. A feasibility study of human leucocyte antigen (HLA) typing for dried bloodstains. *Journal of Forensic Science* 28(3), 608–614, July.

Nelson, M., Turner, L., and Reisner, E. 1980. A feasibility study of human leucocyte antigen (HLA) typing from dried bloodstains. *Journal of Forensic Sciences,* Vol. 25, No. 3, pp. 479–498.

Ni, J.T., et al. 1983. Application of disc electrophoresis with polyacrylamide in the examination of haptoglobins in bloodstains. *Chung-Hua I Hsueh Tsa Chih* 63(5), 274–277, May (China).

Nickolls, L.C., and Pereira, M. 1962. A study of modern methods of grouping dried bloodstains. *Medicine, Science, and the Law* 2, 172–179.

Nicolas, G., et al. 1969. Importance of blood groups in the medicolegal study of bloodstains. *Rev. Franc Transfus.* 12 (Suppl.), 169–182 (France).

Nikolenko, O.V. 1975. Determination of haptoglobin groups in bloodstains—2. *Sudebno-Metitsinskaia Ekspertiza* 18(1), 39–41, January–March (Russia).

Noppinger, K.E., et al. 1981. The determination of carbonic anhydrase—2 phenotypes in dried bloodstains by cellulose acetate electrophoresis. *Journal of Forensic Sciences* 26(1), 176–180, January.

Nuorteva, P. 1974. Age determination of a bloodstain in a decaying shirt by entomological means. *Journal of Forensic Sciences* 3(1), 89–94, February.

Oepen, I., et al. 1977. A photometric method for the diagnosis of pregnancy in bloodstains by determination of heat stable alkaline phosphatase (E.C. 3.1.3.1)—a modification of Oya, Asano, and Fuwa's Technique. *Journal of Legal Medicine* 79(2), 83–86, March (Germany).

———. 1978. LDH type determination on bloodstains. *Archiv Fur Kriminologie* 161(3–4), 105–115, March–April (Germany).

———. 1978. Differentiation between the subgroups A1 and A2 on bloodstains. *Archiv Fur Kriminologie* 161(5–6), 153–167, May–June (Germany).

Olkhovik, V.P. 1985. Use of a method of isotachophoresis on cellulose acetate films for detecting agglutinins in traces of blood. *Sudebno-Metitsinskaia Ekspertiza* 28(4), 30–32, October–December (Russia).

Olkhovik, V.P., et al. 1986. Use of anti-A-Hp (helix pomatia) reagent for studying dried blood. *Sudebno-Metitsinskaia Ekspertiza* 29(1), 53–54, January–March (Russia).

Orfanos, A.P., et al. 1986. Microassay for estimation of galactose-1-phosphate in dried blood specimens. *Clin. Biochem.* 19(4), 225–228, August.

Ortho Diagnostics, 1969. "The ABO and Rh Systems." Raritan, NJ: Ortho Diagnostics and Pharmaceutical Co.

Oshima, M., et al. 1982. Identification of species specific hemoglobin by iso-electric focusing. *Forensic Sci. Int.* 20(3), 277–286, November–December.

Ota, S., et al. 1965. Identification of menstrual bloodstains—experimental studies on the detection of glycogen of vaginal epithelial cells. *Japan Journal of Legal Medicine* 19, 300–305, July (Japan).

————. 1979. Increased responsiveness of electric precipitation (electro-synerese) by means of a chemical method. *Journal of Legal Medicine* 83(2), 101–104, July.

Ouchterlony, A. 1949. Antibody—antigen reactions in gels. *Acta Path and Microbiol. Scand.* XXVI, 507.

Owen, G.W., et al. 1975. Blood and semen stains in outer clothing and shoes not related to crime—report of a survey using presumptive tests. *Journal of Forensic Sciences* 20(2), 391–403, April.

Oya, M., et al. 1976. An improved method for the detection of haptoglobin types from bloodstains. *Journal of Legal Medicine* 77, 105–107, February (Germany).

————. 1986. Isoenzyme determinations as aids in the identification of biological traces. *Journal of Legal Medicine* 96(4) 309–312 (Germany).

————. 1975. Demonstration of placental aminopeptidase isozymes by disk electrophoresis and its application to the forensic pregnancy test from bloodstains. *Journal of Forensic Sciences* 6(1–2), 73–81, August–October.

Parkin, B.H., et al. 1975. The typing of esterase D in human bloodstains. *Med. Sci., Law* 15(2), 102–105, April.

Pavlova, A.Z., et al. 1984. Use of chromogens for the identification of bloodstains. *Sudebno-Metitsinskaia Ekspertiza* 27(2), 37–39, April–June (Russia).

Pereira, M. 1972. Recent developments in the analysis of dried bloodstains in England. *Med. Leg. Domm Corpor.* (Paris) 5, 36–39, January–March (France).

————. 1971. Automated Rh genotyping of dried bloodstains. *Technicon Quarterly* 1, III, 16–18.

————. 1963. The identification of MN groups in dried bloodstains. *Medicine, Science, and the Law*, Vol. 18, No. 1, pp. 268–271.

Peters, V.K. 1966. A quick fixative mixture of nikiforev. *Lab. Delo* 2, 119 (Russia).

Pex, J.O., and Vaughan, C.H. 1987. Observations of high velocity bloodspatter on adjacent objects. *Journal of Forensic Sciences*, Vol. 32, No. 6, pp. 1587–1594, November.

Phillips, A.P. 1974. The potential of nephelometric immunoprecipitin quantitation in forensic science. *Journal of the Forensic Science Society* 14(2), 135–136, April.

Phillips, A.P., et al. 1972. Improved Y chromosome fluorescence in the presence of magnesium ions. *Journal of the Forensic Science Society* 12, 361–362, April.

————. 1974. The identification of male bloodstains by Y chromosome fluorescence. *Journal of the Forensic Science Society* 14(1), 47–54, January.

Pirek, A., et al. 1984. Blood glucose monitoring using dried spots. *Vnitrni Lekarstvi* 30(1), 60–65, January (Czechoslovakia).

Pizzola, P.A., Roth, S., and DeForest, P.R. 1986. Blood droplet dynamics—I. *Journal of Forensic Sciences*, Vol. 31, No. 1, pp. 36–49, January.

————. 1986. Blood droplet dynamics—II. *Journal of Forensic Sciences*, Vol. 31, No. 1, pp. 50–56, January.

Platt, S.R. 1982. The effects of the argon ion laser on subsequent blood examinations. *Journal of Forensic Sciences* 227(3), 726–728, July.

Podlecki, M.A., et al. 1985. Detectability of group-specific component (Gc) in aged bloodstains. *Journal of Forensic Sciences* 30(2), 398–404, April.

Pollet, P. 1968. Contribution to the direct determination of erythrocyte group factors in putrified or hemolyzed bloodstains—medicolegal application. *Bruxelles Med.* 48, 165–170, March (France).

Popov, I., et al. 1986. Determination of alpha-fetoprotein in bloodstains. *Sudebno-Metitsinskaia Ekspertiza* 29(1), 31–32, January–March (Russia).

Potapov, M.I., et al. 1981. Serological method of determining bloodstains belonging to fetuses and newborn infants. *Sudebno-Metitsinskaia Ekspertiza* 24(1), 40–42, January–March (Russia).

Potapov, M.I. 1970. Establishing the species origin of rabbit bloodstains using evonymus europaea extract. *Sudebno-Metitsinskaia Ekspertiza* 13, 24–27, January–March (Russia).

————. 1970. Tests on bloodstains and human excreta by means of the group lectin anti-B1 (euonymus alata). *Folia Haematologica* (Leipzig) 93, 458–464 (Germany).

————. 1978. Importance of biological knowledge in the expertise of species blood classification. *Sudebno-Metitsinskaia Ekspertiza* 21(1), 22–26, January–March (Russia).

————. 1984. Determination of GlM(−1) in bloodstains. *Sudebno-Metitsinskaia Ekspertiza* 27(4), 40–41, October–December (Russia).

Race, R.R., and Sanger, R. 1968. *Blood Groups in Man, 5th Edition.* Philadelphia, PA: F.A. Davis Co.

Rand, S., et al. 1986. Systematic aspects of the stain picture in blood spray stains caused by impact. *Beitr. Gerichtl. Med.* 44, 71–80 (Germany).

————. 1985. Morphology of bloodstains. *Beitr. Gerichtl. Med.* 43, 259–264 (Germany).

Randall, T., et al. 1980. A method of phenotyping erythrocyte acid phosphatase by iso-electric focusing. *Med. Sci., Law* 20(1), 43–47, January.

Raszeja, S. 1966. Limits of specificity in estimating the species origin of blood. *Journal of Forensic Science* 13, 138–140, October–December.

Raymond, M.A., et al. 1983. Haemoglobin typing as an aid to species identification. *Central African Journal of Medicine* 29(3), 51–53, March.

Rittner, C., et al. 1974. HLA typing in dried bloodstains—I—specificity and reliability of the inhibition test. *Journal of Immunogenetics* 1(2), 99–111, April.

Romanovski, U. 1985. Effects of ultrasonics on the detection of M and N group antigens in bloodstains. *Sudebno Metitsinskaia Ekspertiza* 28(1), 31–32, January–March (Russia).

Rothwell, T.J. 1985. The frequency of occurrence of various human blood groups in the United Kingdom with observations on their regional variation. *Journal of the Forensic Science Society*, Vol. 25, No. 2, pp. 135–144, March–April.

Rotter, R. 1956. Splenic infarct in sickelemia during flight. *Annals of Internal Medicine* 44:257.

Roychowdhury, A.B. 1974. Triple bonded agglutination in bloodstains on medicolegal exhibits. *Journal of the Indian Medical Association* 63(1), 8–10, July.

————. 1978. Triple bonded agglutination in bloodstains of forensic exhibits. *Journal of the Indian Medical Association* 71(7), 185–188, October.

Rupcheva, L. 1980. Determination of adenylate kinase (AK) phenotypes in bloodstains. *Eksperimentalna Meditsina I Morfologiia* 19(4), 220–224 (Bulgaria).

Sachdeva, M.P., et al. 1984. Esterase D polymorphism in Indians—stability studies in bloodstains. *Med., Sci., Law* 24(2), 142–145, April.

Saenger, M.S., et al. 1975. A cellulose acetate membrane technique for the determination of adenylate kinase types in bloodstains. *Journal of Forensic Sciences* 20(4), 643–646, October.

Sagisaka, K. 1974. MN grouping of bloodstains by the group specific double combination method. *Tohoku Journal of Experimental Medicine* 113(3), 201–211, July.

Sallee, P.J., et al. 1984. Attempts to determine the Lewis phenotypes of dried bloodstains. *Journal of Forensic Sciences* 29(1), 75–79, January.

Saneshige, Y., et al. 1980. Blood typing of bloodstains on sweat stains by the isoagglutinins detection method. *Forensic Sci. Int.* 15(2), 161–168, March–April.

Sant-Paul, M., et al. 1972. Modifications observed by bidimensional immunoelectrophoresis during the putrefactive degradation of serum proteins. *Med. Leg. Domm Corpor.* (Paris) 5, 68–70, January–March (France).

Santini, M., et al. 1964. General and specific diagnosis of bloodstains with immunoelectrophoresis. *Bollettino-Societa Italiana Biologia Sperimentale* 40, 537–538, June (Italy).

Schleyer, R. 1962. "Investigation of Biological Stains with Regard to Species Origin." In *Methods of Forensic Science*, Vol. 1. New York, NY: Interscience Publishing Co.

Schmitter, H. 1980. The ability to prove blood group antigens Gm(1,2,4,10) and InV (1) in bloodstains independently of the protein concentration in the stain extract. *Archiv Fur Kriminologie* 165(1–2), 35–39 (Germany).

Schwerd, W., et al. 1980. Demonstration of ABO substances in blood traces with the absorption-elution method. *Archiv Fur Kriminologie* 165(5–6), 143–147 (Germany).

Schwerd, W. 1978. Determination of blood group N in blood traces using phytaagglutinin. *Beitr. Gerichtl. Med.* 36, 81–83 (Germany).

————. 1978. On the proof of the MN-differentiation from blood samples. *Journal of Legal Medicine* 80(4), 293–298, 31, January (Germany).

————. 1975. Proof of value of blood trace studies. *Beitr. Gerichtl. Med.* 33, 243–246 (Germany).

Schwerd, W., et al. 1977. Influencing factors of previous testing on blood determination. *Journal of Legal Medicine* 80(3), 221–225, 18, November (Germany).

Schwinger, E. 1972. Sex determination from bloodstains. *Beitr. Gerichtl. Med.* 29, 210 (Germany).

Schwinger, E., et al. 1977. How reliable is sex determination in traces of blood? *Beitr. Gerichtl. Med.* 35, 267–271 (Germany).

Seifert, B., et al. 1985. Stability of beta-HCG in old bloodstains. *Journal of Legal Medicine* 95(4), 255–258 (Germany).

Sensabaugh, G.F. 1982. "Biochemical Markers of Individuality." In *Forensic Science Handbook*, Richard Saferstein, Ed. Englewood Cliffs, NJ: Prentice-Hall, Inc.

Shaid, G., et al. 1973. Sex determination in blood samples and bloodstains of male individuals. *Archiv Fur Kriminologie* 151(1–2), 41–48, January–February (Germany).

Shaler, R.C. 1982. Interpretation of Gm testing results—two case histories. *Journal of Forensic Sciences* 27(1), 231–235, January.

Shaler, R.C., et al. 1978. MN determination in bloodstains—selective destruction of cross-reacting activity. *Journal of Forensic Sciences* 23(3), 570–576, July.

Shinomiya, T., et al. 1982. Value of immunoelectrophoresis in expert evaluation of bloodstains in forensic medicine. *Acta Med. Leg. Soc.* (Liege) 32, 605–612 (France).

———. 1978. Immunoelectrophoresis used for identification of bloodstains in forensic medicine. *Journal of Forensic Sciences* 12(2), 157–163, September–October (France).

Shtereva, V. 1975. Determination of antigens M and N in bloodstains by an absorption-elution method. *Eksp Med. Morfol.* 17(4), 227–231 (Bulgaria).

Simeoni, E. 1985. Determination of plasminogen (PLG) phenotype distribution and gene frequency in Schleswig-Holstein trace studies. *Beitr. Gerichtl. Med.* 43, 249–254 (Germany).

Sivaram, S., et al. 1975. Differentiation between stains of human blood and blood of monkey. *Journal of Forensic Sciences* 6(3), 145–152, December.

Smerling, M. 1978. Sanguine Propio?—blood trace analysis of a bible handed down by Baron Friedrich von der Trenck. *Beitr. Gerichtl. Med.* 36, 107–118 (Germany).

Smith, F.P. 1981. Detection of amphetamine in bloodstains, semen, seminal stains, saliva and saliva stains. *Forensic Sci. Int.* 17(3), 225–228, May–June.

———. 1981. Detection of digoxin in bloodstains. *Journal of Forensic Sciences* 26(1), 193–197, January.

Smith, F.P., et al. 1980. Detection of drugs in bloodstains II—morphine. *Journal of Forensic Sciences* 25(2), 369–373, April.

Soyama, K., et al. 1981. Sensitive fluoremetric detection of heat stable alkaline phosphatase from bloodstains for the forensic diagnosis of pregnancy. *Forensic Sci. Int.* 18(2), 195–199, September–October.

Stafunsky, M., et al. 1977. Determination of alpha-1-fetoprotein in bloodstains by means of electrophoresis on cellulose acetate. *Journal of Legal Medicine* 79(2), 81–82, March (Germany).

Stajduhar-Caric, Z. 1975. Determination of pregnancy from a bloodstain. *Rad. Med. Fak. Zagrebu* 23, 73–76, 1975 (Scr).

———. 1973. Our experiences in the determination of blood groups from a bloodstain using the chisum rapid method. *Rad. Med. Fak. Zagrebu* 21, 73–77 (Scr).

Stanislavskii, L.V. 1983. Inertial deformation of blood traces—sign of infliction of blows with a specific weapon. *Sudebno-Metitsinskaia Ekspertiza*, 26(4), 16–19, October–December (Russia).

Stedman, R. 1972. Human population frequencies in twelve blood grouping systems. *Journal of the Forensic Science Society*, Vol. 12, pp. 379–413.

———. 1985. Blood group frequencies of immigrant and indigenous populations from southeast England. *Journal of the Forensic Science Society*, Vol. 25, No. 2, pp. 95–134, March–April.

Stegnova, T.V. 1980. Present day potentials for detecting blood and secretions in mixed stains. *Sudebno-Metitsinskaia Ekspertiza* 23(3), 52–53 (Russia).

Stephens, B.G., and Allen, T.B. 1983. Backspatter of blood from gunshot wounds—observations and experimental simulation. *Journal of Forensic Sciences*, Vol. 28, No. 2, pp. 437–439, April.

Stolorow, M.D., et al. 1979. An efficient method to eliminate streaking in the electrophoretic analysis of haptoglobin in bloodstains. *Journal of Forensic Sciences* 24(4), 856–863, October.

Stombaugh, P.M., Jr., et al. 1978. Factors affecting the use of lactic dehydrogenase as a means of bloodstain differentiation. *Journal of Forensic Sciences* 23(1), 94–105, January.

———. 1977. Determination of adenylate kinase variants in two Washington, D.C. population samples—a microcellulose acetate procedure. *Journal of Forensic Sciences* 22(3), 590–595, July.

Strejc, P., et al. 1986. Detection of urinary substances in stains from amniotic fluid, urine, and the blood of pregnant women using thin layer chromatography. *Soud Lek*, 31(1), 5–7, March (Czechoslovakia).

Stuver, W.C., Shaler, R.C., et al. 1975. "Forensic Bloodstains and Physiological Fluid Analysis." In *Forensic Science*, Geoffrey Davies, Ed. American Chemical Society, Washington, DC.

Suleimenova, G.M. 1977. Variants of setting up the comparative agar precipitation reaction for the differentiation of the blood of phylogenetically related animals. *Sudebno-Metitsinskaia Ekspertiza* 20(3), 38–40, July–September (Russia).

Suyama, H., et al. 1976. Identification of blood groups and isoenzymic phenotypes from bloodstains, heart blood, and nervous tissues after transfusion. *Journal of Forensic Sciences* 8(3), 277–280, November–December.

Suzuki, T. 1970. Blood grouping of bloodstains by immuno-electron microscopy. *Tohoku Journal of Experimental Medicine* 101, 1–7, May.

———. 1969. Detection of Gc types of bloodstains. *Med. Biol.* (Tokyo) 79, 159–162, October (Japan).

Suzutani, T., et al. 1979. Studies on medicolegal diagnosis in cold district—bloodshed on the snow. *Hokkaido Igaku Zasshi* 54(5), 461–465, September (Japan).

Svirskii, M.S. 1984. Use of fibrinolysin in studying haptoglobin in bloodstains. *Sudebno-Metitsinskaia Ekspertiza* 27(1), 33–36, January–March (Russia).

———. 1981. Determination of the hemoglobin and haptoglobin fractions in studying bloodstains by electrophoresis on vertical polyacrylamide gel plates. *Sudebno-Metitsinskaia Ekspertiza* 24(2), 41–44, April–June (Russia).

———. 1970. Differentiation of group antigens of sperm and blood in mixed stains by the absorption-elution method. *Sudebno-Metitsinskaia Ekspertiza* 13, 27–29, January–March (Russia).

Sweet, G.H., et al. 1976. Studies by crossed electroimmunodiffusion on the individuality and sexual origin of bloodstains. *Journal of Forensic Sciences* 21(3), 498–509, July.

———. 1976. Human bloodstains—individualization by crossed electroimmunodiffusion. *Science* 192(4243), 1012–1014, June.

Swinburne, L.M. 1962. The identification of skin. *Medicine, Science, and the Law* 3:3.

Szendrenyi, J., et al. 1980. The measurement of testosterone content of bloodstains for the criminalistic determination of sex. *Journal of Legal Medicine* 85(4), 263–267 (Germany).

Tahir, M.A. 1984. Gm(11) grouping of dried bloodstains. *Journal of Forensic Sciences* 29(4), 1178–1182, October.

Tajima, T. 1967. Agglutinin-absorbing latex method for blood grouping of bloodstains and other specimens. *Tohoku Journal of Experimental Medicine* 91, 331–346, April.

Takagi, M.J. 1968. Medicolegal studies on group determination of human blood and saliva stains by the elution method. *Tokyo Med. Coll.* 26, 453–471, July.

Takatori, T., Tustsubuchi, Y., and Terazawa, K. 1987. Lewis typing of human bloodstains by enzyme-linked immunosorbent assay (ELISA) using monoclonal anti-LeA and anti-LeB. *Journal of Forensic Sciences*, Vol. 32, No. 4, pp. 900–905, July.

Tamaki, Y., et al. 1983. Identification of human bloodstains by enzyme-linked immunosorbant assay (ELISA). *Nippon Hoigaku Zasshi* 37(2), 84–87, April.

———. 1984. Identification of human blood with hybridoma derived antibody to human immunoglobin G. *Journal of Forensic Sciences* 29(3), 885–888, July.

Tanaka, N., et al. 1982. Human-type blood group activities in bloodstains and heated liver tissue specimens of some species of vertebrates. *Acta Med. Leg. Soc.* (Liege) 32, 577–580.

Tesar, J. 1967. Immunological pregnancy test on bloodstains using the pregnosticon method. *Zacchia* 3, 84–88, January–March (France).

Tesar, J., et al. 1974. Possibility and sensitivity of M,N determination in bloodstains. *Ceskoslovenska Patologie* 10(3), 17–19, August (Czechoslovakia).

Thomsen, J.L. 1980. An investigation of some of the factors influencing the results of Y chromosome detection in bloodstains. *Forensic Sci. Int.* 16(2), 111–117, September–October.

———. 1980. The effect of temperature on Y chromosome detection in bloodstains. *Forensic Sci. Int.* 16(2), 139–143, September–October.

———. 1978. Influence of the temperature on the detection of fluorescent Y bodies in bloodstains. *Forensic Sci.* 11(2), 123–126, March–April.

———. 1975. An improved method for the determination of Y chromosomes in bloodstains. *Journal of Legal Medicine* 76(2), 81–86, November (Germany).

Thomsen, J.L., et al. 1985. The effect of various fixatives on Y-chromosome detection in leucocytes. *Forensic Sci. Int.* 29(1–2), 21–27, September–October.

Thorwald, J. 1966. "Forensic Serology." In *Crime and Science.* New York, NY: Harcourt, Brace, and World Co.

———. 1964. *Century of the Detective.* New York, NY: Harcourt, Brace, and World Co.

Tobe, S. 1966. Identification of human blood by means of fibrin plate method—using cloths stained with blood but washed with cleansers. *Japan Journal of Legal Medicine* 20, 466–476, September.

Tomita, K. 1967. On the detection of blood groups from bloodstains containing detergent. *Hiroshima Journal of Medical Sciences* 16, 67–80, March.

Troger, H.D. 1973. Modified absorption-elution method for rapid determination of the ABO group in bloodstains. *Beitr. Gerichtl., Med.* 30, 445–448 (Germany).

Troger, H.D., et al. 1981. Serological tests in a case of so-called faith healing. *Beitr. Gerichtl. Med.* 39, 243–245 (Germany).

———. 1974. Time limits of Y chromosome determination from bloodstains and hair. *Beitr. Gerichtl. Med.* 32, 159–162 (Germany).

Tsutsumi, A., et al. 1983. Determination of the age of bloodstains by enzyme activities in blood cells. *Nippon Hoigaku Zasshi* 37(6), 770–776, December.

———. 1983. Heat stability of Y-chromatin in blood smears. *Nippon Hoigaku Zasshi* 37(6), 777–782, December.

Tumanov, A.K., et al. 1974. Determination of phenotype of the Gc system in bloodstains. *Sudebno-Metitsinskaia Ekspertiza* 17(4), 18–21, October–December (Russia).

Tumosa, C.S. 1982. The reaction of human anti-A and anti-B sera with animal bloodstains. *Journal of Legal Medicine* 89(2), 101–104 (Germany).

Turebaev, O.N. 1985. Establishment of the time of the formation of bloodstains. *Sudebno-Metitsinskaia Ekspertiza* 28(4), 29–30, October–December (Russia).

———. 1986. Establishment of the time of formation of bloodstains. *Sudebno-Metitsinskaia Ekspertiza* 29(1), 47–49, January–March (Russia).

———. 1986. Determining the dynamics of lactate dehydrogenase isoenzymes in bloodstains. *Sudebno-Metitsinskaia Ekspertiza* 29(2), 45–46, April–June (Russia).

Turowska, B. 1969. Group specific protein and enzyme systems in human bloodstains. *Folia Medica Cracoviensia* 11, 411–445 (Poland).

Turowska, B., et al. 1966. Preliminary studies on the determination of pseudo-cholinesterases C5+ and C5− in bloodstains. *Przeglad Lekarski* 22, 597–599 (Poland).

———. 1968. Serum cholinesterase type C5+ and C5− in human bloodstains. *Acta Medica Polona* 9, 213–215 (Poland).

Tyler, M.G., et al. 1986. Human bloodstain identification and sex determination in dried bloodstains using recombinant DNA techniques. *Forensic Sci. Int.* 31(4), 267–272, July.

Uhlenhuth, P.A. 1961. A method of differentiating blood groups. *Deutsche Medizinische Wochenschrift* No. 6, 7.

Uhlir, P. 1979. Decrease in the alcohol level in blood and urine stains. *Soudni Lekarstri* 24(1), 15–16, February (Czechoslovakia).

Umetsu, K., et al. 1984. Species identification of old bloodstains (approximately 60–670 years old) using anti-sera to human Hb and serum. *Nippon Hoigaku Zasshi* 38(2), 195–198, April (Japan).

Vagina, N.N. 1985. Stability of species-specific antigenic properties of serum proteins in bloodstains. *Sudebno-Metitsinskaia Ekspertiza* 28(1), 39–41, January–March (Russia).

———. 1986. Effect of cleansing agents on the detection of individual serum proteins in bloodstains. *Sudebno-Metitsinskaia Ekspertiza* 29(1), 32–33, January–March (Russia).

Vereshchaka, M.F. 1975. Sequential determination of A, B, H, P, and S antigens in a single incisure from a bloodstain. *Sudebno-Metitsinskaia Ekspertiza* 18(2), 47–48, April–June (Russia).

Villanueva, E., et al. 1972. Study of the degradation of certain proteins (albumin, transferrin, haptoglobin, and IgG immunoglobulin) during bloodstain aging. *Med. Leg. Domm Corpor.* (Paris) 5, 63–67, January–March (France).

———. 1972. Study of human haptoglobins by means of continuous density gradient polyacrylamide gel electrophoresis. *Med. Leg. Domm Corpor.* (Paris) 5, 48–51, January–March (France).

———. 1972. K-L quotient of K and L type chain immunoglobulins of Bence-Jones proteins—possibility of a medicolegal application to the individual diagnosis of blood. *Med. Leg. Domm. Corpor.* (Paris) 5, 57–62, January–March (France).

Watanabe, H. 1969. Ultraviolet spectrophotometric analyses of HbF and medicolegal identification of foetal bloodstains. *Japan Journal of Legal Medicine* 23, 170–178, March (Japan).

Weber, K. 1966. The use of chemiluminescence of luminol in forensic medicine and toxicology—I, identification of bloodstains. *Deutsch Z Ges, Gerichtl. Med.* 57, 410–423 (Germany).

Weiner, A.S. 1961, 1965. *Advances in Blood Grouping*, Vols. 1, 2. New York, NY: Grune and Stratton Co.

Welch, S.G. 1972. Glutamate-pyruvate transaminase in bloodstains. *Journal of the Forensic Science Society* 12, 605–607, October.

Werrett, D.J., et al. 1976. The detection of allergen—associated antibodies in bloodstains. *Journal of the Forensic Science Society* 16(2), 121–126, April.

———. 1976. Allergy profiles from bloodstains. *Clinical Allergy* 6(1), 75–77, January.

Westwood, S.A., et al. 1986. The typing of group-specific component in case bloodstains using narrow pH interval isoelectric focusing gels. *Journal of the Forensic Science Society* 26(4), 267–274, July–August.

White, R.B. 1986. Bloodstain patterns on fabrics—the effect of drop volume, dropping height, and impact angle. *Journal of the Canadian Society of Forensic Science*, Vol. 19, No. 1, pp. 3–36.

Whitehead, E.M., et al. 1983. The detection of fetal hemoglobin in bloodstains by means of thin layer immunoassay. *Journal of Forensic Sciences* 28(4), 888–893, October.

Whitehead, P.H. 1977. Crossed electroimmunodiffusion and bloodstain investigation. *Science* 198(4315), 427, 28 October.

Whitehead, P.H., et al. 1979. New information from bloodstains. *Naturwissenschaften* 66(9), 446–451, September.

———. 1969. Improved technique for the typing of haptoglobins in bloodstains. *Journal of the Forensic Science Society* 9, 129–130, December.

———. 1973. Assay of soluble fibrinogen in bloodstain extracts as an aid to identification of menstrual blood in forensic science: preliminary findings. *Clinical Chemistry* 19, 762–765, July.

———. 1974. A micro-technique involving species identification and ABO grouping on the same fragment of blood. *Journal of the Forensic Science Society* 14(2), 109–110, April.

———. 1974. The identification of the species origin of bloodstains using sensitized latex. *Journal of the Forensic Science Society* 14(2), 103–107, April.

Wiggins, K.G., et al. 1979. The use of hemoglobin F antiserum for the detection of foetal haemoglobin (HbF). *Journal of the Forensic Science Society* 19(1), 49–52, January.

Wigmore, R., et al. 1979. The detection of Y chromosomes in bloodstains—a re-evaluation. *Journal of Forensic Sciences* 24(2), 366–375, April.

Wilkins, R., et al. 1977. Determination of foetal hemoglobin in bloodstains by means of electrophoresis on cellulose acetate. *Journal of Legal Medicine* 79(2), 79–80, March (Germany).

Wilson, F.E., and Schuessler, D. 1985. Automated geometric interpretation of human bloodstain evidence. *I.A.B.P.A. News*, Vol. 2, No. 4, pp. 36–43, December.

Wise, J.B. 1966. Treatment of experimental siderosis bulbi, vitreous hemorrhage and corneal bloodstaining with deferoxamine. *Archives of Ophthalmology* 75, 698–707, May.

Wraxall, B.G. 1972. The identification of foetal hemoglobin in bloodstains. *Journal of the Forensic Science Society* 12, 457–458, July.

Wraxall, B.G., et al. 1976. Erythrocyte acid phosphatase in bloodstains. *Journal of the Forensic Science Society* 16(2), 127–132, April.

Yamakami, K. 1926. The individuality of semen with reference to property of inhibiting specifically isohemoagglutination. *Journal of Immunology* XII, 186.

Yamamoto, Y., et al. 1984. Sex identification of bloodstains by radioimmunoassay of sex hormones. *Forensic Sci. Int.* 24(1), 69–79, January.

Yoshiba, S., et al. 1985. Influence of drying times on the smeared blood in fluorescence microscopic detection of basophilic stippled erythrocytes and its application to a provocation method. *Nippon Eiseigaku Zasshi* 39(6), 873–885, February (Japan).

Yuasa, I., et al. 1976. ABO grouping of bloodstains by rapid mixed agglutination without first washing. *Yonago Acta Med* 20(1), 11–18, April.

———. 1985. Esterase D phenotyping of bloodstains and hair roots by low voltage isoelectric focusing. *Forensic Sci. Inter.* 28(1), 63–67, May.

Zajac, P.L., et al. 1978. Problems of reliability in the phenotyping of erythrocyte acid phosphatase in bloodstains. *Journal of Forensic Sciences* 23(3), 615–618, July.

———. 1975. Typing of phosphoglucomutase (PGM) variants in dried bloodstains by the Grunbaum method of cellulose acetate electrophoresis. *Journal of the Forensic Science Society* 15(1), 69–74, January.

Zaretskaia, E.F. 1984. Determination of glyoxalase I in bloodstains. *Sudebno-Metitsinskaia Ekspertiza* 27(4), 38–40, October–December (Russia).

Zipser, S. 1966. Liability for negligence in blood transfusions. *Federal Insurance Quarterly* 16:3, 9.

Zucchelli, G.C., et al. 1982. Radioimmunoassay of trypsin-like immunoreactivity in dried blood spots. *Journal of Nuclear Medicine* 26(1), 35–39, January–March.

Index